D0445574

Mar 2016

# American
# Character

ALSO BY
Colin Woodard

*Ocean's End*

*The Lobster Coast*

*The Republic of Pirates*

*American Nations*

COLIN WOODARD

# American Character

A History of the Epic Struggle
Between Individual Liberty
and the Common Good

VIKING

VIKING

An imprint of Penguin Random House LLC

375 Hudson Street

New York, New York 10014

penguin.com

Copyright © 2016 by Colin Woodard

Penguin supports copyright. Copyright fuels creativity, encourages
diverse voices, promotes free speech, and creates a vibrant culture.
Thank you for buying an authorized edition of this book and
for complying with copyright laws by not reproducing, scanning,
or distributing any part of it in any form without permission.
You are supporting writers and allowing Penguin
to continue to publish books for every reader.

Map illustration by Sean Wilkinson

ISBN: 978-0-52542-789-6

Printed in the United States of America

1   3   5   7   9   10   8   6   4   2

Set in Baskerville
Designed by Amy Hill

*For my son, Henry Skillin Woodard,*
*who let me write this,*
*when he really wanted me to play with trains*

# Contents

# American
# Character

# CHAPTER 1

# Maintaining Freedom

I t was cold, much colder than the passengers crowded aboard the *Mayflower* had expected. A long beach curved before them, its high dunes protecting them from the open Atlantic beyond, where they had nearly perished amid the Nantucket Shoals. Delayed by storms and business troubles, many of the 101 colonists were now sick, especially the children, their coughs echoing in the fetid hold, itself dangerously bare of supplies. Some of the rest, surly young men who had come on the voyage at the insistence of senior investors in their colonial project, hinted at mutiny. The New England winter would soon be upon them, yet they had no shelter, no livestock, no gear to catch smaller fish, nor harpoons to hunt the hundreds of whales that greeted them in the bay that first morning. All of their lives were in danger. Something had to be done.

They had sailed out of the English Channel two months before, leaving a war-torn continent to port, a depression-ravaged England to starboard. The original party had consisted of Pilgrims, Calvinist separatists seeking a new life in the Virginia Company's lands, which on paper extended all the way to the mouth of the Hudson, where they had obtained permission from King James to settle. Lacking the capital to finance their transatlantic migration, the Pilgrims had turned to a shady group of investors led by a ne'er-do-well alum smuggler who was himself one step from insolvency. With them, they formed a common stock company that would own the colony's land, buildings, tools, and trading profits for seven years, at which point the company would be liquidated and its assets divided among the shareholders. The capital investors had shares in proportion to their investment, but the colonists received one share each, their sweat equity in the venture.

Now they had arrived, in the chill air of November 1620, but not at the mouth of the Hudson. Frightened by their near deaths on the shoals south of Cape Cod, they had turned north instead, to lands owned, on paper, by Sir Ferdinando Gorges, in a place that would later be called Massachusetts. They were trespassers, in both English and Native American eyes.[1]

Most aboard the *Mayflower* knew they would need to cooperate or all would perish. Yet the would-be mutineers had pointed out that their royal charter of government was for the lands of Virginia, not Gorges's New England. They threatened "that when they came ashore they would use their own liberty, for none had the power to command them." To rectify the situation, others quickly drew up a document and called all the adult men together, from the lowliest laborers to the swashbuckling military man Myles Standish. Modeled on an English town charter, the document committed its signatories to "covenant and combine ourselves together into a civil body politic, for our better ordering and preservation." Together they would create such laws, constitutions, and offices as were needed to secure "the general good of the colony." The men endorsed this Mayflower Compact by at least a nine-to-one margin, pledging their "due submission and obedience" to their improvised body of self-government. Twelve years before the birth of John Locke, the Pilgrims had effectively realized the philosopher's imaginings of how human government had first been formed: as the voluntary act of freeborn individuals to "unite into a community, for their comfortable, safe, and peaceable living one amongst another, in a secure enjoyment of their properties, and a greater security against any that are not of it."[2]

Struggling to find an appropriate town site as winter closed in, they didn't start construction on their first shelter at Plymouth until December 24. Rain, wind, and sickness delayed its completion until the middle of January, at which point many of the settlers were already doomed. "There died sometimes two or three of a day in [January and February so] that of 100 and odd persons, scarce fifty remained," recalled William Bradford, who would later be elected governor. "In the time of most distress there was but six or seven sound persons." Thankfully the following autumn their first harvest of corn and barley was good, and they celebrated with a three-day feast of Thanksgiving, at which they were joined by ninety members of the Wampanoag tribe who had helped them in their distress. "Although it be not always so plentiful, by the goodness of God, we are so far from want," colonist Edward Wilson wrote friends in England shortly thereafter, "that we often wish you partakers of our plenty."[3]

★

Three hundred and eighty-nine years later, one of America's most popular talk radio personalities, Rush Limbaugh, was telling millions of listeners the "true story" of Thanksgiving and the Pilgrims, part of an annual ritual on his program. "It was a commune, folks," he told his followers. "It was the forerunner to the communes we saw in the sixties and seventies out in California—and it was complete with organic vegetables, by the way."

In Limbaugh's telling, the colony's stockholding company and its corporate property were portrayed as a communist experiment, each individual colonist's single share in the venture evidence of productivity-killing collectivism. "That's right. Long before Karl Marx was even born, the Pilgrims had discovered and experimented with what could only be described as socialism," Limbaugh continued. "And what happened? It didn't work! They nearly starved! . . . They did sit down and they did have free-range turkey and organic vegetables, but it was not the Indians who saved the day. It was capitalism and Scripture which saved the day."[4]

Limbaugh, broadcasting in 2010, was drawing on a narrative tradition more than half a century old, and one already widely disseminated among the radical libertarians of the Tea Party movement. In 1951, as U.S. civil defense authorities were preparing Americans to survive a nuclear exchange with the Soviet Union, popular historian Bradford Smith published a biography of his ancestor, Governor Bradford, lionizing him for overthrowing Plymouth's "communist society." The Pilgrims' story, Smith advised, was "a true parable of the American faith in the dignity of labor and the rights of the individual . . . the course [America] still defends against all assaults." In the 1960s, libertarian journalist Henry Hazlitt, a personal friend of Ayn Rand and the economist Ludwig von Mises, tied the storyline to Thanksgiving, urging readers to be "thankful for this valued lesson from our fathers—and yield not to the temptations of socialism." By 2005, anticommunist Christian conservative senator Jesse Helms of North Carolina was arguing that the Mayflower Compact had created a "share the wealth" society and thus "Communism came over on the *Mayflower*." The Pilgrims starved, he observed, "then they turned to God for an answer—and they got it."[5]

This twentieth- and twenty-first-century revisionism built its case from Governor Bradford's account of a change in policy at Plymouth in 1623, two years after the first Thanksgiving. Faced with the need to boost food production, Bradford's advisers convinced him to assign each family a plot where it could grow its own food, rather than have the entire colony farm the company's fields and deliver the production to its storehouse. The families didn't own the plots, just the food they produced, but self-interest did the trick. "It made all hands very industrious, so as much more corn was planted than otherwise would have been by any means the Governor or any other could use, and saved him a great deal of trouble," Bradford later recalled, referring to himself in the third person. Tenant farming "was found to breed much confusion and discontent, and retard much employment that would have been to their benefit and comfort." As originally planned, Plymouth continued on as a shareholding company, its assets and property—save food harvests—held in common until 1627, when settlers were given ownership of twenty-acre lots.[6]

Settled by devout Calvinists, profit-seeking in its purpose and corporate in organization, Plymouth was never a communist enterprise. If there is a historical lesson to be drawn from the colony's early history, it's that a band of people cast upon an unknown shore, short of resources and surrounded by potential enemies, needed to cooperate to survive, while respecting and rewarding individual initiative. Yet for the better part of a century the Pilgrims have been made pawns in a rhetorical struggle between champions of individualism and those of the common good, a conflict so elemental to the American experience that it has consumed even Thanksgiving.

★

Political conflict in the United States is often said to be between "liberals" and "conservatives," or between "elitists" and "hardworking Americans," or between Democrats and Republicans. History has demonstrated that all of those terms simply sow confusion. Since 1930, the Democrats and Republicans have swapped their agendas and, since 1960, their entire constituencies. In the early twentieth century Democrats were the party of white southerners and northern blue-collar workers, while a century later those groups are key pillars of the Republican coalition. During Teddy Roosevelt's administration, Republicans were a coalition of Yankees and black southerners, two groups that haven't supported the GOP for decades. If our conflict is really a populist one, which elite is it that ordinary people are seeking to take their country back from, the educated middle- and upper-middle-income professionals who staff our hospitals, schools, universities, and government laboratories, or the multimillionaires and billionaires who control much of the economy and some 40 percent of the nation's wealth while making up 1 percent of the population? What would Edmund Burke, the great eighteenth-century champion of conservatism—a man who valued the wisdom of received institutions and practices and foresaw the excesses of the French Revolution's Reign of Terror—make of the demands of early twenty-first-century "conservatives" to immediately dismantle the century-old constitutional, institutional, and philosophical legacies of the Progressive and New Deal eras on the basis of an abstract theory of human nature? What would the seventeenth-century political theorist John Locke make of people who would have proudly called themselves "liberals" in his day—and "libertarians" today—forging a political coalition with religious fundamentalists who seek government enforcement of their social, spiritual, and moral beliefs and practices on a majority of people who don't share them? Burke might well judge the Democrats to be the party of conservation, just as Locke, scratching his head, might pronounce Newt Gingrich and Paul Ryan to be liberals.[7]

Throughout the history of our republic, the real and abiding conflict has been not between these shape-shifting political camps, but over competing definitions of freedom. There are two distinct visions, each with a full spectrum of adherents, from radical revolutionaries to pragmatic centrists. At the middle, they are differentiated by their answer to the question "When individual liberty and the common good come into conflict, with which principle will you side?" On one near flank are individualists, who prioritize the freedom of the individual, on the other, communitarians who emphasize the freedom of the community. Together they span the ideological distance between Thomas Jefferson, who imagined a self-regulating republic of independent producers led by enlightened landed gentlemen like himself, and Alexander Hamilton, who envisioned a vigorous national government staffed by the best and brightest, committed to promoting the public interest by building institutions and infrastructure, and strong enough to defend the Constitution from enemies foreign and domestic. Between 1945 and 1979, governance was shared between these centrist camps while hard-liners stewed on the edges, sometimes vocal but marginalized from the conversation.

Moving further apart on the spectrum, one reaches libertarians, who seek a laissez-faire world in which government acts only to defend private property and enforce contracts, and social democrats, who would build a comprehensive social welfare state possibly featuring centralized industrial planning. Both of these philosophies have been put into practice in our history. Laissez-faire economic libertarianism was the ruling ideology of the United States from the period between the assassination of Abraham Lincoln in 1865 and the rise of the Progressives at the turn of the twentieth century and again through the 1920s; it wrought a wildly oscillating economy, inequality sufficient to forever kill the Jeffersonian dream, the rise of an oligarchy that threatened freedom itself, and a worldwide economic meltdown that ended liberal democracy in Germany and nearly in America as well. In the aftermath of that collapse, Franklin Delano

Roosevelt dabbled in social democracy with his National Recovery Administration, micromanaging prices, the distribution of raw materials, and industrial production, and then resurrected it again to fight and win the Second World War. However effective it may have been in a national emergency, this level of government intrusion into the workings of the marketplace was soundly rejected by peacetime electorates. America, as we will see, is far too individualistic to tolerate social democracy, let alone socialism.

At the farthest extremes of the spectrum, one encounters tyrannical realms. On one hand are the radical libertarians, anarcho-capitalists and followers of Ayn Rand, who want government to wither away and for "free" individuals to engage in unfettered competition without public obligations. On the other hand are radical collectivists, who would ensure "freedom" by turning all wealth and power over to the all-knowing benevolence of the state, Fatherland, or party. These ideas have not been tried in the United States, but have resulted in the deaths of tens of millions around the world, from the killing fields of Cambodia and Soviet Ukraine to the gas chambers of Nazi Germany and the victims of the death squads of the Salvadoran, Honduran, and Guatemalan oligarchies. Since the collapse of the Soviet Empire, no one in the United States has taken radical collectivism seriously. Unfortunately, radical libertarians abound at the highest levels of government in the early twenty-first century, including several fringe presidential candidates, a House speaker and recent vice presidential nominee, and a longtime chairman of the Federal Reserve. Here lies the greatest present threat to individual freedom and America's world-changing, 250-year experiment with liberal democracy.

*American Character* will argue that sustaining liberal democracy requires balancing those two essential aspects of human freedom: individual liberty and the freedom of the community. Sacrifice one, and you are on the road to oligarchy or anarchy; lose the other, and the shadow of collectivist dictatorship looms. You simply can't have one without the other. The reasons for this go deeper than logic and philosophy. They're literally encoded in *Homo sapiens*'s DNA.

★

Many of the underlying ideas we have about how to achieve human freedom come from a handful of English political thinkers who lived in the seventeenth and eighteenth centuries. They were writing at a time when the easy assumptions of the medieval era—the divine right of kings, the inerrancy of the Bible, the natural subjugation of humans to their superiors—were coming apart. Their theories of liberal government were built on their imaginations of what life was like before governments existed. Thomas Hobbes, John Locke, and Adam Smith all assumed that humanity in its natural state consisted of solitary individuals, each free to eke out an existence on his or her own. This environment, while free of government oppression, was presumed to be unpleasant. Hobbes famously described it as a perpetual "war of every man against every man" in which individuals lived in "continual fear and danger of violent death; and the life of [each was] solitary, poor, nasty, brutish, and short." To bring some measure of relief from the uncertainties of this anarchic world, the philosophers argued, humans consented to form governments, but remained, by their very natures, self-interested individuals.

At the time they were put forth, these were radical notions, as they challenged fifteen hundred years of Western thinking centered on the collective nature of human existence whereby humans thought of themselves not as individuals but as parts of a great social organism headed by a monarch chosen by God. The intellectual battle over these competing ideas about the human condition and their implications for government was being fiercely fought while the east coast of North America was being colonized; the American Revolution was the first real-world application of the principles of liberal government.[8]

As a factual matter, however, both parties were wrong. Human nature is not fundamentally individualistic or fundamentally collectivist. It's both.

Edward O. Wilson, the founder of social biology and one of the world's leading experts on biological evolution, has made the case that *Homo sapiens* is unique in this regard, and that it is that quality that has made us so successful. All other advanced social creatures— ones that organize themselves in colonies featuring the cooperative care of unrelated young, a division of labor, and multiple generations living together—compete at the group, not the individual level. Ants, bees, and termites don't compete with one another as individuals; they compete against other colonies and hives, and are willing to sacrifice themselves for the success of their super-organism, itself an extension of their queen's genome. Similarly, we humans are genetically hard-wired to be tribal and join groups and, having done so, to consider them superior to others. Our groups—whether small bands, tribes, societies, or nations—compete with one another for dominance, with individuals sometimes willingly giving their lives for the group, even when it consists of unrelated people, as in a fire team of U.S. Marines. Yet, unlike our hive-dwelling friends, we also compete for survival and reproduction within groups via individual selection. The human condition, Wilson concluded in his 2012 book *The Social Conquest of Earth,* is largely a product of the tension between these two conflicting impulses:

> The dilemma of good and evil was created by multilevel selection, in which individual selection and group selection act together on the same individual, but largely in opposition to each other. Individual

selection . . . shapes instincts in each member that are fundamentally selfish with reference to other members. . . . Group selection shapes instincts that tend to make individuals altruistic toward one another (but not toward members of other groups). Individual selection is responsible for much of what we call sin, while group selection is responsible for the greater part of virtue. Together they have created the conflict between the poorer and the better angels of our nature.[9]

For our purposes, the point is that our fundamental nature is conflicted on the question of individualism versus collectivism. We're torn on how to balance these forces, and while most of us teach our preschoolers to share their toys and show kindness to others, we hope they will be at the top of their high school graduating class. As Wilson puts it, there's an iron rule to genetic social evolution: "Selfish individuals beat altruistic individuals, while groups of altruists beat groups of selfish individuals." Our curse, as it were, is to forever strive to keep these forces in equilibrium:

> The victory can never be complete; the balance of selection pressures cannot move to either extreme. If individual selection were to dominate, societies would dissolve. If group selection were to dominate, human groups would come to resemble ant colonies.[10]

Far from being naturally solitary, humans have always existed in a social state. Our evolutionary ancestors, *Homo erectus*, were using fire a million years ago, a game-changing innovation that led them to live in group campsites; share tasks, responsibilities, and resources; and, eventually, forge metal tools. Groups whose members cooperated well tended to defeat or outcompete dysfunctional ones and isolated family units alike, which led to "altruistic" genes becoming more prevalent over the course of time. By the time the first *Homo sapiens*

appeared some forty thousand generations later, they already belonged
to bands, and depended on such groups for survival. From infancy they
were predisposed to interpret the intentions of other humans, and from
early childhood cooperated closely with others to build tools and shelter, to acquire and prepare food, to watch after young and old. Re-
searchers who study animal intelligence—in chimpanzees, gorillas,
dogs, or crows—have found again and again that its biggest difference
from our own is its failure to allow as intensive collaboration for shared
goals. Pursuing the "common good" isn't some imagined ideal but one
of the essential qualities that has always defined our species.[11]

Indeed, communalism—not individualism—was the natural state
of humans for most of recorded history. From ancient Babylonia to
medieval Europe to imperial China, people lived in societies in which
individual freedom wasn't even part of their conceptual framework.
Medieval Europeans conceived themselves as being members of one
or another organ of a great, harmonious super-organism. John of Salis-
bury, the great twelfth-century English philosopher and bishop, described the commonwealth as a body, with the prince serving as the
head, the sheriffs and judges as the senses, the army as one hand and
the tax collectors as the other, the artisans and peasants as the feet
"who erect, sustain, and move forward the mass of the whole body."
(The clergy, standing slightly apart, guided the entire organism as the
soul.) While everyone had his or her place, John wrote, all members of
society were to "keep watch over the public advantage," which included "mutual charity reigning everywhere." Society was hierarchical, but it wasn't intended to be exploitative; lords didn't own their
property, they had been appointed custodians of it by their king and
had duties to the serfs and citizens living on it. Medieval life was intel-
lectually stifling, oppressive to the individual, and often unjust, but it
was premised on a theory of the common good that was thought to be
the will of God. In much of Europe, this general model endured into
the eighteenth century.[12]

In England, however, the medieval model, so dismissive of individual aspiration and expression, came under sustained attack in the seventeenth century. When King Charles I asserted that he had absolute, divinely ordained political power, much of the gentry (who controlled all representation in the country's ephemeral parliament) rose up against him in a civil war that lasted from 1642 to 1651. King Charles lost the war and his head, clearing the way for England's first and only republic, under Oliver Cromwell, an event that shook the foundations of Anglo-American political culture. The feudal system of land tenure and mutual obligation was done away with, making nobles landowners instead of tenants of the Crown and dispossessing the rural poor from their customary rights to use the land. Thomas Hobbes, who spent the war in exile in the Netherlands, wrote *Leviathan* (with its line about anarchic life being "nasty, brutish, and short") in an effort to justify an absolute monarchy with logic, as the beheading of the king had undermined the previous reliance on biblical authority. John Locke, whose father had fought on the side of Parliament in the civil war, became famous by developing a set of political theories that validated the aristocracy's rebellion and property seizures in the name of something new: individual rights.

Locke's ideas formed the foundations of what Europeans still call "liberalism" and is known today in America as "libertarianism." They would have a powerful influence on the thinking of America's founding fathers. Locke, like so many Enlightenment philosophers, imagined the first humans as having been free and solitary individuals, happily going about creation and, through the sweat of their own labors, creating the first properties. Those who worked hardest claimed the most property. To defend it, they created the first governments, which were tasked for that purpose by contract. If a government violated this social contract by seizing property as Charles had tried to do through taxation, property owners were justified in overthrowing it. At the time Locke formulated these ideas, the great property owners were engaged in an ongoing struggle with the restored monarchy over the further dismantling of a highly collectivized order and the carving out of an important zone of individual freedom. It is essential to understand, however, that Locke and his successors—Adam Smith and John Stuart Mill—were primarily concerned with the struggle between the Crown and the English elite. The broad mass of people—the ones who had been forced off the lands they had farmed for countless generations and were now called the "surplus population"—were universally regarded as a nuisance to be suppressed.

The classical liberals therefore imagined that the sole threat to individual freedom was the state, and that the two were locked in a zero-sum game for control: The greater the sphere of the state, the less freedom there would be for the individual. This made sense from the perspective of, say, Locke's employers and patrons, men like Sir John Popham and Lord Shaftesbury, whose freedom would be constrained by a strong state. From the perspective of the vast majority of England's people, however, a strong state was the only thing standing between them and oligarchy. The result was, in eighteenth- and nineteenth-century Britain, not a liberal democracy but a liberal autocracy, a government where individual rights were secure, but meaningful freedom and political participation remained the privilege of the upper classes. It was the world of Charles Dickens's novels, not the utopia of classical liberal promise. It also provided the foundation for the essential culture of the Chesapeake region of the American colonies, with lasting effects on the future trajectory of the United States.

★

The reason classical liberal theory didn't deliver freedom's promise is simple: The struggle for freedom is not bilateral, but instead triangular. The participants are the state, the people, and the would-be aristocracy or oligarchy. Liberal democracy, an incredible historical and cultural accomplishment that allows for mass individual freedom, relies on keeping these three forces in balance.

There is no doubt that the state can be tyrannical and oppressive; history is replete with examples, from the ancient Maya to the Soviet Empire. However, a weak state doesn't necessarily ensure freedom, as it typically ushers in the tyranny of the oligarchy. Hans Morgenthau, father of the realist school of international relations, reflected on this liberal blind spot back in 1957:

> The autonomous forces of society, left to themselves, engendered new accumulations of power, as dangerous to the freedom of the individual as the power of the government had ever been. And while liberalism had assumed that the weakness of the government assured the freedom of the individual, it now became obvious that it also assured the unhindered growth of private power, destructive of individual freedom. . . . The solution . . . demands an answer to the question as to how the state can be made strong enough to limit the concentrations of private power in order to protect the freedom of the many without becoming so strong as to be able to destroy the freedom of all.[13]

Francis Fukuyama, the neoconservative political scientist, came to similar conclusions in his two-volume, sixteen-hundred-page history of the state. He highlighted the example of medieval Hungary, where the nobility succeeded in putting restraints on the king, eliminating taxes on themselves, and forcing the peasantry back into serfdom. The Hungarian state became so weak that it wasn't able to defend itself when the Ottoman Turks attacked, precipitating its destruction and a century and a half of Ottoman rule. "Constitutional limits on a central government's power do not by themselves necessarily produce political accountability," Fukuyama concluded:

The "freedom" sought by the Hungarian noble class was the freedom to exploit their own peasants more thoroughly, and the absence
of a strong central state allowed them to do just that. . . . The twentieth century has taught us to think about tyranny as something per-
petrated by powerful, centralized states, but it can also be the work
of local oligarchs. . . . It is the responsibility of the central government to enforce its own laws against the oligarchy; freedom is lost
not when the state is too strong but when it is too weak.[14]

A comparable situation occurred in the Deep South before the Civil
War and in early twenty-first-century El Salvador and Honduras, where
a handful of families control not only the wealth, banks, and news media
of their nations, but the government, courts, and army as well. The only
challenges to the rule of El Salvador's "Fourteen Families" and the "Ten
Families" of Honduras have been communist-minded peasant insur-
gencies born of despair in the 1970s and 1980s and, more recently, the
rise of violent drug cartels, who've taken advantage of the weakness of
the state. Neither nation offers meaningful freedom for their citizenries,
who live in what are among the most violent societies on earth.[15]

The founding fathers well understood that the struggle for freedom was three-cornered. In *Federalist* No. 17, Alexander Hamilton
counseled that the federal government would usurp state government's powers only if the latter failed to retain the confidence of its
citizens. By way of analogy, he raised the feudal system of the Old
World, where the king was locked in a power struggle with his vassals. "The power of the head of the nation was commonly too weak
either to preserve the public peace or to protect the people against
the oppressions of their immediate lords," Hamilton wrote. "In those
instances in which the monarch finally prevailed over his vassals, his
success was chiefly owing to the tyranny of those vassals over their
dependents. The barons, or nobles, equally the enemies of the sover-

eign and the oppressors of the common people, were dreaded and detested by both."[16]

James Madison, making his famous argument for the separation of powers in *Federalist* No. 51, emphasized the dangers of an unchecked oligarchy or an unrestrained majority:

> It is of great importance in a republic not only to guard the society against the oppression of its rulers, but to guard one party of the society against the injustice of the other part. Different interests necessarily exist in different classes of citizens. . . . Justice is the end [i.e., the purpose] of government. It is the end of civil society. It ever has been and ever will be pursued until it be obtained, or until liberty be lost in the pursuit. In a society under the forms of which the stronger faction can readily unite and oppress the weaker, anarchy may as truly be said to reign as in a state of nature, where the weaker individual is not secured against the violence of the stronger.[17]

John Adams, traditionally associated with "elitism," was in fact extremely concerned about the need to constrain oligarchic ambition, which—unlike Madison and Hamilton—he believed to present a greater danger to the Republic than the unwashed masses. "The aristocracy is always more sagacious than an assembly of the people collectively, or by representation, and sooner or later proves an overmatch in policy," he warned in 1778.

> It is always more cunning, too, than a first magistrate [i.e., a chief executive], and always makes of him . . . a mere ceremony, unless he makes an alliance with the people, to support him against it. What is the whole history of the wars of the barons but one demonstration of this truth? . . . The standing armies in Europe . . . were all given to kings by the people, to defend them against aristocracies.

It was with this in mind that Adams called for aristocrats and their influence to be isolated in one chamber (an "ostracism" was how he put it) and for the creation of a monarchical president who would be "the natural friend of the people, and the only defense which they or their representatives can have against the avarice and ambition of the rich and distinguished citizens." The founders, in short, were well aware of the threat unchecked private power posed to human liberty.[18]

They were also clear about the purpose of their unprecedented experiment. Its aim was not to remove every feasible impediment to individual desire, but rather to promote human happiness and the common good. The goal of government, Madison wrote, "is the happiness of the people" and "the public good, the real welfare of the great body of the people." He argued that the 1789 Constitution—which created a stronger, not a weaker federal government than had existed under the Articles of Confederation—was necessary to ensure this ideal. The Preamble of the Constitution itself stated its purpose: "to form a more perfect Union, establish Justice, insure domestic Tranquility, provide for the common defence, promote the general Welfare, and secure the Blessings of Liberty to ourselves and our Posterity." Our task as a nation, in other words, was the common good, shared and fostered across generations.[19]

★

The advent of liberal democracy is one of humanity's most remarkable achievements. Far from representing a "natural" state of being, it is a complex and delicate work of art, the creation of which took our species eons of preparation and four centuries of awkward experimentation. Its gift is the erection of a framework that allows, for the first time in the history of complex human societies, the possibility of individual freedom on a nearly universal basis. Maintaining this situation, which defies thousands of years of human experience, requires maintaining the balance between the freedom of the government (or the state), the powerful (the oligarchs-in-waiting), and the people.

In the Anglo-American context, restraints on the state's power came first. In 1215, the nobility imposed certain restrictions on the power the Crown held over them via the imposition of the Magna Carta, and they furthered and confirmed these with the execution of Charles I and, in 1688, the deposition and replacement of his son, James II. While eighteenth-century Britons celebrated their rights under common law—which protected individual property rights and certain civil liberties—only 2 percent of the adult male population was allowed to vote or otherwise participate in politics. It was a liberal state, but not a democratic one, and its liberties were mostly conferred on a property-owning elite. In colonial America, where there was a sparse population and a great deal of Indian-held land that could be bought or seized, a majority of families could acquire property, greatly enlarging the proportion of people who could be granted political rights. The American Revolution started as a series of wars of liberation, as each regional colonial culture sought to protect its distinctive way of life from imperial centralization, but in some regions it unleashed democratic forces that insisted on the equality and political rights of all adult white men.[20]

The French Revolution provided a cautionary tale for populist democratizers. France's impoverished masses overthrew and executed their king and queen, abolished the monarchy, and then set about making the world anew. The radical revolutionaries renamed the months, beheaded over sixteen thousand alleged enemies, engaged in the summary execution of priests, arrested their electoral opponents, and drove the country into such chaos that its people rallied around a military leader, crowned him emperor, and launched a war against their neighbors. Democracy in the hands of the illiberal, humans have since learned, brings not freedom but tyranny, the "illiberal democracy" of Slobodan Milošević's Serbia and Franjo Tuđjman's Croatia, which engaged in popularly sanctioned repression and genocide; Vladimir Putin's murderous and authoritarian regime, which is enthusiastically endorsed by the Russian electorate; and the terrorism of Hamas, voted into power by the traumatized people of the Gaza Strip. "Democracy without constitutional liberalism," Fareed Zakaria, the public intellectual who popularized the term "illiberal democracy," proclaimed in 1997, "is not simply inadequate, but dangerous, bringing with it the erosion of liberty, the abuse of power, ethnic divisions and even war." Democracy itself can't protect freedom in a society in which most people endorse terror, tyrants, and dictatorship.[21]

A liberal democracy requires a citizenry prepared to exercise liberty. As the former George W. Bush speechwriter Michael Gerson and a colleague stated, "Responsible, self-governing citizens do not grow wild like blackberries, which is why a conservative political philosophy cannot be reduced to untrammeled libertarianism. Citizens are cultivated by institutions and families, religious communities, neighborhoods and nations." The goal of liberal democracy isn't to allow everyone to do whatever he or she wants, but to create and maintain a society in which all people can be free and self-governing. Doing so requires a preponderance of autonomous individuals who are committed not just to their own selfish ends, but to sustaining an environment conducive to every child having the tools for and a fair chance of also becoming autonomous. Without such customs, without a commitment to the public goods and civic institutions that foster the attainment of individual freedom for those who are not so well-born, without a citizenry interested, informed, and engaged in civic affairs, liberal democracy cannot be sustained.[22]

Alexis de Tocqueville, the insightful and much-quoted nineteenth-century French observer of Americans in the early Republic, underscored this point above all others: that the customs and habits of the people were far and away the most important factor in understanding the success and survival of their democracy, more so than the details of their constitution or their fortuitous geographical circumstances. "I am convinced that the most advantageous situation and the best possible laws cannot maintain a constitution in spite of the customs of a country; while the latter may turn to some advantage the most unfavorable positions and the worst laws," he concluded in *Democracy in America*. "So seriously do I insist upon this head that, if I have hitherto failed in making the reader feel the important influence of the practical experience, the habits, the opinions in short, of the customs of the Americans upon the maintenance of their institutions, I have failed in the principal object of my work." Those customs, especially the wide dissemination of public education in the Northeast, and the direct and widespread participation of most adult males in local politics in New England and New England–settled upstate New York, supplied the social capital that enabled them to govern well. Coming from a feudal country where the vast majority of the population was illiterate, Tocqueville was shocked to find the learned and literate even in the rudest, most primitive frontier huts. "Everything about him is primitive and wild," he said of the backwoods American, "but he is himself the result of the labor and experience of eighteen centuries . . . speaks the language of cities . . . is acquainted with the past, curious about the future, and ready for argument about the present."[23]

These "habits of the heart" that underpin liberal democracy include a degree of restraint and civic-mindedness, an ethic of internalized altruism and trust in others that limits the need for public authority and state intrusion, and a personal commitment to liberal

values. This is why, at the outset of a treatise on representative government, the classical liberal theorist John Stuart Mill wrote, "A
people may prefer a free government, but, if, from indolence, or
carelessness, or cowardice, or want of public spirit, they are unequal
to the exertions necessary for preserving it; . . . they are unlikely to
long enjoy it." The paradox of broad individual freedom is that it
requires individuals to act altruistically and the successful to be willing to "pay it forward" to support the institutional and cultural achievements that made their own ascent possible.[24]

★

If sustaining freedom is ultimately a matter of balancing individual
liberty and the common good, where does the "sweet spot" lie? The
answer is context dependent: Every society is going to have a slightly
different set of coordinates where their people feel their happiness is
best secured. Some liberal democracies, such as Japan and South
Korea, will strongly favor social harmony and collectivist values. Most
of our West European peers have chosen a social democratic position
that prioritizes the common good more than most Americans would
be comfortable with. The United Kingdom, Canada, Australia, and
New Zealand have each staked a position between social democracy
and the current neoliberal orientation of the United States, which is
an individualistic outlier among liberal democracies. What works for
one political culture doesn't necessarily fit for another.

Consider the social welfare democracies of Western Europe.
They have shown that a large and activist government and a thriving private economy can go hand in hand. The libertarian Frasier
Institute publishes annual ratings of economic freedom in the world,
based on rule of law, access to sound money, freedom of trade, and
regulation. In aggregate, in 2014 the United States finished behind

Finland and Switzerland, and only slightly ahead of Denmark, Sweden, and Norway, because the raters penalize states with high taxation and regulation. Despite their commitment to both, however, many welfare states finished far ahead of the United States in rule of law and free trade, with big-spending Denmark, Finland, and the Netherlands near the top of the world lists for both. The governments of Australia, the Netherlands, and Norway all spent a higher proportion of their country's overall consumption than the United States did, and yet all ranked higher on the United Nations Human Development Index, which compares life expectancy, living standards, literacy, education, and quality of life to measure overall well-being. On that list, Norway finished first, the United States fifth, and all the West European welfare states in the top twenty-five. Social democracy—which couples capitalist enterprise with high taxes, ample regulations, and comprehensive services and benefits (including free and high-quality health care, higher education, and child care, monthlong annual vacations, and yearlong maternity leave)—isn't incompatible with liberal democracy or the accumulation of wealth. Nonetheless, it has never had broad-based support in the United States.[25]

The struggle to define freedom has been particularly fractious in the United States for a simple reason. Unlike Norway, Sweden, South Korea, or Japan, we're not a unitary state with a common culture, but rather a coalition of nearly a dozen regional cultures, most of which trace their origins and fundamental characteristics back to one of the colonial clusters founded on the eastern or southern rims of what is now the United States. As we will discuss in chapter 3, each of those regional cultures has and has always had a different answer as to where the balance point lies on the individualist-communitarian spectrum. Some have always been more inclined toward the common good, others to individual liberty. (Even Tocqueville remarked on this, contrasting the civic-minded Northeast with the libertarian and aristocratic South.) All have been more individualistic than, say, modern-day Scandinavians, and some continue to fight for a radical libertarian vision of society that, if implemented, would spell the end of liberal democracy.

The balkanized nature of our federation has made constructive discussion of this essential issue extremely difficult. It confounds efforts to articulate a common vision for American freedom, a set of ideals from which our political parties would draw their specific policy stances on everything from taxes to regulation to welfare. It confuses efforts to assess our historical record, to understand what we've tried before, where it led us, and how we might apply these lessons to the problems and challenges of contemporary life. It leaves us reeling, unable to gain our collective bearings, to agree about the direction our country should take and how we are to achieve the happiness of our people. The Republic stumbles through a haze, or stands paralyzed, its compromise-dependent institutions frozen, its lifeblood draining into a pool of debt that threatens to drown the future.

This book aims to help find the answers, to locate our balance point, to restore our civic strength and unity of purpose. It begins with two cautionary tales, one of collectivist excess, the other libertarian, because it is essential to understand what the single-minded pursuit of either has wrought.

# CHAPTER 2

# Two Paths to Tyranny

In early September 1989, I was a twenty-year-old student on my first trip outside of North America, jet-lagged, laden with luggage, and aboard a train bound for Budapest, where I was to enroll as an exchange student for a semester at what was then called the Karl Marx University of Economics. I was majoring in East European history and had been studying Eastern Bloc politics, but I'd never before set foot in a country that wasn't a liberal democracy. The prospect of living on the other side of the Iron Curtain—in a region many had died trying to escape from, where secret police might be listening to your phone calls and opening your mail, and where the nuclear missiles that had cast an apocalyptic shadow over two generations of children were pointed toward our homes—was an intimidating one. That the Hungarian language tapes I had been listening to featured conversations where people cheerily said things like "You don't have to eat meat every day, once or twice a week's enough" and "Were there eggs at the store today?" suggested an austere world quite different from the late-1980s United States. I expected to learn a great deal about what it was really like to live in authoritarian and totalitarian societies, in an economy where shortages, not demand, conditioned individual economic behavior, and civil liberties did not exist.

I did not expect, however, to also witness the collapse of communism.

My train originated in Vienna and crossed the frontier between Austria and Hungary on September 10, 1989, at just about the time the reform communist government in Budapest made a decision that would crack the foundations of the Eastern Bloc. It opened its border fences and let East Germany's people go.

As my train rolled toward Budapest's cavernous Keleti station, thousands of East Germans were fleeing in the opposite direction, part of an exodus to freedom in the West that grew so large it forced regimes in Moscow, East Berlin, Prague, and Budapest to make a decision: call in the military or capitulate to popular will. For Hungary, the most open, politically relaxed, and consumer-oriented member of the bloc, a nation that resented the ongoing Soviet occupation and longed to become a neutral state like Austria or Yugoslavia, the decision was a relatively easy one. Their citizens were already allowed to travel to the West, and that night they decided to let the sixty thousand East German "tourists" who had flooded the country that summer—in reality families seeking to escape through Hungary's recently defortified frontier—do so as well. The East Germans had known that if they made it to Austria, they would be allowed to travel on to West Germany, whose constitution already considered them citizens. Taking advantage of the fact that Hungary was one of the few places in the world their regime permitted them to visit, tens of thousands had booked their summer vacations there, but had no intention of ever coming home.

By the end of the day, more than ten thousand East Germans had escaped to the West. Journalists at the main receiving center in Passau, West Germany, reported that nearly all the escapees were under forty years of age, and half of them were in their twenties. Almost nine in ten had professional jobs: doctors, dentists, industrial engineers, and the like. Two-thirds had owned cars, a luxury item in East Germany. They were, put simply, some of the most valuable and irreplaceable citizens of a country that already had such an acute labor shortage it had imported one hundred thousand guest workers from Vietnam and other developing nations just to keep its industries going.[1]

Over the coming weeks, the hemorrhaging worsened, as citizens long deprived of a say in the affairs of their country voted with their feet. Tens of thousands left their homes in September, even after their government stopped issuing exit visas to Hungary. With the Hungarian escape route closed, they made their way instead to the only foreign country they could still easily travel to, Czechoslovakia. Nearly three thousand sought refuge in West Germany's embassy in Prague, hoping to be allowed to emigrate to the West. A thousand more risked swimming to Hungary across the broad, dangerous Danube River, which formed a section of that country's border with Czechoslovakia. Emboldened by the regime's impotence, large anti-government demonstrations broke out in Dresden and Leipzig. In mid-October, East Germany's seventy-eight-year-old leader, Erich Honecker, was removed from power by his own politburo, which made a futile attempt to win back the people's confidence by pledging to lift travel restrictions; nobody believed they would. In the first week of November alone, more than sixty thousand additional people fled the country. Soldiers were deployed to relieve growing labor shortages in factories, where remaining workers were putting in seventy-hour weeks. Small towns found themselves without doctors or dentists. There were shortages of clothing, fruit, lumber, and spare parts. Days later, the beleaguered regime accepted the inevitable, opening the country's borders with West Germany and West

Berlin. Millions poured out, and by December the Eastern Bloc had effectively ceased to exist.[2]

⭐

I traveled throughout the region in those final months of the Soviet Empire, from Berlin and Warsaw to central Romania and Yugoslavia's Dalmatian coast. I witnessed the privations and tyranny of the collapsing order, a system whose alleged purpose was the promotion of the common good, but one that yielded instead collective misery.

Romania was the worst. Nicolae Ceauşescu, general secretary of the Romanian Communist Party for a quarter century, had sunk the country deeply into debt to finance absurd projects: a useless canal off the Danube River; a misguided scheme to turn Europe's greatest wetland, the Danube Delta, into a rice-growing region, which would help trigger a biochemical disaster that killed off much of the life in the Black Sea while failing to produce much rice; the bulldozing of great swaths of historic Bucharest to build the hideous Palace of the People, which at 3.77 million square feet was the second-largest administrative structure on the planet after the Pentagon in Washington, D.C.; a nuclear power plant whose construction was so flawed that many viewed its possible completion as a threat to the safety of southeastern Europe. Having accumulated an enormous foreign debt—the palace alone cost $4 billion—Ceauşescu had suddenly become obsessed with paying it all back as quickly as possible. The resulting policy was *Totul Pentru Export*—"Everything for Export"— under which everything possible was sold abroad for hard currency, regardless of the needs of Romania's twenty-three million people. The result was tragic.[3]

In a country in possession of one of Europe's largest oil fields, people now had to wear winter hats and jackets in offices and hotel lobbies. A nation of farmers stood in long lines to buy pig snouts and feet, the intervening parts of the animals having been sold abroad. At dusk, Braşov, the city I visited that October, descended into darkness: By law, each room of a home or business could have just one forty-watt bulb to conserve electricity, and police made random checks to ensure compliance, as every watt consumed by Romania's people reduced the stock of energy that could be exported. The power shut off entirely an hour after sunset, forcing guests at my unheated hotel to feel their way along the stairway walls in total darkness to reach the lobby. Outside, teams of policemen stood on each street corner toting machine guns and accompanied by German shepherds, their silhouettes outlined in the ghostly glare of the only source of light: spotlights bouncing off great rooftop billboards declaring the greatness of Ceauşescu, "Genius of the Carpathians" and, as one ironically put it, founder of the "Epoch of Light."

In Czechoslovakia and East Germany people occasionally took a second glance at foreigners in their midst; in Ceauşescu's Romania they stopped in their tracks and stared, unblinking, as if we had dropped from the moon. At the bus stop in front of the station, commuters formed a silent semicircle around my two American traveling companions and myself, everyone gaped in silence. Nobody would return greetings.

Then, after ten minutes had passed, as if responding to a starting gun, everyone rushed inward toward us, faces desperate, wads of greasy, decomposing currency in their hands, pleading urgently to buy most anything: food, cigarettes, candy. We gave what we had of the latter, handing chocolate bars to grasping hands, refusing pay until—as suddenly as it began—everyone swooped away, back into their silent semicircle. An electric trolley bus finally dragged itself painfully up the street to our stop, three of its four tires completely flat.

Ceauşescu had built a cult of personality modeled on that of North

Korea's Kim Il Sung and backed by the Securitate, a secret police force believed to have Orwellian omnipresence. Some Securitate officers were said to have been recruited when young from Romania's massive population of abandoned children, itself a direct product of Ceaușescu's rule. Possessed with the notion that Romania's national greatness would grow in direct proportion to its population size, he had banned abortion and the import or sale of any form of birth control, slapped taxes on couples with few children, and instituted surprise examinations to detect illegal terminations of pregnancy. The result was a flood of unwanted babies, one hundred thousand of whom wound up in horrifying conditions in overtaxed, undersupplied state orphanages. I encountered a party of them when we returned to the train station to catch the overnight to Budapest. The station's cavernous interior was blacked out, and in the shadows hundreds of people lay on the floor, waiting for trains. One boy who looked to be six or seven took notice of our foreignness and struck up a conversation in Romanian, unperturbed and apparently uninterested in the fact that we couldn't understand him. He had a small flashlight that he kept pointed in his own face, flicking it on and off. He laughed in a sort of maniacal way from time to time for no apparent reason. Everyone else in the station was afraid to speak to us—the invisible presence of informants was reflected in their body language—but eventually a young man sitting beside us asked the boy a few questions and whispered a translation, while pretending to look the other way. "He is going to a school for hopeless children in Moldavia, alone. He is sick. He is actually eleven years old. Yes, he is small, because of his sickness." The man added that he could be arrested just for talking to us. "I want to leave Romania," he said, before stating the obvious. "There is no freedom here."[4]

The surveillance state was ubiquitous. Classrooms and offices were bugged. All typewriters had to be registered with the police, and photocopying machines were banned outright. One in four people was said to be an informant. Many Romanian professionals believed that even the political jokes whispered from person to person—that human flesh was being sold at restaurants for lack of ordinary supplies, or that Ceaușescu's wife, Elena, dined on the blood of children—were actually circulated by the Securitate for conspiratorial reasons of their own.[5]

Like those of the Soviets before him, Ceaușescu's development policies were based on the forced industrialization of the country, which he believed would foster the creation of a "new socialist man." There was a twist, however. Ceaușescu and his wife (and heir apparent) had both been raised in small village peasant families and were fundamentally distrustful of cities and urban dwellers. To the greatest extent possible, they wanted to industrialize without urbanizing. Ceaușescu ordered large factories to be built in remote areas of the countryside and assigned workers to man them, but didn't provide the housing, schools, hospitals, roads, sewage, or water systems necessary to support new residents. Instead, members of peasant families commuted from area villages or moved into jerry-built factory dormitories lacking heat, electricity, or flush toilets. To discourage individual independence and character, Ceaușescu bulldozed the centuries-old cottages in the villages along with their garden plots, forcing their inhabitants to be relocated into drab multistory concrete blocks. Seven thousand villages were slated for destruction, though only a few dozen were demolished before the December 1989 uprising ended the regime.[6]

Two months after my visit the Ceaușescus were dead and the lights were back on. Hungary had left the Warsaw Pact, Czechoslovakia's regime had surrendered to the Velvet Revolution, and the Berlin Wall had fallen. Through it all, Soviet leader Mikhail Gorbachev never rolled the tanks. Two years later, even his country had ceased to exist.

★

For a period of forty years in occupied Eastern Europe—and seventy in the Soviet Union—authorities in Moscow had attempted to build a utopian society devoted, in theory, entirely to the common good. Individuals would have no meaningful rights. Virtually everything was to be owned by the state: factories, farms, and power plants; banks, railroads, and airlines; newspapers and television stations; restaurants and bars; shops and supermarkets; children's summer camps and adult sport teams. The nonprofit sector and civic associations were eliminated and, in the more hard-line countries, weren't reestablished until after 1989. Any organization that stood between the state and the individual—whether Boy Scouts or Rotary Clubs, foundations or charities, labor unions, private schools or village churches—was disbanded or replaced with state- or party-controlled entities.

Soviet communism was forced upon the countries of Eastern Europe and the Balkans at gunpoint at the end of World War II. On a psychological level, it demanded that every individual abandon his or her own superego—the part of our psychical makeup that acts as our conscience and moral compass and arbiter of social norms in battles with the primal urges of the id—and replace it with that provided by the Communist Party. The system, Czechoslovak dissident Václav Havel attested in a 1978 essay that landed him in jail, "draws everyone into its sphere of power, not so they may realize themselves as human beings, but so they may surrender their identity in favor of the identity of the system, so they may become agents of the system's general automatism and servants of its self determined goals."[7]

John Kósa, a Harvard Medical School sociologist who experienced the Soviet takeover of his native Hungary, wrote poignantly about how the Soviets sought to accomplish this. Every group—

whether country club, fishing party, or street gang—has its own collective superego, a set of values, goals, etiquette, and norms accepted by the group. "Through membership, a person accepts the norms of the group as part of his individual superego; in other words, he 'internalizes' them," Kósa wrote in 1962. "Some people cooperate sincerely and eagerly, some more or less reluctantly. . . . Those who seem to follow the superego most perfectly usually become leaders of the group."[8]

In a liberal democracy like the United States, individuals are members of many groups simultaneously, including churches, social classes, ethnic groups, sports fandoms, political parties, and the firms where we are employed. A person might say, "I'm a father, an employee of GM, a Republican, an Orioles fan, a Catholic, a trout fisherman, volunteer fireman, and retired marine of middle-class upbringing," and balance the degree to which and contexts in which he identifies with each.

In the radical collectivism of the Soviet system, none of these countervailing allegiances were allowed. Every individual was to take on the Soviet communist superego as his or her own, and could face derision, punishment, and even death if he or she faltered for even a moment. The Communist Party claimed the sole right to formulate society's norms, goals, and values, and permitted no criticism or competition. It is telling that upon securing control of Russia in the aftermath of the 1917 Revolution, the Bolsheviks didn't just liquidate the tsar's family, the aristocracy, and Russia's handful of industrialists; they also ruthlessly dismantled independent professional, occupational, and intellectual associations; labor unions; and even the centuries-old collective farming institutions of the Russian peasants (the *mir*) that some had thought would be the natural building blocks of a communist society in a country lacking an industrial working class.

In the early days of Soviet communism, even the family was targeted for destruction. Parents were encouraged to let the state raise their children, and anyone could permanently deposit his or her offspring in state-run *detskie doma* ("children's houses"), which were in effect poorly staffed and underresourced orphanages. Divorces and abortions were made legal and easy to obtain not because of respect for the autonomy and will of individual adults, but as a means of weakening their loyalty to the family, the only remaining rival to the communist state. State nurseries, kindergartens, schools, and youth organizations were established to co-opt as many family functions as possible, and to increase the state's ability to shape the next generation.[9] New housing—and there was a desperate need for it after the destruction of World War I and the revolution—consisted of communal apartments where unrelated strangers were forced to share crowded kitchens, bathrooms, and living spaces. Children were encouraged to spy on their parents and report any deviant actions or speech to the authorities. Only when the party discovered it lacked the resources and capacity to achieve its vision—many of the children under its care grew to become misfits and criminals—did it concede early child rearing to the family, though it continued to seek to penetrate and condition the Soviet household.[10]

Another key goal of the regime was to create what it called a "New Socialist Man," a selfless, collective-minded, austere, hardworking, and obedient "man of the future" who would help build and sustain the communist utopia. Joseph Stalin, who ruled the Soviet empire from 1924 to 1953, thought young people could be molded into such New Men like clay, through propaganda, education, and experience. Embracing the pseudoscientific theories of Trofim Lysenko, the head of the USSR's Institute of Genetics, Stalin believed that these attributes could be inherited by the conditioned people's children, permanently transforming the character of the Soviet people. (Questioning

Lysenko's anti-Darwinian theory was against the law.) Children were taught not to question the party's analysis of reality and to let the party serve as their moral arbiter. "The scheme," as Kósa would put it, ". . . reduces the individual essence of personality and aims for a society of spirited ants and intelligent robots who work, build, fight, marry, and multiply, but in all their actions miss an essential human trait: the labors of conscience."[11]

Soon after taking power in Russia and, later, Eastern Europe, the Soviets had expelled, imprisoned, or executed all their real internal enemies, so the regime had to find scapegoats within the party itself to blame for its mistakes. Under Stalin and Ceaușescu, purges were common. The best course for anyone who was accused was to immediately accept his or her guilt, and perhaps even confess to additional crimes that he or she had not committed. Arguing one's innocence was tantamount to suggesting that party authorities had erred, which of course was impossible; punishment was much more severe for anyone who did so. When census takers in 1937 diligently and accurately tabulated the population of the USSR, they inadvertently exposed the fact that six to eight million people had vanished—people who had in fact starved to death in the state-engineered famines of 1932 to 1933. The census administrators were charged with sedition, and dozens were shot or imprisoned for having done their assigned task.[12]

By eliminating individual agency, the Soviet system planted the seeds of its own destruction. Since everything was collectively owned, there were no market mechanisms, no supply and demand to organize economic production and social relations. The government had to plan every decision: what to invest in, what resources to extract and where to send them, what farmers should grow and where the produce would be sold, wages and prices, what science should be funded, what the media would report, what artists could create, where each person would live, and how much food their community would receive. If any one part of a supply chain failed, the effects would ripple through the entire system. Innovation, be it to create a better process or an improved product, was discouraged because it might disrupt the carefully laid details of the ongoing five-year economic plan. Meeting production targets was usually more important than producing quality products, or even those that people actually needed. Since these goals were generally increased with every new five-year plan, managers had a strong incentive to hoard inputs against future quotas, further constricting economic activity. Shortages became endemic, as unforeseen events undermined central planners' assumptions, throwing supply chains into disarray.

The judiciary was simply an arm of the secret police and thus under the direction of senior party officials, meaning there was no established rule of law; the law was whatever the party cadres determined at any given moment. Soviet Bloc parliaments had no independent existence either, and even the party congresses where policies were supposedly set were in reality theatrical stages, where key decisions that had already been made in private by senior leaders at their hunting lodges were presented.

The most devastating critique of this tyrannical system came from Milovan Djilas. A Yugoslav communist who had risked his life fighting a guerrilla war against the Nazis, he'd met repeatedly with Stalin to coordinate military strategy and postwar policy. He had helped build the Federal People's Republic of Yugoslavia, served in its politburo, and in the early 1950s was considered to be Josip Broz Tito's likely successor. Then, in 1953, Djilas began protesting the increasingly undemocratic nature of the Yugoslav system, the increasing opulence in which its leaders were indulging, and their refusal to allow a rival socialist party to stand in elections. He was imprisoned for a year and a half, and again shortly after his release for writing in

support of the 1956 Hungarian uprising, in which reform communists tried to assert independence from Moscow. While in jail he
wrote a full-throated denunciation of what Soviet and Yugoslav communism had become, *The New Class: An Analysis of the Communist
System,* which was published abroad in 1957 and translated into numerous languages. "Bureaucrats in a non-Communist state have political masters, usually elected, or owners over them, while Communists
have neither," Djilas wrote. "The bureaucrats in a non-Communist state
are officials in modern capitalist economy, while the Communists
are something different and new . . . a new owning class." At its
core were "the all-powerful exploiters and masters" who had monopolistic control over all material assets, and showered themselves with
exorbitant salaries, second homes, access to special stores, spas, and
facilities, and, of course, the best housing, furniture, food, and automobiles. Its "methods of rule fill some of the most shameful pages of
history," he charged. "When the new class leaves the historical scene—
and this must happen—there will be less sorrow over its passing than
there was for any other class before it. Smothering everything except what suited its ego, it has condemned itself to failure and shameful ruin."[13]

⭐

This system not only killed tens of millions and scarred hundreds of
millions more but also had direct and consequential effects on political developments in the United States, where émigré Russian and
East European intellectuals and other witnesses of the horrors of radical collectivism formed a radical counterreaction, championing an
extreme form of individualism and denouncing any response that
was more moderate as a slippery slope to slavery.

Perhaps the most militant political philosopher among the Soviet

refugees was Ayn Rand, who was born Alisa Zinov'yevna Rosen-
baum in Saint Petersburg in the closing years of tsarist Russia.
Her parents' steady upward rise was cut short by the 1917 Revolution, and she watched Red Army soldiers loot her father's pharmacy
at gunpoint, seal the doors, and shut it down. Her private school
was closed, and the family maid and nurse were let go. It became
difficult to find food and essentials, and "class enemies" were being
rounded up. Her best friend, Olga Nabokov, Olga's soon-to-be-
famous older brother Vladimir, and their aristocratic family fled the
country, ending Rand's visits to their Florentine mansion, where the
girls had been attended by butlers, governesses, and cooks. Rand's
own family evacuated to the Crimea for three years until it too fell to
communist forces. When they returned to Petersburg, they discovered that the family home and business had been expropriated
and that all their savings—hoarded in tsarist rubles—had become
worthless. Rand enrolled at Petrograd University, where the works
of Friedrich Nietzsche were among her favorites, and in a lucky break
received a visa to visit relatives in the United States in 1924. She
never returned.[14]

From this traumatic experience, Rand would rise to become the
founder and proponent of an extreme individualist creed, which she
called "Objectivism." It insisted that people should not be limited by
moral concerns and should embrace their rapacious self-interest.
Greed was good, and altruism—which she thought the primary
motivating impulse of the Bolsheviks—was the stuff of evil. Talented,
hardworking people like her parents and grandparents had been
forced to sacrifice to support the weak, stupid, and lazy. Even when
Stalin took power in the USSR, eliminating invented enemies, mur-
dering millions on a whim, and building a cult of personality unri-
valed in history, Rand proclaimed the egomaniacal Soviet leader's
regime to be an example of being too "altruistic." Man's "highest

moral purpose," she once told broadcaster Mike Wallace when asked to describe her philosophy, "is the achievement of his own happiness . . . each man must live as an end in himself, and follow his own rational self-interest."[15]

Her influence on radical individualism in America is hard to overstate. Her novel *The Fountainhead* (1943), a story of individual genius struggling against collective mediocrity, became a bestseller and was made into a movie with Gary Cooper. Shortly thereafter she became a lifelong friend and mentor to a young economic analyst named Alan Greenspan, who embraced and practiced her philosophy—with ultimately disastrous results for the U.S. economy—as the second-longest-serving chair of the Federal Reserve in history. Her second novel, *Atlas Shrugged* (1957), championed the Nietzschean Superman against "the mob" and approvingly described a train full of less libertarian-minded passengers being gassed to death in a tunnel accident. The book was panned by critics on the left and right—the *National Review*'s Whittaker Chambers denounced its gas chamber allusions—but it nonetheless became another bestseller and continues to sell staggering numbers of copies. Shortly after it was published Greenspan defended the book in a letter to the *New York Times,* calling it "a celebration of life and happiness. . . . Creative individuals and undeviating purpose and rationality achieve joy and fulfillment. Parasites who persistently avoid either purpose or reason perish as they should." The book was later championed by 2012 Republican vice presidential nominee and future House speaker Paul Ryan—author of a budget that would have slashed social services to pay for tax cuts for billionaires—and embraced by his myriad followers. Rand is also an influence of former Texas congressman Ron Paul, hero of the early twenty-first-century libertarian right, and his son, Rand Paul, U.S. senator from Kentucky. As former *BusinessWeek* investigative reporter Gary Weiss wrote in the aftermath of the 2008 financial collapse, when her followers stopped meaningful Wall Street reform, "Rand had become the Tom Joad of the right. One could almost hear her saying: 'Wherever there's a fight where rich people can get richer, I'll be there. Wherever there is a regulator beating up on a banker, I'll be there.'"[16]

Rand was not alone in her problematic reaction to the despotic collectivism of the Soviet Union. Wichita oil magnate Fred Koch made his initial fortune in the early 1930s upgrading Soviet oil refineries for Joseph Stalin. He was shocked at the conditions he found in the USSR: the food rationing, the shoddy clothes, the constant surveillance. As he put it, it was "a land of hunger, misery, and terror." Over the next twenty years, many of the Soviet engineers he worked with were executed or deported to Siberia. Even his official minder—who had constantly boasted of Soviet plans to infiltrate the American government—was shot for allegedly plotting against the regime. "What I saw there convinced me that communism was the most evil force the world has ever seen and [that] I must do everything in my power to fight it," he observed. Fight it he did, writing pamphlets and giving speeches across the country warning of an internal communist plot and denouncing U.S. nonprofits, foreign aid programs, labor unions, civil rights leaders, and the United Nations as agents or expressions of the Soviet plot to bring totalitarian collectivism to America. Koch became one of the founders of the John Birch Society, the extreme anti-communist group that regarded water fluoridation programs as "a tool of Communist dominion" and suspected President Dwight Eisenhower of being a dedicated communist. Government handouts, Koch warned, turned people "into dependent creatures without them knowing it. The end result is a human race as portrayed by Orwell—a human face ground into the Earth by the large boot of benevolent Big Brother." For Fred Koch, public-mindedness would lead inexorably to a Soviet-style dictatorship of the collective.[17]

He also inveighed against communism at his own dinner table, attempting to instill his worldview in his children, with mixed success. While sons Frederick and Bill would stay clear of politics, Charles, the second eldest, absorbed his father's views, establishing a John Birch Society bookstore in Wichita and giving speeches warning of the dangers of communism. Another son, David, would later say his father was "paranoid about communism," but he still adopted his father's strong views about the evils of government and primacy of the individual. Together David and Charles would spend decades and hundreds of millions of dollars in an attempt to create a libertarian American movement committed to cutting taxes and regulations and ending government entitlement programs, bailouts, deficit spending, and efforts to confront global warming. They showered resources on the libertarian Cato Institute and the Heritage Foundation and founded the Mercatus Center at George Mason University, which issued reports advocating the privatization of Social Security, cuts to social welfare programs and Medicaid, and inaction on climate change. When the Tea Party movement emerged in 2009, the Koch brothers helped fund and organize its largest rallies via their advocacy group, Americans for Prosperity, events at which their father might have felt at home, with speakers denouncing the UN's alleged plot to bring a one-world government and President Barack Obama's supposed aim to institute "socialism." By 2011 the Kochs had become possibly the most powerful force in bankrolling conservative politics.[18]

Reacting to a genuinely despotic form of collectivism, Ayn Rand, Fred Koch, and their acolytes built a powerful countervailing force arguing for an extreme form of individualism. But, fixated as they were on the dangers of an overarching state, they failed to see that the alternative system they were advocating had been tried before, and had also led to its own brand of tyranny.

★

Advocates of extreme individualism often fail to recognize that while an unrestrained state can indeed become a tyrannical force, so too can private individuals. Throughout human history, societies with weak states have become despotisms because they have been unable to prevent wealth, power, and privilege from becoming concentrated in the hands of an elite who are then able to use their influence to seize control of the economy and the state itself. Such elites—the nobility of medieval Hungary and Poland, the ruling families of late twentieth-century Guatemala or El Salvador, for example—can establish near-monopolistic control of the market, national wealth, the courts, the army, and the administrative and lawmaking functions of government, shifting burdens of taxation onto others and expenditures toward themselves. Absent a sense of social responsibility—and the most radical individualists like Ayn Rand demand that they have none—the self-interested individuals at the top will remake society to serve themselves. As the most powerful individuals maximize their liberty, everyone else sees theirs disappear. The result is not unlike the late-stage Soviet system, where a small elite diverted all of society's wealth, power, and privilege to themselves.

Just as unchecked collectivism is destructive of the common good, unchecked individualism eventually leads to a society in which individual freedom is impossible for all but a handful of people at the top. It's no accident that radical libertarianism—unlike communism—has never been put into practice: it's almost entirely unworkable. While critics of radical collectivism can point to dozens of cautionary examples in real-world societies—North Korea, Nazi Germany, the Soviet Union—critics of radical individualism are forced to resort to places like early twenty-first-century Somalia, where state authority has vanished and individuals are "free" to pursue their self-interest, resulting in anarchy and terror, the "state of nature" imagined by Thomas Hobbes, in which life is nasty, brutish, and short. But that's not really fair. The situation in Somalia—or in Albania in 1997, or Sierra Leone and Liberia in the 1990s—didn't come about as the result of excessive devotion to individual liberty, but rather from the collapse of a regime with little interest in such. For a more plausible real-world example of applied radical individualism, one has to look back in time, to America, or rather to one of the Americas that formed on the eastern seaboard in the colonial period.

★

Its founders arrived by sea, anchoring off what is now Charleston in 1670. Like the founders of New England, the Delaware Bay colonies, and the Virginia Tidewater country, they were English, but unlike the others they had not been raised in the British Isles, but rather in England's colonies in Barbados and the Leeward Islands of the Caribbean. Their mission was not to build a Calvinist utopia (like the New Englanders), nor a Quaker one (as in Pennsylvania), nor even to replicate the semifeudal manorial society of the English countryside (as the Tidewater gentry had). Instead, they were transplanting a fully formed social model, an entrepreneurial and capitalistic society emphasizing the liberty of the individual property owner and the vigorous defense of property rights. Their constitution was written by John Locke himself. They championed the republicanism of classical antiquity, of ancient Greece and Rome, where a small elite had the liberty of practicing democracy, while subjugation and slavery were the natural lot of the many. Their new settlement was indeed a slave society, and it would spread its gospel of inequality and hierarchical privilege across the vast region it would colonize: most of what is now South Carolina, Georgia, Florida, Alabama,

Mississippi, and Louisiana; East Texas and the southwestern half of Arkansas; the Mississippi shore of Tennessee; and the creeks of southeasternmost North Carolina. Its hostility to collective values and the ethic of equality placed it on a collision course with other regions of what would become the United States, triggering the most horrific war in our history and political and social conflicts that continue to be fought today.

At the time the Deep South was founded, Barbados was the most wealthy, populous, and controversial English colony in the Americas. It originated in 1627 as a simple community of peasant farmers eking out an existence growing poor-quality tobacco, cotton, and pigs. But in the 1640s, Dutch traders showed the Barbadians how to plant sugar, and took some of them on tours of plantations in Dutch-controlled northern Brazil, where chain gangs of African slaves did the backbreaking work of tending and harvesting the cane fields in the broiling equatorial sun. Sugar, unlike tobacco, fetched a high price in both England and the Netherlands, and gave those who first mastered its production the means to buy up much of the remaining land on the twenty-one-by-fourteen-mile island. Labor was a problem, however. In Virginia, for example, indentured servants were willing to toil under often brutish masters for years because of the promise of receiving land when their contracts expired. In Barbados, however, there was no more land to be had, so English, Welsh, and Scottish servants avoided the place. Most of the laborers who wound up on the island had come involuntarily, Irish deported by English authorities either because they were prisoners of war, petty criminals, or simply vagrants. When this supply ran out, merchants took to kidnapping children, which resulted in "Barbadozz'd" having the same meaning in the late seventeenth century as "shanghaied" would in the early twentieth. On the island they were abused, cheated, and even murdered by their masters, whose kin and social peers were in charge of law enforcement and the courts. There were frequent servants' revolts, including one in 1649 that nearly put an end to the planters' regime. A new labor source had to be found.[19]

Fortunately for the Barbadian planters, they were by now wealthy enough to be able to purchase and import hundreds of slaves to work the fields—men and women treated not as servants but as property. As such, their slaves had no rights or "liberties" under the slave codes the Barbadians invented, which became the template for English colonies elsewhere. Blacks were "heathenish, brutish and an uncertaine, dangerous kinde of people," the law stated. They could be beaten, tortured, or worked to death if the planters pleased, and sugar was so profitable that it often made economic sense to do so. "Our English here doth think a Negro child the first day it is born to be worth £5," a visitor to the island in 1655 reported. "They cost them nothing to bring up, they always go naked. . . . They sell them from one to the other as we do sheep."[20]

The great planters became staggeringly rich and earned a reputation throughout the English empire for immorality, arrogance, and excessive displays of wealth. John Dickinson of Pennsylvania, one of the founding fathers, dismissed the Barbadians as "cruel people . . . lords vested with despotic power over myriad vassals and supported in pomp by their slavery." Other visitors to the island observed that the local gentry lived more sumptuously than their counterparts at home, while commenters in England complained that they were buying up knighthoods and estates. Many indeed returned to England to become absentee landowners and effective lobbyists at Parliament and the Court, which allowed them to impose stiff property requirements to vote or hold office. The social realm on the island was also highly libertine in this profit-driven society. "Paying but scant attention to religion or other social and cultural institutions, Barbados and the Leeward Islands were notorious for their riotous and abandoned styles of life," as historian Jack Greene put it. "The entire society was organized for profit."[21]

However, by the late 1660s, with no land left for new plantations in Barbados or the Leeward Islands, the planters' younger sons had to leave home to find their fortunes. Hundreds of them accordingly emigrated to the new colony that English officials and cartographers were already calling "Carolina in the West Indies."

In what is now Greater Charleston, they replicated the slave society they had left behind, but on the subtropical shores of a continent with plenty of room for expansion. The Carolina colony's founding constitution was written by Locke and envisioned a multitiered society of gentlemen and serfs, with the former granted "absolute authority over his slaves." Under the charters of government, slaveholders were ensured to have the largest landholdings, as the document provided that they would receive 150 acres for each servant or slave they brought to the new colony. By the mid-1680s, three-quarters of the colony's plantations were held by Barbadian families, with the highest concentrations in the most valuable areas around Charleston and Goose Creek. On the eve of the American Revolution, per capita wealth in the Charleston area, concentrated in the hands of the planter elite, was a staggering £2,338, more than quadruple that of the Chesapeake colonies and six times that of New York or Philadelphia. Like Barbados, it was a materialistic, grasping, and individualistic place, with the gentry aggressively competing with one another for dominance, and the merchant classes striving to join the elite. "Their whole Lives are one continued Race: in which everyone is endeavoring to distance all behind him; and to overtake or pass by, all before him. . . . Every Tradesman is a Merchant, every Merchant is a Gentleman, and every Gentleman one of the Noblesse," the *South Carolina Gazette* observed in 1773. "Between Vanity and Fashion the species is utterly destroyed."[22]

★

The society the Barbadians established spread across America's subtropical lowlands, creating a distinct Deep Southern regional culture that persists to this day. The Deep South in the antebellum period was an extreme individualist's dream. The purpose of the state was limited to the protection of private property through the provision of courts, circumscribed police functions, and military defense. Individuals at the top of the social pyramid were highly protective of their own liberties, uninterested in those of others, and hostile to the notion of human equality.

Taxes were extremely low, and were designed to spare those most able to pay them. The slave lords who controlled the colonial South Carolina legislature taxed merchants and other townspeople on the actual value of their property and assets, but imposed a flat tax on rural land based on its acreage, not its worth, meaning that a poor farmer with a hundred acres of forest in the hilly frontier paid the same tax as a planter with a highly profitable hundred-acre rice-growing plantation and manor house. Under pressure, legislators undid this disparity after the Revolution, but planters refused to allow assessors to examine their manors to determine the true value of their holdings.[23]

With scant taxes collected, there were very few public services. Taxpayer-financed public schools had been established across New England in the early seventeenth century; in the colonial Deep South they did not exist at all, and in some states were not established until the 1870s, largely because of the strong individualistic spirit of the white, property-owning heads of household who were the only people allowed to vote there. As Clement Eaton, a mid-twentieth-century historian of the American South, explained, "It was regarded as the duty of the individual and not of the state to see that his children were educated." Members of the planter oligarchy hired tutors for their children and sent them to private academies, preferably the elite ones back in England, and secured public funding for the colleges their children later attended. Most lower- and middle-class whites received the educations they could afford. As late as 1850 only 10 to 16 percent of white children in the seven states dominated by the Deep South were enrolled in public school, compared to 60 to 90 percent of children overall in the United States. As a consequence, white adult illiteracy in the Deep Southern states stood at 13 to 26 percent (and 53 to 63 percent for all adults); in Massachusetts— the least literate New England state—the overall rate of illiteracy was less than 5 percent, while in New Hampshire it was 1.7 percent. The Deep Southern elite considered an uneducated population to be a good thing, and actively blocked efforts to increase the literacy of poor whites. When settlers in the uplands of South Carolina, which had been settled by independent Scots-Irish farmers and herders, asked state legislators in 1855 to grant their communities the right to tax themselves to provide common schools for their children, the planters who controlled the body refused on the grounds that only they had the power to impose taxes.[24]

Because state law enforcement, courts, and prisons were so underfunded, people took the law into their own hands, and security and police work were largely carried out by privately organized militias, plantation overseers, and lynch mobs. On the eve of the Civil War, Florida's white-on-white murder rate reached a shocking 86 per 100,000 inhabitants—higher than the overall rate in the world murder capital in 2009, Honduras (66.8), and nearly twenty times the adult rate in the United States in 2012 (4.7). For decades, Deep Southern voters and legislators resisted spending money to build state penitentiaries because of their preference for violent punishments and their deep-seated suspicion of government power; in 1860,

South Carolina was the only state not to have built a single one. Across the Deep South, slaves were overwhelmingly tried in private settings by their masters, who were allowed to punish or even kill them (but had to pay penalties if they maimed or killed those belonging to someone else).[25]

As Deep Southern governments were forbidden to interfere in the economy or society, economic and social relations were almost entirely unregulated. A glaring exception to this official lack of involvement was the aggressive criminalization of speaking, writing, or disseminating any ideas that questioned the ownership of property in the form of other humans. Under an 1830 Louisiana law it was illegal to say anything from the pulpit, bar, bench, or stage that might produce discontent among the enslaved. In Georgia, Governor Wilson Lumpkin spoke in support of a similar bill, warning legislators that if they did not use force against antislavery writers, "have we not reason to fear that their untiring efforts may succeed in misleading the majority of people . . . and finally produce interference with the constitutional rights of the slaveholders?" The "freedom to own slaves"—an assertion of the individual rights of the property holder—trumped the freedom of speech in the Deep South and even on the floor of the U.S. House of Representatives, where South Carolina congressmen successfully imposed a "gag rule" on antislavery speeches or petitions, which remained in place for six years.[26]

The oligarchy's fixation on individual liberty and the sanctity of property was so extreme that it handicapped the Confederacy's ability to defend itself and its political system. Faced with an existential crisis, the government of the Confederate States of America attempted to take emergency measures to ensure the survival of the newly minted nation, but ran afoul of Deep Southern taboos against empowering government or circumscribing individual property rights. As the Civil War dragged on, food supplies dwindled, including those for soldiers in the field, but many planters refused official requests to grow grain instead of their primary cash crop, cotton. Confederate officers begged planters to loan the army slaves to build critical fortifications, but were rebuffed. Forced in the spring of 1862 to pass a conscription law, the government in Richmond was roundly attacked by Deep Southern governors and even Confederate vice president Alexander Stephens of Georgia, who wrote that the measure made it "a mockery to talk of states rights and . . . constitutional liberty." (The law was quickly amended to exempt one able-bodied male on any plantation with twenty or more slaves.) In 1863, with a full-scale Union invasion well under way, the CSA empowered the army to seize grain and other goods for the war effort; when an officer presented South Carolina planter James Henry Hammond with an order for a share of his corn, he tore it up, tossed it out the window, and declared that submitting to it meant "branding on my forehead 'Slave.'" Richmond, others said, should make fewer, not greater demands on the slave lords, as they would provide for the nation's defense only voluntarily. "The sacrosanctity of slave property in this war," Assistant Secretary of War John A. Campbell observed, "has operated most injuriously to the Confederacy."[27]

★

Because of their focus on the state as the sole agent of tyranny, libertarians and Ayn Randers would expect a society so committed to small government and private property to have been the epitome of individual freedom and prosperity. This was of course not the case. While a weak state will never become a collectivist dictatorship like the Soviet Union or Nazi Germany, it will also prove no match for another common source of tyranny: the rich and powerful, who in the effort to maximize their own freedom will quickly deprive most everyone else of the same, either by monopolizing the means of advancement or by explicitly redefining who is entitled to the benefits of being a free individual. The result, for the Deep South and so many other societies, past and present, is a despotism of the elite, where an oligarchy is free to do what they will to everyone else.

The Deep Southern oligarchy was passionate about a certain type of individual freedom: their own. Over time they developed an increasingly restrictive definition of which individuals had the capacity to live free. Drawing on the West Indies precedent, they denied those of African descent individual rights on grounds of racial inferiority. They saw no contradiction between their love of individual liberty and rejecting it for others. "That *perfect* liberty they sigh for," Abraham Lincoln observed in 1854, was "the liberty of making slaves of other people." South Carolina's firebrand senator John C. Calhoun would not have disagreed. "Liberty when forced on a people unfit for it would instead of a blessing be a curse . . . the greatest of all curses," he wrote, adding that "nothing can be more unfounded and false" than "the prevalent opinion that all men are free and equal."[28]

Using this logic, the Deep Southern elite progressively narrowed the set of people considered capable of practicing and enjoying individual freedom. With the weak Deep Southern colonial and state governments entirely under their control—and the U.S. Bill of Rights held to constrain only the federal government—there was no one to stop them from doing so. A person of African descent was from the outset considered incapable of self-rule, and by the early nineteenth century was believed to benefit greatly from slavery, without which, South Carolinian intellectual William Gilmore Simms asserted, he would return "to the condition of cannibal Africa from whom he has been rescued." By the 1850s, blacks were deemed to be not fully human under the pseudoscientific theory of "polygenesis," which held that the various races were in fact separately evolved species, and the negro was the most inferior of them all. The "great truth," Alexander Stephens would assert, is "that slavery, subordination to the superior race, is [the Negro's] natural and moral condition."[29]

This point of view was vigorously and publically refuted at the time by educated African Americans who had either been born in or escaped to regions where slavery was illegal. The most famous of them, the fugitive Tidewater slave Frederick Douglass, spoke against slavery across Britain, returning to the United States after abolitionists there purchased his freedom from his former master. He then published an abolitionist tract and went on a speaking tour across the northernmost tier of the country, arguing that the immorality of slavery was self-evident. "What, am I to argue that it is wrong to make men brutes, to rob them of their liberty, to work them without wages, to keep them ignorant of their relations to their fellow men, to beat them with sticks, to flay their flesh with the lash, to load their limbs with irons, to hunt them with dogs, to sell them at auction, to sunder their families, to knock out their teeth, to burn their flesh, to starve them into obedience and submission to their masters?" he asked white audiences. "Must I argue that a system thus marked with blood, and stained with pollution is wrong? No . . . I have better employments for my time and strength." The Constitution was a "glorious liberty document," he asserted, and thus its very spirit prohibited slavery. Others rejected racial categorization altogether. "We rejoice that we are colored Americans, but deny that we are a 'different race of people,' as God has made of one blood all nations that dwell on the face of the earth and hence has no respect of men in regard to color," a large group of New York City's residents wrote Abraham Lincoln in 1862 to protest his support for a postwar deportation of black Americans to Africa. Such arguments, moral, racial, or constitutional, were controversial in the northern nations, but they could not even be discussed in the Deep South.[30]

As the Deep South's planters accumulated wealth and power during the eighteenth-century rice boom and nineteenth-century cotton one, they continued to maximize their individual liberty by constraining everyone else's. In most of the colonies in the region, there were stiff property requirements to be allowed to vote, and progressively more stringent ones to stand for various levels of office, under the theory that the people who owned the country should be the ones to govern it. South Carolina maintained this exclusionary system right up to the Civil War. Power was concentrated in the state legislature, but the districts were designed so that the plantation parishes received nearly all the representation, and the increasingly populous backcountry of yeoman Scots-Irish farmers got very few seats. To run for legislature in the early nineteenth century, one had to have five hundred acres and ten slaves or real estate valued at £150 after debts; at a time when a typical American laborer made the equivalent of £20 a year, state senators needed a £300 estate, and governors a £15,000 one. In turn, this planter-dominated legislature—not the public—chose all state and local officers, the state's two U.S. senators, and delegates to the electoral college to choose the president.[31]

Facing increasing criticism of slaveholding in the mid-nineteenth century, Deep Southern leaders developed an elaborate defense for human bondage, one that did not limit itself to blacks. James Henry Hammond, a former governor of South Carolina, published a seminal book in 1845 arguing that enslaved laborers were happier, fitter, and better looked after than their free counterparts in Great Britain and the northern states. The latter, Hammond said, were ruthlessly exploited by industrial capitalists who, unlike slave lords, were under no obligation to look out for the interests of people they did not own. Since the working classes of the North weren't kept in bondage, they also posed a risk to society, ever ready to rise up in support of populist political causes, strikes, or possibly revolution, threatening "Republican institutions." Enslaved labor, by contrast, was docile and disenfranchised, the "foundation" of what Hammond termed a "well-designed and durable 'Republican edifice.'" The white poor and laboring classes, Hammond asserted in an argument widely embraced among the Deep Southern oligarchs, should be enslaved for their own good, and would find it "a most glorious act of emancipation." One wonders, if the Confederacy had avoided the war and gone its own way, whether this theory might have been put into practice.[32]

But when South Carolinians foolishly fired on the American flag at Fort Sumter, previously sympathetic or ambivalent regions of the country turned on the Deep South and rallied to the Union cause, triggering a war that otherwise might not have taken place. The result was a disaster for the federation, and especially the Confederacy, resulting in hundreds of thousands dead, cities in ruins, the destruction of the Confederate economic system, and a Yankee occupation that sought to "reconstruct" the South in their own image. The Yankees would fail in that effort, and the former Confederacy would restore and defend a racial caste system right into the 1960s. In the Deep South, the oligarchs would return to power, forming a determined voice for laissez-faire economic and social policy that continues to shape American politics today.

As different as they were, the Soviet and antebellum southern systems had several things in common. They were profoundly undemocratic, distinctly illiberal in their lack of interest in the civil rights and liberties of the vast majority of their citizenries, profoundly unfair in their distribution of national wealth, and ultimately unable to compete, economically, militarily, or diplomatically, against less autocratic external rivals. Each society denigrated one or the other of the two vital components of mass human freedom—individual rights in the case of the Soviet Union, the collective good in the case of the Deep South—putting each on an inevitable track to tyranny.

Their lesson for humanity is that liberal democracy requires balance between freedom's competing mandates. For Americans, however, negotiating this balance is complicated by the fact that we are not one nation, but several, each with its own views on where the balance point should lie. The first step in finding a solution to our national deadlock is to understand these divides.

# CHAPTER 3

# The Rival Americas

If both individualism and collectivism, taken to extremes, lead to tyranny, how do we build and maintain a free and good society? The answer, of course, is to achieve balance between these two forces. There is a happy equilibrium point out there for any society, where government is accountable to its people and respectful of individual rights and yet strong enough to maintain the free markets and structural equality that nourish liberal democracy.

Every liberal society has a different "sweet spot." Japan and South Korea emphasize the common good far more than the United Kingdom or Canada, where individualism is broadly celebrated. The United States as a whole is one of the more individualistic places on earth, with a pantheon of rugged individualists—Davy Crockett, Horatio Alger's characters, John Wayne—at the heart of its national mythos and a welfare system much weaker than that of any of its peer nations. But the American effort to achieve consensus on the appropriate balance between individual and collective freedom is hampered by the simple fact that America is not a unitary society with a single set of broadly accepted cultural norms, like Japan, Sweden, or Hungary. It's a contentious federation comprising eleven competing regional cultures, most of them centuries old, each with a different take on the balance between individual liberty and the common good. This makes understanding the debates in our country—past as well as present—unusually difficult, especially as few are aware of the true contours of our fractious regional cultures and the conditions in which the dominant ethos of each was forged.

We're accustomed to thinking of American regionalism along relatively straightforward Mason-Dixon lines: North against South, Yankee blue against Dixie gray or, these days, red. The reality is more complicated than that, and not just because this paradigm excludes the western half of the country. In the East alone there are massive, obvious, and long-standing cultural fissures within states like Maryland, Pennsylvania, Delaware, New York, and Ohio. Nor are cultural fault lines reflected in the boundaries of more westerly states. Northern and downstate Illinois might as well be different planets. The coastal regions of Oregon and Washington have more in common with each other and with the coasts of British Columbia and Northern California than they do with the interiors of their own states. Austin may be the state capital, but Dallas, Houston, and San Antonio are the hubs of the Three Texases, while citizens of the Two Missouris can't even agree on how to pronounce their state's name. The conventional, state-based regions that are the basis for much of our political and social discussion—North, South, Midwest, Southwest, West—are inadequate, unhelpful, and ahistorical.

The real, historically based regional map of our continent respects neither state nor international boundaries, but it has profoundly influenced our history since the days of Jamestown and Plymouth, and continues to dictate the terms of political debate today. I spent years exploring the founding, expansion, and influence of these regional entities—stateless nations, really—while writing a previous book, *American Nations: A History of the Eleven Rival Regional Cultures of North America*. It demonstrated that our country has never been united, either in purpose, principles, or political behavior. We've never been a nation-state in the European sense, but rather a federation of nations, more akin to the European Union than the Republic of France, and this confounds collective efforts to find common ground and campaigns to force one component nation's values on the others. Once you become familiar with the real map (see pages 60–61), you'll see its shadow everywhere: in linguists' dialect maps, cultural anthropologists' maps of the spread of material culture, cultural geographers' maps of religious regions, and the famous blue county/red county maps of nearly every hotly contested presidential election of the past two centuries. Understanding America's true component "nations" is essential to comprehending the Tea Party movement, just as it clarifies the events of the American Revolution or the Civil War.[1]

Our regional divides stem from the fact that the original clusters of North American colonies were settled by people from distinct regions of the British Isles—and from France, the Netherlands, and Spain—each with their own religious, political, and ethnographic characteristics. For generations, these discrete Euro-American cultures developed in remarkable isolation from one another, consolidating their own cherished principles and fundamental values, and expanding across the eastern half of the continent in nearly exclusive settlement bands. Some championed individualism, others utopian social reform. Some believed themselves guided by divine purpose; others espoused freedom of conscience and inquiry. Some embraced an Anglo-Protestant identity, others ethnic and religious pluralism. Some valued equality and democratic participation, others deference to a traditional aristocratic order modeled on the slave states of classical antiquity. Throughout the colonial period and the early

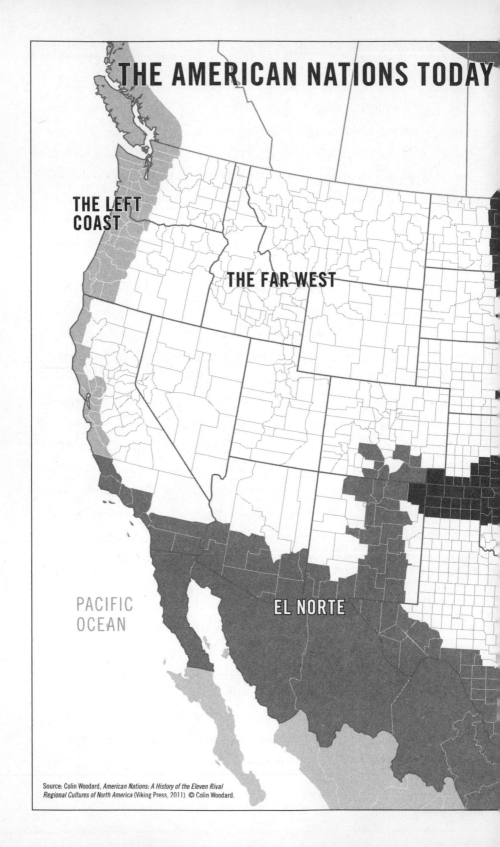

# THE AMERICAN NATIONS TODAY

THE LEFT
COAST

THE FAR WEST

PACIFIC
OCEAN

EL NORTE

Source: Colin Woodard, *American Nations: A History of the Eleven Rival Regional Cultures of North America* (Viking Press, 2011) © Colin Woodard.

Republic, they saw themselves as competitors—for land, settlers, and capital—and even as enemies, taking opposing sides in the English Civil War, the American Revolution, and the War of 1812. Nearly all of these regional cultures would consider leaving the Union in the eighty-year period after Yorktown, and two went to war to do so in the 1860s. There's never been an America, but rather several Americas, and today there are eleven.

★

Founded on the shores of Massachusetts Bay by radical Calvinists as a new Zion, since the outset the nation I call **Yankeedom** has put great emphasis on perfecting earthly society through social engineering, individual self-denial for the common good, and the aggressive assimilation of outsiders. It has prized education, intellectual achievement, community (rather than individual) empowerment, and broad citizen participation in politics and government, the latter viewed as the public's shield against the machinations of grasping aristocrats, corporations, and would-be tyrants. From its New England core, it has spread with its settlers across upper New York State; the northern strips of Pennsylvania, Ohio, Illinois, and Iowa; parts of the eastern Dakotas; northward into the upper Great Lakes states; and eastward across much of the Canadian Maritimes.

The early Puritans believed they had a covenant with God, that they were a chosen people tasked with creating a more perfect society here on earth, a "city upon the hill," a beacon for humanity to follow in troubled times. From the beginning, they attempted to accomplish this through collective institutions, with the common good invariably taking precedence over individual freedom when the two came into conflict. The point of the New England experiment was to maintain the freedom of the community, which to the region's founders meant remaining ever vigilant against the formation of an aristocracy, which in turn demanded restraint on the avarice of individuals.

Early Yankees tended to settle areas not as individuals, but as family units traveling with groups of friends and neighbors, sometimes as a "village on the move," often led by their Puritan, Congregational, or Presbyterian preacher. On arriving at the frontier—eastern Massachusetts in the early seventeenth century, western New York a half century later, the Western Reserve of Ohio in the late eighteenth century, or Michigan in the early nineteenth—they divided the land nearly equally among themselves, levied taxes, and promptly constructed a public school, meetinghouse, and common pasture. Each town was from the outset a tiny republic onto itself, wherein elected committees decided everything from where the public roads, churches, town greens, and schoolhouses would be located to how to levy, collect, and spend taxes, and to raise and organize the militia. The local church congregation was also completely self-governing, with no external hierarchy to which to report. Whereas in other regions, counties held considerable power and towns had little, if any, in New England and much of Yankeedom counties had few powers at all so as to confound the emergence of unaccountable political forces. To this day, many small towns in New England maintain a town meeting form of government, where the people themselves assemble as legislators and vote on all substantive decisions directly. Government, to the Yankee mind, was conceived not as the enemy but rather as an embodiment of its citizenry.[2]

Indeed, Yankees would come to have a faith in government and public institutions to a degree that was unimaginable to the people of other regions. Government, New Englanders believed from the outset, could defend the public good from the selfish machinations of moneyed interests. It could enforce community standards through

the prohibition or regulation of undesirable activities, from adultery
and swearing in the sixteenth century to slavery and drinking in the
nineteenth. It could create a better society through public spending
on infrastructure and schools. Even the pursuit of profit—a subject
with which the Yankee elite was obsessed—was conceived as being
not a private endeavor but a civic responsibility, part of the continu-
ing duty of building the New Zion promised by Puritan founder John
Winthrop in the sermon he gave upon stepping off the boat in 1630.
"Wee must be knitt together in this work as one man," Winthrop
preached. "Wee must be willing to abridge our selves of our superflu-
ities, for the supply of others necessities . . . uphold a familiar Commerce together . . . delight in eache other, make other's conditions our
owne, rejoyce together, mourne together, labour and suffer together,
allwayes haveing before our eyes our Commission and Community
in the worke, our Community as members of the same body."[3]

Here was a society that prized the common good, distrusted the
selfish motivations of individuals, and aspired to lead America and
the world to the light.

Established by the Dutch at a time when the Netherlands was the most
sophisticated society in the Western world, the regional culture I call
**New Netherland** has displayed its salient characteristics throughout
its history: a global commercial trading culture—multiethnic, multireligious, and materialistic—with a profound tolerance for diversity and
an unflinching commitment to the freedom of inquiry and conscience.
Today it comprises Greater New York City, including northern New
Jersey, western Long Island, and the lower Hudson Valley. Like seventeenth-century Amsterdam, it emerged as a leading global center of
publishing, trade, and finance, a magnet for immigrants, and a refuge

for those persecuted by other regional cultures, from Sephardim in the seventeenth century to gays, feminists, and bohemians in the early twentieth. Not particularly democratic or concerned with great moral questions—it tolerated slavery and defended the Deep South until the 1861 attack on federal troops at Fort Sumter—it nonetheless has found itself in alliance with Yankeedom in defense of a shared commitment to public-sector institutions and a rejection of evangelical prescriptions for individual behavior.

The early New Netherlanders, to a remarkable degree, struck a balance between individualistic aspirations and the common good. A colony founded, owned, and ruled by a corporation, the Dutch West Indies Company, it was organized to earn profits for its shareholders. When some of its early directors tried to rule as authoritarian bosses, treating its polyglot inhabitants as employees, the citizenry would have none of it. The "establishment of an arbitrary government among us," they wrote in a 1653 protest, "crushed our spirits and disheartened us in our labors and our callings so that we, being in a wilderness, are unable to promote the good of the country with the same zeal and inclination as before." Dutch authorities, they insisted, had the duty "to promote the welfare of their subjects," and therefore had to uphold the civil liberties of "every freeborn man" against the company's governor. They won the day.[4]

Unlike the English Puritans in New England, the New Netherlanders didn't expect much self-government—there were no representative assemblies and, for much of the Dutch period, no municipal government—but they did expect what did exist to provide for the common good. Their successful protests against the authoritarian rule of the West Indies Company argued that without change "this country will never flourish." As soon as they won the right to establish a municipal government in 1653, they undertook a series of public works projects—the creation of a wall against the English (where

Wall Street now lies), the paving of the streets with cobblestones, the building of a proper canal through the middle of the settlement, and a wharf for the oceangoing ships upon which the colony's prosperity depended. A series of laws were passed that coerced individuals on behalf of the common good: Thatch roofs had to be converted to tiles (to prevent major fires in the densely packed town), and street-front chicken coops and pigsties had to be removed (for aesthetic and health reasons). As New York grew in the late eighteenth and early nineteenth centuries, public works and ordinances became all the more essential to maintaining safety and prosperity in an increasingly crowded city.[5]

More important, New Netherlanders constrained their government with strong and explicit protections of individual liberties, which they believed to be their birthright. The 1653 protestors asserted their rights as "freeborn" men to assemble and to protest against the company boss's violations of property rights. When England conquered New Netherland—first in 1664 and permanently in 1674—its people managed to negotiate guarantees for a long list of individual liberties: protections against the arbitrary seizure of property and the quartering of troops in homes, guarantees of trial by jury, and the freedom of religion. In the aftermath of the American Revolution, residents of the New Netherland section of New York spearheaded the passage of a state law granting additional rights, including free elections, freedom of speech for legislators, and the guarantee that any new taxes could be imposed only by the people's legislative representatives. Not surprisingly, it was New York that insisted on the inclusion of a Bill of Rights to the proposed U.S. Constitution. A multireligious society with a tradition of free presses and a historical experience of foreign occupation and authoritarian-minded corporate governors, New Netherlanders were—and remain—attuned to the importance of protecting civil liberties in maintaining a free society.[6]

Finally, New Netherland was, perhaps more than any other colonial culture, a socioeconomically mobile society. The elite families who became dominant in the late seventeenth century hadn't inherited their privileges from forebearers, but had been founded by what was then a particularly Dutch type of personality: the self-made man. The founder of the Van Cortlandt dynasty arrived as a soldier, took up carpentry, and eventually became the city's mayor. Frederick Philipse was a butcher turned pawnbroker who died the wealthiest man in the city, with a slave plantation in Barbados and a manor home in Yonkers. The first Vanderbilt was an indentured servant and the first Van Burens were tenant farmers, yet those individuals begat the wealthiest family in history and the first self-made man to be elected president, respectively.[7]

As members of a highly mobile, outwardly oriented trading society, New Netherlanders have long recognized the need to have both an involved government tasked with looking out for the common good and clear protections for the freedom of the individuals living under it. "Shut your eyes, at least not force people's consciences, but allow everyone to have his own belief, as long as he behaves quietly and legally, gives no offense to his neighbors and does not oppose the government," Governor Peter Stuyvesant was directed in 1663 by his superiors in Holland. "Your province . . . would be benefited by it."[8]

★

**The Midlands**, America's great swing region, was founded by English Quakers, who believed in humans' inherent goodness and welcomed people of many nations and creeds to their utopian colonies on the shores of Delaware Bay. Pluralistic and organized around the middle class, the Midlands spawned the culture of Middle America and the heartland, where ethnic and ideological purity have never been a priority, government has been seen as an unwelcome intrusion, and political opinion has been moderate, even apathetic. An ethnic mosaic from the start—it had a German rather than British majority at the time of the Revolution—it shares the Yankee belief that society should be organized to benefit ordinary people, but rejects top-down government intervention. From its cultural hearth in southeastern Pennsylvania, southern New Jersey, and northern Delaware and Maryland, Midland culture spread through central Ohio, Indiana, and Illinois; northern Missouri; most of Iowa; southern Ontario; and the eastern halves of South Dakota, Nebraska, and Kansas, sharing the border cities of Chicago (with Yankeedom) and Greater St. Louis (with Greater Appalachia).

Like Yankeedom, the Midlands got its start as a utopian project, but one with an entirely different character. With their optimistic take on human nature, William Penn and the early Quaker founders saw little need to coerce individuals to act for the greater good. Indeed, the Quakers themselves were opposed to authority and hierarchy, refusing to address gentlemen and nobles with their honorific titles or to doff their hats to them. As pacifists, they would eventually lose control of the colony's government for their refusal to undertake the most basic of government functions: the defense of the colony from destruction (in their case, from an Indian attack that threatened Philadelphia itself). Whereas early Yankee towns were nucleated to buttress community unity, cohesion, and discipline, Penn allowed colonists to settle in separate tracts, resulting in a dispersed pattern of farms. Settlers from a particular religious sect or part of the world— Welsh or Mennonites, or German Palatines—were allowed to form their own communities to actively practice and preserve their separate identities. In his original constitution for Pennsylvania, Penn vested most power in a large annual legislative assembly, and very little in the governor, reflecting the egalitarian structure of the Quakers' meetings. Order was expected to occur naturally as the result of each person observing the golden rule: to do unto others as you would have done to yourself. Government was relatively weak, and taxation rates among the lowest in colonial America.[9]

The underlying ethos of the Midlander colonies was egalitarian. Family farms—individual and independent—were the primary driver of their rapidly growing economy and the home to most of their population. There were very few large-scale farms. In the 1760s, a time when most plantations in the South Carolina lowlands measured between five hundred and one thousand acres, the average farm size was just 125 acres in southeastern Pennsylvania and in New Jersey, the southern half of which was settled by Midlanders. Inheritance laws encouraged equal partition of estates, discouraging the formation of a Midlander aristocracy.[10]

Here was a community-minded society distrustful of strong government, a nation where people assumed the best in people and therefore could do without one. If the Midlander ethos were to be stated in a single sentence, it would be, "Government, let our communities alone to get on with building a better place."

⭐

Built by the younger sons of southern English gentry, **Tidewater** was meant to reproduce the semifeudal manorial society of the countryside they'd left behind, where economic, political, and social affairs were run by and for landed aristocrats. These self-identified "Cavaliers" largely succeeded in their aims, turning the lowlands of Virginia, Maryland, southern Delaware, and northeastern North Carolina into a country gentleman's paradise, with indentured servants and, later, slaves taking the role of the peasantry. Tidewater has always been fundamentally conservative, with a high value placed on respect for authority and tradition, and very little on equality or public participation in politics. The most powerful nation in the seventeenth and eighteenth centuries, today it is a nation in decline, having been boxed out of westward expansion by its boisterous Appalachian neighbors and more recently eaten away by the expanding Midlands.

The society that took hold in the Chesapeake country in the aftermath of the English Civil War is best described as hierarchically libertarian, a liberal autocracy not unlike that which was taking shape back in England as the divine right of kings was discredited. Landed gentlemen, many aspiring to nobility, had a near-monopoly control over property, power, religious institutions, and the law. They were the masters of their estates, the "heads" with the intellect and wisdom to control the "hands" of their lessers: wives and children, laborers and servants, paupers and slaves. They enjoyed "liberties"—that is, privileges—that others did not, including the avoidance of taxes and corporal punishment, and the ability to stand for public office. These came, however, with the responsibility to guide society, to provide for one's inferiors, and, later, to uphold liberal republican principles.[11]

In England and much of colonial America, it was believed that in a republic, the common good could be entrusted only to extremely wealthy people, on the assumption that since they wanted for nothing, they were naturally possessed of "civic virtue," the ability to act selflessly for the common good. (That landed aristocrats might also make decisions based on their self-interest never seems to have occurred to anyone.) Indeed, being a gentleman meant, by definition, having a steady source of income—preferably in the form of the reliable revenues of a landed estate—that allowed one to live without working. Ungenteel people—even those rich individuals who had to attend to their businesses to keep their income flowing—were believed incapable of rising above their self-interest and so were denied the privilege of standing for office. Thus Virginia and Maryland set stiff property prerequisites for anyone seeking to take part in the election of legislators: a hundred acres of undeveloped land or twenty-five acres, a home, and a working farm in Virginia's case. Another of the hallmarks of a gentleman was a liberal education, which was seen as a requirement for being able to understand the public policy issues of the day.[12]

The role of the wider public was to elect leaders who embodied these virtues. "I go on this great republican principle, that the people will have virtue and intelligence to select men of virtue and wisdom," James Madison would write. "If there be sufficient virtue and intelligence in the community, it will be exercised in the selection of these men; so that we do not depend on their virtue, or put confidence in our rulers, but in the people who are to choose them." Madison and other Tidewater revolutionaries had faith in the common person's ability to vote wisely, and also to have the good sense not to try to stand for office himself. When this faith was shaken in the decades following the Revolution, many of them despaired that much of what they fought for had been lost.[13]

This conception of "republican virtue" helps explain how the enlightened Tidewater gentlemen who played such a decisive role in the American Revolution—George Washington, Thomas Jefferson, James Madison—could at the same time be slaveholders. Slaves had helped them achieve their "virtue" so that they could guide society to everyone's supposed benefit. The "indispensable working class existed as property beyond the realm of politics," the *Atlantic's* Ta-Nehisi Coates observed in a celebrated 2014 essay, a situation that left slaveholders "free to trumpet their love of freedom and democratic values." This conceptual framework also explains why Washington made such displays of disinterest in being elected or reelected president, much less being crowned king. He made himself a living embodiment of classical virtue, resigning his generalship at the end of the Revolution and stepping down at the end of his presidency, both times to return to his manorial duties at Mount Vernon. The key point of all of these gestures was that the objective of government was the pursuit of the public good, not private interest. Theirs was an aristocratic collectivism, a seventeenth-century version of *Downton Abbey,* where the good of the community was foremost but the elite's right to lead was supposed to go unquestioned.[14]

⭐

Founded in the early eighteenth century by wave upon wave of rough, bellicose settlers from the war-ravaged borderlands of Northern Ireland, northern England, and the Scottish lowlands, **Greater Appalachia** has often been lampooned as the home of rednecks and hillbillies. In reality, it is a transplanted culture formed in a state of near-constant warfare and upheaval, characterized by a warrior ethic and a deep commitment to personal sovereignty and individual liberty. From south-central Pennsylvania, it spread down the Appalachian Mountains and out into the southern tiers of Ohio, Indiana, and Illinois, the Arkansas and Missouri Ozarks, the eastern two-thirds of Oklahoma, and on down to the Hill Country of Texas, clashing with Indians, Yankees, and Mexicans along the way. Intensely suspicious of lowland aristocrats and Yankee social engineers alike, Greater Appalachia has shifted alliances based on whoever appeared to be the greatest threat to its freedom; since Reconstruction and, especially, the upheavals of the 1960s, it has been in alliance with the Deep South in an effort to undo the federal government's ability to overrule local preferences.

Generations of Americans have been raised with the myth that our country was founded by highly individualistic frontiersmen, men in coonskin caps and, later, cowboy hats who survived and prospered based on their bravery, hard work, and self-sufficiency. Living in log cabins, defending their families from Indians with their own weapons and courage, they neither sought nor relied on government assistance or the comforts of cities. While this account is entirely untrue for much of what is now the United States, it is an accurate description of the Greater Appalachian frontier, which was dangerous, far removed from the centers of government, and populated by people who treasured their individual liberty and were suspicious of ordering institutions of any kind.

The Scots-Irish and other borderland settlers embraced an extreme libertarian definition of freedom: the right to rule oneself with as little intrusion by law enforcement, courts, and other political institutions as possible. They practiced an "eye for an eye" form of justice in which a wronged party was expected to punish his transgressor himself. As a backcountry proverb brought from north Britain put it, "Every man should be a sheriff on his own hearth"; the corollary to this, as historian David Hackett Fischer has pointed out, was that government institutions, including the actual sheriffs, had relatively little to do. Vigilantes and lynch mobs—the latter named for one Charles Lynch, who dispensed frontier justice upon loyalists in Virginia's Appalachian region in 1789—were socially accepted right into the middle of the twentieth century. Settlements were few and far between for much of the colonial period, the settlers preferring to live on isolated homesteads, and schools, courts, libraries, and other public institutions were correspondingly rare. Leaders— the local elite—relied on their reputations rather than social rank to attract a personal following, usually by having displayed bravery and decisiveness. The inhabitants of this region neither sought nor received much from their governments, and wished to keep it that way.[15]

Moreover, Greater Appalachians were willing to stand up for

their rights, even against powerful opponents. Throughout the colonial era, much of the region was part of one or another colony controlled by the Tidewater or Deep Southern aristocracies. These oligarchs—hierarchical in their thinking, contemptuous of the baser people of the backcountry and highlands—refused to give their Appalachian regions proper representation in the legislatures and passed taxation policies that shifted the burden from wealthy planters to impoverished farmers and herdsmen. In North Carolina during the 1760s, Tidewater counties received ten times the per capita legislative representation as the state's large and rapidly growing Appalachian sections; the backcountry settlers reacted by forming bands of "Regulators" who seized control of their region for three years, beating lawyers, sacking courthouses, and expelling tax collectors, until they were put down in a pitched battle with Tidewater militia. Similar resistance movements formed across the Appalachian frontier, and during the Revolution past grievances fueled a horrific civil war in both Carolinas and Georgia, with ample atrocities. Life on the frontier was, right up into the nineteenth century, strikingly reminiscent of that of the war-torn British borderlands from which the region's settlers had come.[16]

The region's religious heritage buttressed its individualism. When the "Second Great Awakening" spread across the American frontiers in the years after the American Revolution, millions of Americans embraced novel religious forms, inventing new Protestant sects and weakening the established churches—Anglican, Puritan Congregational, Presbyterian, or Quaker—that had been brought from Europe. But while Yankee frontiersmen created collectivist religions aiming to fashion more perfect earthly societies—Millerism, Mormonism, Seventh-day Adventism—Greater Appalachia's people embraced individualistic creeds whereby each person might meet God personally, be spoken to by him or his son, and be guided without the mediation of institutions, a clerical hierarchy, or literary interpretation. In Greater Appalachia—and indeed among the nonelite of the Deep South—the emphasis has been not on improving this world, but on one's personal salvation in the hereafter.

Unruly, populist, and highly libertarian, Greater Appalachia has historically been a cauldron for individualistic political efforts, be it the Regulator movement or the Tea Party one.

⭐

Established by slave lords from Barbados as a West Indies–style slave society, the **Deep South** has been a bastion of white supremacy, aristocratic privilege, and a version of classical republicanism modeled on the slave states of the ancient world, where democracy was the privilege of the few and enslavement the natural lot of the many. It spread apartheid and authoritarianism across the southern lowlands, ultimately encompassing most of South Carolina, Georgia, Alabama, Mississippi, Florida, and Louisiana, plus western Tennessee and southeastern Arkansas, Texas, and North Carolina. Even after its slave and caste systems were dismantled by outside intervention, it has continued to fight for rollbacks of federal power, taxes affecting capital and the wealthy, and environmental, labor, and consumer safety protections.

Described in detail in the previous chapter, the Deep South is a hierarchical libertarian nation. It differs from the Tidewater in that its oligarchy has never had a sense of obligation or responsibility to the rest of society, but rather believes that society exists for and should be structured to suit them. While it shares Appalachia's emphasis on individualism, it is decidedly not egalitarian. If Appalachian people see the world as a battleground in which only the fittest will survive, the Deep Southern oligarchy believes those battles were fought centuries ago, and that their families won. To the victors—society's fittest—therefore go the spoils.

⋆

The oldest of the Euro-American nations, **El Norte** dates back to the late sixteenth century, when the Spanish Empire founded Monterrey, Saltillo, and other outposts in what are now the Mexican-American borderlands. Today this resurgent culture spreads from the current frontier for a hundred miles or more in both directions, taking in South and West Texas, Southern California and the Imperial Valley, southern Arizona, most of New Mexico, parts of Colorado, and the six northernmost Mexican states. Most Americans are aware that the region is a place apart, where Hispanic language, culture, and societal norms dominate; few realize that among Mexicans, *norteños* have a reputation for being more independent, self-sufficient, adaptable, and work-centered than their central and southern countrymen. Long a hotbed of democratic reform and revolutionary sentiment, various parts of the region have tried to secede from Mexico to form independent buffer states between the two federations. Today it has come to resemble Germany during the Cold War: two peoples with a common culture separated from one another by a large wall.

Seventeenth- and eighteenth-century Spain, unlike England and the Netherlands, was an unenlightened, unreconstructed despotism, a centralized monarchy wherein neither the mother country nor its staggering array of American colonies had any representative legislative bodies of any sort. Trade and manufacturing were highly regulated, with special licenses required to engage in most activities—if they were permitted at all—and prices fixed by central officials. Most of El Norte, the far-flung frontier of the empire's already far-flung Mexican viceroyalty, was settled as if it were a lunar base: by militarized missions of farmers, ranchers, servants, and soldiers sent to establish remote installations. Most of the region was ruled by military officers or other outsiders appointed by the distant bureaucracy.[17]

Even when Mexico became independent in 1821, the parts of El Norte that are now in the United States all lacked full statehood and thus institutions of self-government. Under Mexico's regressive 1836 constitution, state legislatures were eliminated, state governors were appointed in Mexico City, and only the wealthy were allowed to stand for office. In Alta California, a Mexican cavalry officer reported that "allowances should be made" because not a single person had "the capital indicated by law in order to become governor, senator, or deputy." Courts remained physically out of reach to the region's people, as serious cases could only be heard by making a journey of several weeks, and local judicial bodies were handicapped by a lack of literate lawyers or judges. "The government of California," an American visitor reported in the 1840s, was "very lax and inefficient . . . and infinitely worse than none." The region's political heritage, right up to the U.S. annexations, was of centralized and completely ineffective government.[18]

More than any other part of Mexico, however, the North aspired to a more democratic future. Life on the arid frontier was less stratified than in central Mexico, and individuals had greater opportunities to engage in entrepreneurship, even if they had to do so through illicit trade with their Deep Southern neighbors over the U.S. border. Disgusted with the centralized authoritarianism of central Mexico, parts of the region attempted to secede to form the Republic of the Rio Grande and, later, the Republic of Texas, intended to be buffer states between the U.S. and Mexican federations. The parts of El Norte that remained in Mexico provided the resistance to turn-of-the-twentieth-century dictator Porfirio Díaz, and many radical exiles fled over the U.S. border to foment extreme leftist ideas of revolution among working-class Hispanics who were by then exploited by a racial caste system imposed by the new American state governments, many of which were dominated by immigrants from the Deep South and Appalachia.[19]

Since the 1960s, El Norte's Spanish-speaking majority has reasserted itself, helping topple the region's caste system and reclaiming its political rights. Its inherited legacy, as Chicano scholar Juan Gómez-Quiñones once put it, is of being "leery of government" while also maintaining "the fairly continuous expectation that government should provide for the general welfare, combined with the practical awareness that it provides for a select number." In El Norte, where family and church ties are strong, and the collectivist impulses of the Catholic Church remain influential, government is seen as an agent of the common good, even if there is little expectation that it will be able to perform its role without prejudice in favor of the region's elites. El Norte is theoretically a swing region, so long as its nonwhite, Spanish-speaking culture is accepted by the competing political actors.[20]

★

Two other regional cultures were established much later—in the mid- and late nineteenth century—and were founded not by European colonizers, but by people from the older, aforementioned regional cultures. Their histories are much shorter, and until the twentieth century, settler populations were sparse, resulting in a lighter cultural footprint. That footprint does, however, exist and exerts a powerful influence on the political ideals of half of what is now the United States.

The first of these areas to be settled was **the Left Coast**, a Chile-shaped nation wedged between the Pacific Ocean and the Cascade and Coast mountain ranges and stretching from Monterey to Juneau. This region was originally colonized by two distinct groups: merchants, missionaries, and woodsmen from New England (who arrived by sea and dominated the towns) and farmers, prospectors, and fur traders from Greater Appalachia (who generally arrived by wagon and controlled the countryside). Yankees expended considerable effort to make it "a New England on the Pacific" but were only partially successful: The Left Coast remains a hybrid of Yankee idealism, faith in good government, and social reform and the Appalachian commitment to individual self-expression and exploration. The staunchest ally of Yankeedom, it battles constantly against Far Western sections in the interior of its home states.[21]

The Left Coast culture defines the common good differently from Yankeedom, as the project of creating a nurturing support system for individual actualization, rather than one to create an ordered community that will keep individual avarice in check. It is, however, very much a communitarian culture, especially in regard to that ultimate common good, the environment. Prior to the first Earth Day in 1970, the entire American environmental movement was based in the more collectivist nations—Yankeedom, New Netherland, the Midlands, and, most of all, the Left Coast. The Sierra Club, the nation's first grassroots group, was founded in San Francisco in 1892; Greenpeace, which spearheaded environmental activism in the 1960s and 1970s, was established in Vancouver, the Sea Shepherds in coastal Washington State, and the Friends of the Earth in the Bay Area. In 1975 the science-fiction writer Ernest Callenbach imagined this part of the world breaking off to form its own state called Ecotopia, where people lived in a steady-state equilibrium with their environment—an idea still nurtured by idealistic separatists today.[22]

★

**The Far West**, the other second-generation nation, is the one part of the continent where environmental and geographic factors trumped ethnographic ones. High, dry, and remote, the Far West stopped the

expansions of the eastern nations in their tracks and, with minor
exceptions, was colonized only via the deployment of vast industrial
resources: railroads, heavy mining equipment, ore smelters, dams,
and irrigation systems. As a result, settlement was largely directed
and controlled by large corporations headquartered in distant New
York, Boston, Chicago, or San Francisco, or by the federal government itself, which controlled much of the land. Because the region
was exploited as an internal colony for the benefit of the seaboard
nations, its political leaders have focused public resentment on the
federal government (on whose infrastructure spending they depend)
while avoiding challenges to the region's corporate masters, who
retain near Gilded Age influence. The Far West encompasses nearly
all of the North American interior west of the 100th meridian, from
the northern boundary of El Norte to the southern frontier of First
Nation, including much of California, Washington, Oregon, British
Columbia, Alaska, Colorado, and Canada's Prairie provinces and all
of Idaho, Montana, Utah, and Nevada.

The Far West's much-celebrated libertarian streak—embodied in
the image of the cowboy individualist, alone against nature and the corruption of distant urban interests—is tempered by the region's dependence on enormous public works projects and government-supported
industries. Massive irrigation, dam, and water transfer projects enabled
cities and water-intensive farms to exist in an arid region. Federally subsidized railroads and, later, highways and airports linked it to distant
markets. World War II and Cold War military spending—from the
nuclear weapons labs of Los Alamos, New Mexico, and Hanford, Washington, to the nuclear missile silos of western Nebraska, and dozens of
military bases in between—became vital to its economy.[23]

The Far West is also a region whose exploiters have been private
as well as public. In the nineteenth and early twentieth centuries,
Anaconda Copper literally ran Montana, buying off judges and pub-

lic officials and dictating rules and regulations that enriched its owners and executives. Logging interests clear-cut the region's federally
owned forests for next to nothing, while oil and gas companies pros-
pected on federally administered Indian reservations, often without
the required royalties ever being paid out to the tribes.

Having thus been exploited, Far Westerners have been highly
attuned to issues of economic fairness. As a result this individualistic
frontier culture was also a hotbed of economic populism, labor
unionism, and other "common good" concerns right up until World
War II. It elected progressive senators like Burton Wheeler of Montana or Idaho's William Borah and enthusiastically endorsed FDR
and the New Deal. Today the region's people are mobilized against
another perceived tormenter, the federal government, led by politicians who promise to get the government out of the way of prosperity and self-reliance by reducing regulations and oversight.

It is, in short, a schizophrenic political culture shaped by colonial
exploitation, one that values civil liberties and seeks a fair shake for
individuals, but also a level playing field and an open public purse for
spending that buttresses the economy. Egalitarian and individualistic—
but not strenuously so—it is in many ways the analog of the Midlands,
only with libertarian rather than communitarian leanings.

★

Two other nations—the Inuit-dominated **First Nation** in the far
north and Quebec-centered **New France**—are located primarily in
Canada and are peripheral to this discussion. Their U.S. enclaves in
northern and western Alaska and southern Louisiana, respectively,
have scant electoral power and little influence on the ongoing
national struggle over individual and collective interpretations of
freedom. Each is on the verge of establishing a nation-state of its

own—Greenland for First Nation, Quebec for New France—and each would be strongly collectivist. Since reasserting their identity in the not-so-quiet Quiet Revolution of the 1960s, the Québécois have built a European-style welfare state, and leveraged Canada to do the same; the province has powerful unions and an economy dominated by huge state-owned companies like energy giant Hydro-Québec. Greenland's Inuit people don't even have private property: All land is collectively owned, and individuals lease the land upon which their homes or businesses are built. Once sufficient oil and mineral resources are discovered to pay for the country's Danish-provided cradle-to-grave welfare state, Greenlanders intend to rule their own lands for the first time in more than three hundred years.[24]

★

The presence of these separate regional cultures—these rival "nations"—has greatly complicated Americans' effort to come to any consensus on where the proper balance should lie between individual freedom and the public good. Most of the other free societies that emerged in the eighteenth and nineteenth centuries each comprised a single dominant culture—the Netherlands or Denmark, for instance— or just two or three, as in Belgium, Switzerland, or the United Kingdom. Reaching a common understanding of how to weigh individual and collective concerns was relatively easy in these less heterogeneous places, to say nothing of later entrants like Japan or South Korea, where social conformity and harmony are themselves cherished values. In America, the differences between our separate cultures on these issues are enormous, which is why we ended up with such a complicated federal constitutional arrangement to begin with.

The tensions that have arisen as a result of these clashing notions of freedom—from the radically egalitarian individualism of Greater

Appalachia to the fundamentally communitarian outlook of Yankeedom or the hierarchical libertarianism of the Deep South—have brought our nation's people to war with one another, and not just in the U.S. Civil War. When the English king and Parliament went to war over the future of republicanism in the 1640s, the Tidewater gentry and Yankee Puritans took opposing sides. When the American Revolution broke out, Midlanders and the Deep Southern oligarchs wanted nothing to do with it, while New Netherlanders rallied behind the empire for fear their individual rights would be trampled on by the unbridled Yankee communitarians who would likely control New York's government if royal authority was overthrown. Yankees themselves would seek to leave the Union during the War of 1812, which came to symbolize their loss of control over federal affairs to the libertarian-minded Tidewater elite. Such tensions continue today, in the battle lines between the regions seen on electoral maps or the geographical plotting of the voting records of members of Congress.[25]

These regional differences divided the founding fathers and created fear and uncertainty in the early years of the Republic, in turn prompting the drafting of a constitution that sought to balance the freedoms of the government, the elite, and the people. Even the genius of men like Thomas Jefferson, James Madison, John Adams, and Alexander Hamilton, however, could not contain these divisions for the next two centuries and beyond. Indeed, even a terrible war and an extended military occupation would prove unable to resolve them.

# CHAPTER 4

# The Elite and the Masses
# (1607–1876)

The people of England's American colonies were subjects of a peculiar regime: a monarchical republic, free in many ways, unfree in others. England itself had a hybrid political culture that dated back to the Norman invasion of 1066, when aristocratic noblemen from what is now France conquered the more egalitarian Anglo-Saxons, who regarded themselves as a "freeborn" people. While the American colonial projects were getting under way, England's monarchs were delivered two major setbacks—losses in the English Civil War of the 1640s (which resulted in a short-lived, rather gruesome republic) and the Glorious Revolution of 1688–89 (when an increasingly despotic king was overthrown and replaced). Royal power had been checked by the vigorous assertion of English liberties, not so much by "the people" but by the kingdom's landed aristocracy. This gave a particular bent to the republican ideas that would be fervently discussed—and ultimately acted upon—by Americans of the Revolutionary era.

John Locke supplied much of the intellectual ammunition for the cause. Locke was a child of the English Civil War, son of a country lawyer who fought against the king as a cavalry officer under Sir John Popham, a West Country aristocrat whose family had led an unsuccessful colonization attempt in Maine in 1607. After the war, Popham took a teenaged Locke under his wing, sponsoring his education at Oxford during Oliver Cromwell's republic. There Locke found an even more powerful aristocratic patron, Ashley Cooper, First Earl of Shaftesbury, who raised Locke to high government positions and recruited him to help write the constitution for one of his properties, the new Carolina colony. As England convulsed between the authoritarian ambitions of the Restoration kings and the modernizing forces of the gentry, Cooper became a major figure in the fight against absolutism, even as he served in the royal court. Locke's political philosophy was literally drafted in the halls of Cooper's home and reflected the concerns of the British aristocracy: that "government"—that is, the monarchy and its bureaucratic appendages—and "the people" were engaged in a zero-sum struggle for the apportionment of liberty. The more liberty and freedom the king had, the less the "people" would possess. By the "people," however, Locke didn't mean everyone living in the realm, but rather the men of property who were capable of exercising freedom: the great nobles, the landed gentry, wealthy merchants, and perhaps the independent farmers who owned their land outright. Such individuals, possessing the prerequisites of what would come to be called "republican virtue," were capable of rational thought and could and should govern themselves. In doing so, Locke argued, they would create a good society.[1]

Of course, that left unsettled the question of what to do about the poor and unvirtuous who formed the majority of the population of the British Isles. At the time, nobles were expelling millions of peasants from their ancestral lands to make way for large commercial farms and sheep pastures. This termination of the mutual obligations of the medieval system made feudal lords into landed aristocrats and turned millions of self-sufficient peasant farmers into landless paupers. Without land, members of this "surplus population" were forced to hire themselves and their children out as laborers at rates so low that most became, in the words of Sir Francis Bacon, little more than "housed beggars." Many streamed to the cities. Stunted by malnutrition—on average they stood six inches shorter and lived half as long as their middle- and upper-class countrymen—they came to be looked upon by the virtuous as an inferior race, their poverty explained by their supposed laziness or immorality rather than their dispossession from the lands their families had likely farmed for dozens of generations. This submerged half of the population had, by definition, no virtue, status, or political rights and were regarded as a nuisance horde that had to be constantly coerced and disciplined. "Everyone but an idiot knows," said eighteenth-century social commentator Arthur Young, "that the lower classes must be kept poor or they will never be industrious."[2]

Seventeenth- and early eighteenth-century English republicans feared their calls for individual freedom and political equality might be seized upon by these unwashed masses, who could, by virtue of their numbers, destroy a nascent republic by pressing for political and economic changes that would supposedly reward sloth, laziness, and criminality. Thomas Gordon and John Trenchard, authors of *Cato's Letters,* one of the most famous arguments for political equality of the time, vehemently opposed the charity schools that allowed a handful of poor children to receive an education, because they "were breeding up beggars to be what are called scholars . . . putting Chimeras and angry notions into the heads of those who ought to have pickaxes in their hands." Locke himself wrote that the causes of

poverty were not the "scarcity of provisions or the want of employment" but "the relaxation of discipline and corruption of manners,
virtue and industry . . . and vice and idleness." His solution, proposed
to the government in 1697, was a new law to arrest all able-bodied
male beggars aged fourteen to forty-nine and to keep them "at hard
labour" until they could be put aboard a naval vessel for three years'
service; maimed men aged fifty and older caught begging would be
imprisoned and "kept at hard labour for three years," while begging
children of either gender would be "soundly whipped." Paupers'
children aged three to fourteen would be sent to special schools to
learn to work—and only to work—where they would be fed a "belly-
ful of bread daily" and "in cold weather, if it be thought needful, a
little warm water-gruel; for the same fire that warms the room may
be made use of to boil a pot of it." Their wages would be withheld to
cover the cost of the gruel. Other passionate republicans had even
more drastic proposals. James Burgh and Andrew Fletcher—both
held in high esteem by Thomas Jefferson—called for the enslavement of the poor, foreshadowing the arguments of the hierarchical
libertarians of the Deep South in the Civil War era.[3]

Such was the intellectual climate in which the founders' generation came of age, where individualism, political freedom, and basic
civil rights were limited to men of property and thus virtue. But by
the 1760s and 1770s, America's regional cultures had wide differences in the proportion of their respective populations that consisted
of aristocrats, lesser propertied families, or the great unwashed. Not
surprisingly, this shaped distinct sets of values in each region in
regard to the aims and legacy of the War of Independence.

The Tidewater gentry's view of the republican question was identi-
cal to that of the English republicans, only they were in a much bet-

ter position to act on it. Their society was very similar to that of provincial England: A handful of allied aristocratic families controlled political and economic affairs, sharing power only with the wealthier members of the small merchant class. The biggest difference from rural England concerned the nature of "the masses." The colonies' poor white population consisted almost entirely of indentured servants or their descendants and was in any case not numerous enough to present a threat to the gentry. Below them was the black laboring class that was of course already enslaved, allegedly for its own good as well as that of society. Indeed, as a result of this arrangement, the Tidewater planters were the most active proponents of republicanism in the British Empire. They had nothing to fear from below, and had been raised to embody the "civic virtue" of classical republican thinking. Republicanism and slavery, as historian Edmund Morgan long ago pointed out, weren't in conflict; under the thinking of the day, they complemented each other. "Virginians could outdo English republicans as well as New England ones, partly because they had solved the problem," Morgan writes. "They had achieved a society in which most of the poor were enslaved."[4]

The Tidewater gentlemen's unique status was threatened by London's efforts to centralize and standardize its colonial empire. Having for generations enjoyed a near monopoly on the politics, courts, and Anglican church vestries of their region, they saw their powers undermined by the arrival of British-appointed bishops and the imposition of new taxes that reduced the profitability of their plantations. Confident of their ability to rule themselves and aware of the vast potential of the expanding frontier, the aristocrats of the western-facing Piedmont—Richard Henry Lee, Patrick Henry, George Washington, and Thomas Jefferson of Virginia, and Thomas Johnson of Maryland—were particularly keen on securing independence from Crown and empire. They would lead the patriot charge, speaking in the language of classical republicanism, and often serving on the battlefield as gentlemen officers. They were soon joined by their more ambivalent lowland peers after Virginia's royal governor, John Murray, issued a proclamation offering freedom to the colony's slaves if they took up arms for the king. (Some ten thousand of these "black loyalists" would ultimately accept this offer, and some would relocate to Nova Scotia and other British colonies at the end of the war.) This represented a manifold threat to the Tidewater aristocracy: an attack on their property rights, a blow to their economic base, a dangerous security threat, and a terrible strike on what, by their thinking, was the underpinning of their own liberty.[5]

The oligarchs of the Deep South, pleased with their social positions within the empire, were generally hostile to revolutionary ideas. Outnumbered by their slaves by three to one—and in parts of South Carolina by nine to one—the slave lords saw British power as their best guarantor of internal and external security. "Independence is not [a] view of America . . . a sober sensible man wishes for," South Carolina planter Henry Laurens wrote in January 1775, adding that his class sought only "reasonable liberty" within the empire. After hostilities broke out in distant Lexington, a wave of fear descended on the region, with newspapers imagining imperial conspiracies to arm the slaves. South Carolinians took control of the colony by simply ignoring the royal governor, but they remained ambivalent about the independence movement. "A republican government is little better than a government of devils," Georgia's delegate to the Continental Congress, John Zubly, declared. Ultimately, Deep Southerners would back independence in order to protect slavery, only to be invaded and occupied in 1779–80, with Georgia even being formally reabsorbed into the empire. But the backcountry of their respective colonies was another matter altogether.[6]

For the Yankees of New England and upstate New York, the classical republican concerns had been successfully addressed. In their well-ordered communities, where individuals had long been compelled to place the public interest ahead of their private ones, Yankees had no hereditary lords, no landed aristocrats, no indentured servants, and vanishingly few slaves. Broadly speaking, most of the population was already in the middle of the social strata: propertied, frugal, hardworking, and "virtuous" in the republican sense. There were no masses to fear or enslave, no lords to force one into tenancy. Its communities were rigorously self-governing. Revolutionary New Englanders, seeing themselves as the hope for humanity, wanted to protect this social order. They were the first to rise up against the British, who had revoked Massachusetts's governing charter and put Boston under martial law. Organized in citizen-led public militia units directed, in Massachusetts, by a newly created provincial assembly, the people of New England were so united in their resistance that the British immediately lost control of the entire region outside occupied Boston. By the spring of 1776, New Englanders had essentially won their independence. Left to their own devices, that might have been the end of their revolution.[7]

Two other regional cultures were not desirous of independence. Midlanders were perfectly happy with London's centralization effort, and the region's multiethnic population saw no advantage and possible danger in their states becoming independent, especially as they shared Pennsylvania, Maryland, and Delaware with less tolerant Appalachian and Tidewater sections. The Midland's pacifistic Quaker and Anabaptist majorities had little interest in taking part in a war, and its leaders attempted to remain neutral throughout the conflict. In New Netherland, public opinion was overwhelmingly loyalist, the British Crown being seen as an effective guarantor of the region's cherished stable of individual rights, especially in the Province of New York, a royal colony that would otherwise be under the sway of upstate's Yankee majority. British forces would use New Netherland as their primary base throughout the war.[8]

And so the conflict began as a series of wars of independence, national liberation struggles fought by three of the aforementioned regional cultures. Their goals—and those of the two nations that did not rebel—were not revolutionary but conservative: to maintain the distinct political, economic, and social relationships each of them had forged over the previous century or more. The only "revolutionary" element was the notion that the newly independent colonies might be republics, not monarchies, just as the Dutch Republic, Renaissance Florence, and Oliver Cromwell's England had been.

For one regional culture, however, a real revolution was in fact in order. Indeed, Greater Appalachia was responsible for the radicalism and democratic ethos of the conflict and its aftermath, setting America on an unprecedented and world-changing course.

In the fifty years prior to the Battle of Lexington, America had experienced the greatest wave of immigration the continent had ever seen. Some 250,000 Scots-Irish and other borderlanders flooded into the backcountry, first into south-central and southwestern Pennsylvania, and later into the western sections of Maryland, Virginia, the Carolinas, and Georgia. They had large numbers of children, completely changing the demographic structure of those colonies, and as they were removed from the established communities closer to the seaboard, cultural assimilation and traditional social control became next to impossible. Many of them soon abandoned their Presbyterian faith, embracing individualistic creeds—Baptist and Methodist—that respected no hierarchical authority and reckoned each of its members personally capable of grappling with consequential issues, without benefit of books or bishops. They also had radical ideas about individual self-worth, dangerous notions that ordinary people could rule themselves directly. The seaboard elite—Midlanders in Pennsylvania; Tidewater gentry in Maryland, Virginia, and North Carolina; Deep Southern planters in South Carolina and Georgia—

saw them as a potential threat to republicanism and held on to power by denying the backcountry settlements appropriate representation in legislatures.[9]

When hostilities broke out, the people of Greater Appalachia struck out at their enemies, foreign and domestic. In Pennsylvania, where they dominated the south-central and southwestern areas of the colony, they were the shock troops of revolution. During the conflict, they marched into Philadelphia and overthrew Pennsylvania's timid Midlander elite. Once in control of the colony, their leaders drafted a radical new constitution that granted Appalachian districts effective control exercised through a single-chamber legislature and thirteen-man executive council whose members served short terms; to ensure the popular will was upheld, Pennsylvania was to have no senate or governor at all. In North Carolina, borderlanders marched on the Tidewater gentry's armies, sometimes carrying the banner of Scotland into battle, which occasionally featured the Scottish motto *Nemo me impune lacessit*—loosely translated as "Don't Tread on Me." In South Carolina and Georgia many took up arms against the Deep Southern oligarchs. Both areas descended into civil war when British armies occupied their respective regions, some seeking to toss out the hated redcoats who'd oppressed their forefathers, others wishing to ally with them against the lowland elites. Only in Virginia did borderlanders make common cause with seaboard leaders, forging an alliance to end British rule and joining Yankees in filling the ranks of George Washington's Continental Army.[10]

General Cornwallis's surrender did not put an end to the Appalachian people's fight for freedom as they understood it: a libertarian democracy wherein government was weak, distant, and both beholden to and run by ordinary people. They scoffed at notions of "civic virtue" and "natural aristocracy," rejected property requirements for white men to vote or hold office, and wanted no part in

Yankee visions of "ordered freedom" within tightly bound communities. Appalachian people didn't want a republic at all. They wanted
a democracy.

★

From 1776 to 1789, the United States was little more than a loose
alliance of sovereign states that had agreed to maintain shared, centrally administered defense, foreign, and international trade policies.
State legislatures held all the power, and many were using it in radically democratized ways. Post-1776 legislative assemblies became
much larger, usually featuring one-year terms, expanded electorates, and proper representation for backcountry regions, all of which
facilitated unprecedented turnover and the election of large numbers of representatives of humble origins. Across the new confederation, the newcomers sought not to disinterestedly promote the common
good, but to openly represent the interests of their particular region,
profession, and sometimes themselves. Representatives from Greater
Appalachian sections in particular sought to relieve ordinary debtors, shift taxes onto the wealthy, and strip governors and supreme
courts of their ability to overrule the people's representatives. As the
people of Mecklenburg County, North Carolina, instructed their
delegates to that state's first constitutional convention, "Oppose
everything that leans to aristocracy or power in the hands of the rich
and chief men [and] exercised to the oppression of the poor." The
new government, they said, should be a "simple democracy, or as near
as possible."[11]

After the war, the borderlanders rose up against an appallingly
corrupt financial scheme orchestrated by one of history's more nox-
ious figures, the Philadelphia banker Robert Morris. During the
war, the Continental Army had no money to pay for soldiers' salaries

or for the food and livestock it had seized from farmers, and so had issued a series of IOUs. Under the financial administration of Morris, Pennsylvania announced it would no longer accept these IOUs for payment of taxes, forcing veterans and farmers to sell them to Morris's friends and business partners for as little as one-sixth to one-fortieth their face value. Morris then joined the federal government and, together with his protégé Alexander Hamilton, announced it would make these speculators rich by buying back all the IOUs in precious metals at face value plus 6 percent interest—all paid for by new excise and whiskey taxes designed to fall most heavily on the poor who'd been forced to sell their IOUs in the first place. Those who couldn't pay—and because there was a shortage of currency in the country, few could—had their farms and property seized.

The result was a series of uprisings across Greater Appalachia. In western North Carolina (a region that would later become Tennessee), settlers seceded from their Tidewater-controlled state in 1784 to form the State of Franklin, where apple brandy, animal skins, and tobacco were legal tender and lawyers, clergy, and doctors were excluded from elected office. They applied to join the Union and received the backing of a majority of states, but not the two-thirds required; a renewed war with the Cherokee ended the secession movement. In western Pennsylvania, government offices were sacked, and citizen gangs sprang debtors from prisons and attacked sheriffs, tax collectors, and judges. In 1794, nine thousand Appalachian Pennsylvanians marched on the Midlander city of Pittsburgh and forced it to surrender to them before holding a regional secession conference attended by 226 delegates from western Virginia and Pennsylvania. They designed their own flag and discussed reaching out to Spain and Britain for protection before being dispersed by an army led by George Washington.[12]

By now, however, even New England's leaders had moved to

suppress local democratic uprisings. In 1786, impoverished war veterans in western Massachusetts staged an armed rebellion after authorities tried to foreclose on the homes of farmers who'd never been paid for their wartime service; like the uprisings in Appalachia, this so-called Shays' Rebellion had to be put down by federal forces. In the aftermath of the affair, colonial leaders called for a special meeting of the states—a Constitutional Convention—to suppress the democratic movements and rein in state legislatures by reforming and strengthening the national government. Tellingly, the people of Greater Appalachia were almost entirely unrepresented, apart from a single delegate from Pennsylvania, the only state where they had real power.

Different beliefs about the nature of freedom shaped the deliberations over what became the 1789 Constitution, but the primary debate concerned hierarchy versus egalitarianism. Convention delegates from the Midlands and New Netherland sought only minor changes to the status quo, which encouraged egalitarian democratic outcomes and weak central authority. They were outvoted by elite delegates from Yankeedom, Tidewater, and the Deep South, who sought a stronger central government with an appointed president and Senate. When discussion turned to representation in the Senate, Yankees insisted on equal representation for each state and blocked Deep Southern efforts to have all their slaves included when calculating representation in the House, forcing a compromise in which only three-fifths of a state's slave population would count. Each state then held a ratifying convention to vote on the draft constitution. New Netherlanders refused to vote at all until Congress agreed to add a list of civil liberties protections, the Bill of Rights, modeled on Dutch precedents.

Appalachian delegates voted nearly en masse against the document everywhere save Virginia. In Pennsylvania, the only state where borderlanders had sizable representation, the Midlander majority in the state legislature hijacked the process by scheduling an abrupt election of delegates. Their allies seized all anticonstitutional materials and newspapers in the mails, and the election was held before copies of the draft constitution had even reached the more distant Appalachian parts of the state; a pro-ratification delegation was elected with only 18 percent voter participation, mostly from the Midlands. Appalachian people had opposed the creation of a strong government to check individual freedom; many still do today.[13]

The resulting constitution—with its three separate branches of government and civil liberties protections—has served as an effective check on individualistic democracy ever since, just as it has kept one regional culture from being able to fully dominate the others. It contains bodies analogous to monarchical or central governmental power (the executive branch), aristocratic or oligarchic influence (the Senate), the larger citizenry (the House), and even a detached priestly class (the Supreme Court) that never faces election, serves for life, and is charged with interpreting and conserving the federation's sacred principles. It is, in essence, an attempt to balance the centripetal forces that threatened to tear the American experiment apart.

★

The Constitution contained the tensions between competing visions of freedom, but it did not resolve them. In the first three decades after its passage, the founding fathers struggled with one another over the proper role of the new federal government, and they soon fell into two main camps, one inclined toward libertarian principles of individual autonomy and laissez-faire economics, the other seeking to invest power and resources in the guided development of a society and nation they believed would one day be the hope of and model for the world.

Not surprisingly, the libertarian-minded camp was led by a Tidewater planter with unparalleled Enlightenment credentials, Thomas Jefferson. Like so many of his generation, Jefferson believed that economic independence was a prerequisite for citizenship: Only those who were not dependent on superiors could be expected to make thoughtful and unselfish civic decisions. Fortunately, it seemed to him and his allies, the American Republic was perched on the eastern edge of a vast, sparsely populated continent. In sharp contrast to the Old World, where all land had long since been claimed and concentrated in the hands of a few, America seemed to have enough to go around. Any person who wanted to could become an independent farmer-landowner, self-sufficient and thus blessed with civic virtue. "Kindly separated by nature and a wide ocean from the exterminating havoc of one-quarter of the globe," Jefferson proclaimed, this "chosen country" had "room enough for our descendants to the hundredth and thousandth generation," or about twenty-five thousand years. The Jeffersonian vision was an essentially libertarian one: a republic of free and self-sufficient individuals whose economic and civic decisions would, in aggregate, produce a thriving economy, an ideal society. Not surprisingly, it received enthusiastic backing from the libertarian-minded sections of the country (the Tidewater, Deep South, and Appalachia) and from dissatisfied minorities in the more collectivist ones (the Scots-Irish enclaves in southern New Hampshire and midcoast Maine, the distressed farmers of western Massachusetts, and the artisans of Philadelphia and New York). When speaking for this coalition, Jefferson and other aristocrats cast themselves not as gentlemen slave lords but as "honest farmers."[14]

Opposing the Jeffersonians were advocates of collective, government-facilitated action who came to be called the Federalists (for their support of a stronger federal government) and, later, the Whigs (after the Republican-minded political movement back in England).

They did not believe anything good would come from a laissez-faire order. "This is one of those wild speculative paradoxes which have grown into credit among us," Alexander Hamilton said of these ideas. "It must be rejected by every man acquainted with commercial history." Instead, the federal government should be actively engaged in "the accomplishment of great purposes." It should invest in national highways, bridges, and canals and stand ready to wage war. It should reproduce the sophisticated fiscal machinery of Britain, and with it issue securities, consolidate state-level Revolutionary War debts, and establish a national bank that would issue loans and the country's first standardized banknotes, a mint to produce standardized coins, and national excise and tariffs to help pay for it all. All of this, Hamilton argued, would ensure that the federal government, by engaging in fields "which touch the most active springs of the human heart," would increase "the respect and attachment of the community."[15]

The two camps also disagreed on how the country should expand. The Revolution had opened a great swath of land beyond the Appalachian Mountains to colonization by overturning a ban on white settlement made in accordance with treaties the British had signed with the Indian peoples who lived there. The Federalists hoped this region—which included much of what is now the Upper Midwest and Appalachian states—would become "a mine of vast wealth to the United States," but they wanted to see it settled in a gradual, centrally organized fashion. Land would be purchased from Indian tribes in stages, surveyed and divided into organized townships, and auctioned in parcels of at least 640 acres, with thousands of acres set aside in each township to financially support public schools. Civilized settlers with at least modest capital—many of them presumably coming from overseas—were expected to populate what was then called "the West," bringing with them order, enlightenment,

and community-minded values. It was a communitarian vision, antic-
ipating the spread of the Midlander and Yankee models of respectable
middle-class settlements across the continent.[16]

The Federalists' vision failed. Tens of thousands moved westward, ignoring government plans, decrees, and boundaries to squat
on the land. The majority were from Greater Appalachia and, char-
acteristically, defended their actions based on natural rights. "All
mankind . . . have an undoubted right to pass into every vacant
country and there to form their own constitution," a group of defiant
Ohio squatters proclaimed. "Congress is not empowered to forbid
them [or] . . . to make any sale of uninhabited lands to pay the public
debt." When Congress sent federal troops to Ohio to burn squatters'
settlements, they simply waited until the soldiers departed and rebuilt
them. As George Washington, one of the prominent Federalists, put
it, "Anything short of a Chinese wall or a line of troops" would be insuf-
ficient to stop them.[17]

For their part, the Jeffersonians were pleased to witness the rapid,
barely regulated settlement of the frontier. They saw westward
expansion as vital to the continued survival of the Republic, as only
in this way could most families attain the independence of being
yeoman farmers and thus avoid becoming part of a European-style
mass of wage slaves. The western territories would create, he wrote,
"an empire of liberty." While president, Jefferson seized the opportunity to buy out Napoleon's holdings in the Mississippi Valley, more
than doubling the size of the country, much to the horror of the Federalists. This Louisiana Purchase, Massachusetts Federalist Fisher
Ames lamented, was nothing more than "a great waste, a wilderness
unpeopled with any beings except wolves and wandering Indians"
and a scheme to build an "Imperial Virginia" whose swarming,
slaveholding settlers could allow it to dominate the federation. Josiah
Quincy, president of Harvard, warned it would lead to the "ultimate

predominancy of slave power in the Union." In the aftermath of the 1803 acquisition, many New Englanders considered seceding to preserve their more ordered way of life. Hamilton cautioned them against doing so, as it would offer "no relief to our real disease; which is Democracy."[18]

All of these struggles of the early Republic were in essence both regional and ideological, a fact recognized by the participants. "In the South it is supposed that more government than is expedient is desired by the North," said Hamilton. "In the North, it is believed, that the prejudices of the South are incompatible with the necessary degree of Government and with the attainment of the essential ends of the National Union." More than two centuries later, his statement remains entirely accurate.[19]

★

The physical and demographic expansion of the United States in the early Republic doomed the Federalists to become a regional party, ensconced in New England and New England–settled parts of the Midwest, and otherwise competitive only in New Netherland and the Midlands. Their flirtation with secession during the War of 1812 completely destroyed their party. Amid popular calls for New England and New York to withdraw from the union and create a new "Northern Confederacy," Federalists had met in Hartford in late 1814 and drew up demands for sweeping constitutional changes advantageous to Yankeedom. Unfortunately, they issued their ultimatum just before news broke of General Andrew Jackson's stunning victory over the British at the Battle of New Orleans. The Federalists and their somewhat communitarian agenda were finished. Libertarian individualism—and Andrew Jackson—began a stunning rise, one that would continue until the outbreak of the Civil War.

Jackson was Greater Appalachian through and through. Born to Scots-Irish immigrant parents on the border of the two Carolinas, he had fought in the American Revolution, led the Tennessee militia against the Creek Indians during the War of 1812, and invaded Spanish Florida on his own initiative in 1818 to punish the Seminole tribe for sheltering runaway slaves. A onetime resident of the abortive State of Franklin and, later, Tennessee, he was a country lawyer, Indian-fighter, and slaveholding white supremacist. In office, he fought for minimal government, maximum freedom for individuals, aggressive westward military expansion, and the right of each regional culture to maintain its own traditions (especially slaveholding) without the interference of the others. While president, Jackson ignored a U.S. Supreme Court decision and ethnically cleansed the Cherokee from their ancestral land, killing four thousand during an abominable forced march to Oklahoma. He was unlettered, violent, and entirely fearless.[20]

Jackson won the presidency in 1828 by defeating an incumbent who was his political and social opposite. John Quincy Adams had been a senator and was the son of a president. He was a Harvard-educated diplomat who had grown up in the ordered, community-centered culture of New England. He spoke half a dozen languages and had negotiated peace with Britain in Europe while Jackson was defeating its armies in Louisiana. Voters were offered a choice between an intellectual gentleman and a self-made frontiersman, between a candidate whose values and policies were organized around achieving the common good and one who argued for the maximizing of individual freedom for white males. Predictably, Jackson won with the overwhelming support of Appalachia, Tidewater, and the Deep South; Adams carried wide majorities across Yankeedom and the Midlands, in much the same geographical pattern of his father's electoral loss to Thomas Jefferson a quarter century earlier.[21]

During the period that bears Jackson's name, the years between 1828 and 1850, the federal government took a laissez-faire stance toward the economy, opposed the development of a government-chartered banking system and federal funding for highways and harbors, and, perhaps most significantly, disrupted the development of an independent civil service. While European countries were creating apolitical government bureaucracies made up of career civil servants recruited based on skills and application exam scores, Jackson fired thousands of government employees and replaced them with political loyalists who often lacked the skills or experience for the jobs they were undertaking. "The duties of all public offices are," Jackson claimed, "so plain and simple that men of intelligence may readily qualify themselves for their performance." For the next half century, the reputation and effectiveness of the federal bureaucracy and that of many states would be undermined by the politicization of official appointments, which fostered corruption and led Americans to take a far dimmer view of government employees then their European counterparts did. Not coincidentally, Appalachian men occupied the White House for a majority of the Jacksonian era (two terms for Jackson, one for James Polk, then Zachary Taylor), with Tidewater-born moderate Whig planters (John Tyler and the short-lived William Henry Harrison) and the self-made, Dutch-bred New York political machine boss Martin Van Buren in between.[22]

Their opponents in this era were the often hapless Whigs, a party rooted in the order-seeking, community-minded culture of Yankeedom who continually argued for government-directed "improvement" of the nation. Indeed, early nineteenth-century Whig intellectuals and polemicists looked back to the early Puritans for inspiration and ideals. Men like Daniel Webster, Rufus Choate, and John Quincy Adams sought to create a virtuous community defined by individual industriousness, self-discipline, and devotion to the common good. Commerce and business were endeavors that people should treasure and government should support, not because they could facilitate personal advancement, but because they helped build a strong community, a higher form of civilization. Whigs believed that humans had not arrived into a state of nature as individuals, as Locke had claimed, but as what Whig orator Edward Everett of Massachusetts called "a member of a well-ordered family." Indulging one's impulses was damaging to society, whereas self-control, discipline, and self-denial would build the moral and economic strength of the community. An "organized and prosperous state," Everett argued, was "the way that we are to fulfill our destiny in the world."[23]

The Whigs championed not only investments in infrastructure and financial institutions, but also moral causes like abolishing slavery and enacting temperance and Sabbath laws, all of which limited individual rights (to party on Sundays and drink or own slaves at other times) for the common good (a more healthy and moral society). Their industrialists created utopian manufacturing communities like Lowell, Massachusetts, where Francis Cabot Lowell's textile company not only housed its employees—many of them single women— but provided a hospital, schools, libraries, and churches to improve and monitor their private lives. New Hampshire Whig Daniel Pratt duplicated this model in Prattville, Alabama, a company town he founded to acculturate his Deep Southern white workforce to "the positive New England virtues of sobriety, thrift, and hard work." This model was replicated in other parts of the South, even as the "Lowell Model" spread across New England. Whigs also sought to acculturate immigrant workers and fought to deny full citizenship to anyone who had not joined what one Whig leader called "this Anglo-American family" of people whose habits "have been formed upon our model." Like the Federalists, they opposed territorial expansion, which they felt would delay and distract from the social advancement of the country.[24]

Until midcentury, demographic forces were on the side of the libertarian-minded Jacksonians. Then in the 1850s the tide began to shift against them.

⭐

By 1850, the rapid expansion of the Deep South and Greater Appalachia had ground to a halt. In a little over forty years, the Deep South had absorbed the subtropical lowlands of the Gulf of Mexico, and pushed slave plantation agriculture as far north as southern Missouri and south into central Florida and the edge of the arid range in Texas. Simultaneously, the frontiersmen of Appalachia had colonized the entirety of the southern highlands, the Ozarks and Little Dixie sections of Missouri, the northwesterly half of Arkansas, and the southern tiers of Illinois and Indiana. Then, suddenly, there was nowhere else to go.

The two regional cultures had collided with each other in the south, their Yankee and Midland neighbors to the north, and an unfortunate ecological fact to the west. Beyond the 100th meridian or so, there wasn't enough water to support their crops and associated folkways. Independent frontiersmen confronted a land with few trees or watering holes, while slave lords contemplated a region where cotton and other slave-tended crops could not grow. Meanwhile, to the north, the Yankee, Midland, and New Netherland zones were attracting virtually all of the growing tide of foreign immigrants arriving on America's shores, either because they had ample industrial jobs (all three nations), frontier land suitable to grow crops already familiar to the northern and central European newcomers (Yankeedom and the Midlands), or a tradition of multiculturalism and tolerance (the Midlands and New Netherland). Many of the immigrants also came from more collectivist cultures, but ones where a feudal aristocracy controlled land and politics. For such individuals, the Deep South, Tidewater, and Appalachia offered few attractions and fewer economic opportunities; by 1850 the free states had eight foreign-born residents for every one in a slave state. As a result, the population of the North—including the Yankee-settled northern and Midland-settled heartland of the Midwest—was rapidly outpacing that of the slaveholding nations. The Deep Southern and Tidewater aristocracies could suddenly envision a country where their adversaries had a lock on the House, Senate, and electoral college, where slavery—the basis of their entire economic and social system—might one day be abolished.

The Deep South—by now far and away the most economically and politically powerful nation of the three—first sought to expand by persuading the United States to annex its tropical neighbors, many of them small, fragile states that had just gained independence from the declining Spanish Empire. There were schemes to invade Cuba and all of Mexico, actual occupations of Mexico City and Nicaragua, and plans on paper to conquer much of the Caribbean basin as part of a proposed "Golden Circle" of Deep Southern slavery. When these ideas came to naught, in part because Deep Southerners themselves came to fear the implications of adding millions of nonwhite residents to their domain, there appeared to be but one solution: secession.

The war that followed was fought not for individual liberty, but to protect the slave system upon which the Deep South and Tidewater had built their hierarchical libertarian societies. Slavery, the Deep South's leaders argued at every opportunity, was the basis of a virtuous, biblically sanctioned social system superior to that of the free states. But while most people in Appalachia had no problem with slavery, they were opposed to the hierarchical, aristocratic social order the Deep South and Tidewater espoused. The "libertarian coalition" was shattered in 1860 by this division between the egalitarian borderlanders (who saw life as a meritocratic struggle between freeborn men) and the hierarchical aristocrats of the lowlands (who believed that that struggle had been fought decades and centuries earlier and that their families had been victorious). The Democratic Party Jackson had built formally shattered at its 1860 convention, as delegates from the Deep South and Tidewater marched out of the convention hall while Appalachian and northern delegates remained in their places. Shortly thereafter, Abraham Lincoln won the presidency, and the Deep Southern–controlled states—and only the Deep Southern states—seceded. In February 1861 they held a meeting at which they established the Confederate States of America. Tidewater- and Appalachia-controlled areas, meanwhile, wished to remain in the Union or to join with Midlanders to form a third federation, a buffer state between the Deep Southerners and Yankees. (New York City's mayor, Fernando Wood, proposed seceding as well to create an independent, slave-trading city-state modeled on those of northern Europe's Hanseatic League.)[25]

Had the Deep Southerners not begun attacking federal post offices, mints, and military facilities in April 1861, they likely would have been able to negotiate a peaceful secession from the Union, as only the Yankees wished to use force to stop them. (Even Lincoln, a former Whig born in Appalachia to Yankee and Midland parents, had pledged to avoid war.) But the oligarchs of South Carolina, never known for their self-restraint, launched a deadly assault on Fort Sumter, the U.S. installation in Charleston Harbor, turning every nation save Tidewater against them. Even Appalachia rallied to the Union cause. Western Virginia seceded from Virginia, the new state providing huge numbers of volunteers to the Union army. The people of eastern Tennessee tried to do the same, but were put down by force of arms. Residents of Appalachian northern Alabama established the Unionist State of Winston and fought as Alabama units in the Union army. Appalachian-dominated Kentucky, Indiana, and

Missouri didn't secede at all, and Pennsylvania's Scots-Irish governor, James Buchanan, declared for the Union.

The Confederacy went down in defeat in 1865, and we've seen in chapter 2 how its fixation on oligarchic liberty compromised its ability to defend itself. In the aftermath of the war, Yankee-directed Union forces occupied its cities and tried to carry out a massive state-building project to remake the region along more communitarian lines. With soldiers maintaining order, thousands of Yankee and Midlander schoolteachers, missionaries, businessmen, and government officials were deployed to the occupied regions. They introduced public education, founded elementary schools and even universities for blacks (many of which still exist today), and eliminated laws and practices that reinforced the racial caste system. Fifteen African Americans were elected to the House of Representatives from the former Confederacy between 1870 and 1877, and two represented Mississippi in the Senate, where they vigorously argued for the federal government to smash the caste system. "I can assure that portion of my democratic friends from the other side of the House whom I regard as my social inferiors," representative and former slave John R. Lynch of Mississippi told Congress, "that if at any time I should meet one of you at a hotel or occupy a seat at the same table with you, or the same seat in a car with you, do not think I thereby accepted you as my social equal. . . . No, Mr. Speaker, it is not social rights we desire. . . . What we ask is protection in the enjoyment of public rights."[26]

But Reconstruction ultimately failed, and the Yankee effort to remold Confederate parts of Appalachia ultimately turned that region into an ally of the Deep Southern oligarchs. As soon as the occupation ended in 1876, whites in the "reconstructed" regions abolished public schools, imposed barriers to African Americans exercising their right to vote, and murdered blacks who dared run for office or ignore the strictures of Jim Crow.

But while the Civil War failed to change the more individualistic and libertarian regions of the country, their absence from Congress during that period allowed a flood of communitarian-minded reforms to be adopted by the federal government. The new party of communitarianism, the Republicans, enacted much of the old Whig agenda: a national banking and currency system, tariffs to protect domestic industry, and massive spending on infrastructure. During the bleakest years of the war, Congress created the first federal income tax, established the Department of Agriculture (which helped guide that sector's postwar expansion), passed the Land Grant College Act (which supported the creation of public universities across the country), the Homestead Act (which encouraged yeoman farming in the West), the Pacific Railway Act (which sponsored the building of the first transcontinental railroad, which connected Omaha and San Francisco), and the False Claims Act, which clamped down on fraud by federal contractors. Historian Leonard Curry has said this battery of progressive legislation amounted to the "blueprint for modern America."[27]

Abraham Lincoln, who oversaw most of these progressive reforms, was clear about their purpose: "The legitimate object of government is to do for a community of people whatever they need to have done, but can not do at all or can not so well do for themselves—in their separate and individual capacities," he wrote. Government "is a combination of the people of a country to effect certain objects by joint effort." These objects of collective action included "public roads and highways, public schools, charities, pauperism, orphanage, estates of the deceased, and the machinery of government itself." Nor was he unaware of the financial costs this might entail, writing, "The best framed and best administered governments are necessarily expensive."[28]

During Reconstruction, the Confederate-less Congress also passed three key amendments to the Constitution, which outlawed slavery, prohibited states from denying people citizenship or the right to vote based on race, ensured equal protection for all people under the law, and effectively extended the protections of the Bill of Rights to all individuals, enforceable by the federal government. (Previously the first ten amendments had been interpreted to apply only to the federal government and were even then ignored.) Although it would be another century before they would be fully implemented, the new amendments had been intended to strike a mortal blow to a lowland southern way of life sustained by slavery. They also reduced the freedom of the Deep Southern and Tidewater aristocracy by taking away—on paper at least—the liberty to own slaves and to pass laws denying individual liberties to others. For the Yankee-Midlander coalition that drove these legislative and constitutional changes, the federal government was no longer to be regarded as a potential threat to freedom that had to be kept weak. It was now to be the enforcer of liberty and an agent of national improvement and prosperity.[29]

The stage was set for one of the most dramatic economic expansions in human history, one that would end in a crisis so profound that it caused Americans to reassess their very definitions of freedom and liberty.

# CHAPTER 5

# The Rise and Fall of
# Laissez-Faire (1877–1930)

A sk early twenty-first-century libertarians for a model of the
kind of American policy environment they would like to
see, and they will likely point not to the antebellum South, but to
the Gilded Age, that period between the end of Reconstruction in
1877 and the 1890s, when Progressive Era reformers succeeded in
introducing some rudimentary labor and consumer safety regulations. It was a laissez-faire world, where the federal government
was relatively small and unobtrusive (though bigger and somewhat
more meddlesome then it had been before the Civil War), and the
economy a private, not a public concern, beyond the government
enforcing contracts and property rights. It's a world to which
many prominent libertarians and free-market advocates would
like to return. In early 2010, Jacob Hornberger, founder and president of the Future of Freedom Foundation, wrote in *Reason* in
defense of the achievements of "our American forebears" in that
lost golden age:

Let's consider, say, the year 1880. Here was a society in which people were free to keep everything they earned, because there was no income tax. They were also free to decide what to do with their own money—spend it, save it, invest it, donate it, or whatever. People were generally free to engage in occupations and professions without a license or permit. There were few federal economic regulations and regulatory agencies. No Social Security, Medicare, Medicaid, welfare, bailouts, or so-called stimulus plans. No IRS. No Departments of Education, Energy, Agriculture, Commerce, and Labor. No EPA and OSHA. No Federal Reserve. No drug laws. Few systems of public schooling. No immigration controls. No federal minimum-wage laws or price controls. A monetary system based on gold and silver coins rather than paper money. No slavery. No CIA. No FBI. No torture or cruel or unusual punishments. No renditions. No overseas military empire. No military-industrial complex.

As a libertarian, as far as I'm concerned, that's a society that is pretty darned golden.[1]

Hornberger is by no means alone in his fondness for the Gilded Age, a sentiment that has been shared by libertarian-minded Americans ever since the laissez-faire era collapsed with the stock market in 1929. "I am very gloomy on the political situation," chemical magnate Pierre DuPont despaired in the late 1940s, "and will doubtless remain so until the New Deal is thrown out lock, stock, and barrel by a free vote of the American people." Amity Shlaes, late of the George W. Bush Institute, in 2014 championed the era because "regulators, unions, and lawmakers" hadn't yet been allowed to intrude in labor issues, conditions, and contracts, freeing robber barons like Andrew Carnegie and Henry Frick to do "much for workers, precisely because they felt responsible to their counterparty."[2]

The reality is that the late nineteenth century was considerably less libertarian than the antebellum era that preceded it, in that

property rights in other humans were no longer respected, state officials and local democratic majorities were theoretically prohibited
from denying citizenship to other humans based on race (although
gender was still fair game, and even racial protections were soon
diluted), and the federal government had claimed the right to levy
taxes, regulate commerce, and confound the workings of the invisible hand by subsidizing or building infrastructure projects the free
market would not have created on its own. As we have seen in the
previous chapter, these departures from the purer Jeffersonian and
Jacksonian forms of individualistic republicanism were a reflection
of the fact that this era was inaugurated and largely presided over
by a Yankee elite. At the federal level, they made the fundamental
changes while the Confederates were in Richmond rather than Washington, but Yankee leaders continued to introduce rules and regulations in the states they controlled with the aim of conserving their
"moral community" in the face of the corrosive effects of industrial
laissez-faire capitalism and an influx of foreign immigrants who didn't
share their cultural priorities. The reason present-day libertarians
idealize the 1880s is that by the turn of the century this moral communitarian reform movement started again altering even federal-level
policies, often with the support of their regions' industrialists. By
the early twentieth century, reformers calling themselves the Progressives would be fully ascendant, not least because a predominantly
laissez-faire policy environment had so clearly brought Americans
not greater economic and political freedom, but rather monopoly
and oligarchic tyranny.

★

Between the Civil War and 1899, the American economy expanded
at a staggering rate, spearheaded by a revolutionary technology. Railroads, which first reached the United States in 1830, offered faster,

safer, and more reliable and weatherproof transportation than carts, wagons, canal barges, or steamships, and quickly dominated freight and passenger traffic wherever they operated. They grew rapidly, tripling their overall track mileage between 1860 and 1880, only to triple again by 1920. Assisted by the federal government, lines linked the Atlantic to the Pacific, and nearly everywhere in between. The effect on the nation's economy is inestimable. In 1840, before the arrival of the rails, it took four days to ship goods to Boston from Concord, New Hampshire, and four weeks from Chicago. Ten years later, Boston was a four-hour trip from Concord and just four days from Chicago. The railroads, it was said, had annihilated space and time.[3]

The companies that ran the main lines became by necessity the first large corporations in America, employing thousands across hundreds and sometimes thousands of miles. Their need to synchronize schedules—and not rely on the sun to determine when it was noon in any particular place—led to the establishment of standardized time and time zones. In the West, they founded entire towns along their lines and spent millions recruiting and transporting settlers from as far away as central Europe to populate them. Their voracious hunger for capital and resources prompted the modernization of the stock market and the consolidation of Wall Street banks and the coal, steel, copper, oil, and glass sectors. The transportation networks they created facilitated the concentration of other industries, and soon a handful of companies controlled the nation's sugar, meatpacking, and agricultural machinery markets. Artisans—self-employed tailors, cobblers, blacksmiths, glassmakers, and the like—had difficulty competing with their industrial counterparts and often gave up, becoming wage laborers. Small farmers in places with inferior soils and growing seasons, such as northern New England or the hills of Pennsylvania, went bankrupt as produce from larger, more fecund, and once-distant farms reached their markets; they followed their children and grandchildren to towns and cities to seek work in the expanding factories.[4]

This presented a challenge to traditional republican thinking, wherein freedom and liberty were tied to the economic security and independence that accompanied owning one's property or, at the very least, the means of one's livelihood. The availability of cheap or free land in North America had given the founders hope that most white Americans would be able to achieve this form of freedom, thereby circumventing the formation of those impoverished, unpropertied, dependent masses that threatened to undo republican liberty in Britain and had turned France's revolution into a bloodbath and its republic into a despotic, expansionistic empire. Yet millions of landless wage laborers were now crowding into the textile mills, coal mines, and factories of the industrial age, without economic freedom and thus civic virtue. Unlike artisan apprentices of the past, young workers could not expect to learn the skills that would enable them to graduate to being self-employed specialists; wage labor was no longer a stepping-stone to "independence" (as traditionally defined), but a permanent condition. Simultaneously, the frontier had officially closed in 1890, the Census Bureau having determined that all land was now essentially claimed, closing with it the Jeffersonian dream of indefinite agrarian expansion.

Meanwhile, the same processes had made a small group of individuals extremely wealthy—wealthier indeed than even the largest antebellum planters had been. In 1890, the richest 1 percent of Americans had the same combined income as the bottom 50 percent and owned more property than the other 99 percent. With such incredible resources they had an overwhelming influence on the economy, presiding over monopolies, vertically integrated corporations, and the activities of the politicians they placed in office. Not surprisingly, many of them embraced individualism and used their power to champion and propagate a conception of freedom that justified a situation that was serving them very well.

Starting in the 1870s, this emerging oligarchy established the notion that what freedom really meant in America was the "freedom of contract." So long as labor contracts were "freely" signed by both parties, everything that followed from them had to be just and proper as well: young children working long hours around dangerous machinery, miners toiling with open flames amid flammable gases in shafts frugally built with but a single exit, factory workers paid not with money but with company scrip that could be used only in company stores where the goods were overpriced. So long as consumers were not compelled to buy a particular product or service, the fact that that product might be poisonous or that service incompetent or life-threatening was of no public concern; anyone could call himself a medical doctor and prescribe patent medicines that would never deliver on the promises made on their labels. People, in short, had to remain free to be exploited.

Indeed, the nation's courts used this reasoning to block legislative efforts to improve labor standards by prohibiting abuses. Courts in many states ruled that laws establishing maximum working hours and safe working conditions were unconstitutional because they interfered with the workers' rights to labor under any conditions to which they might agree. In 1885, New York's highest court struck down a law prohibiting the manufacture of cigars in tenements on the grounds that it deprived workers of their "fundamental rights of liberty," including being able to "work where they will." The following year, Pennsylvania's supreme court struck down a law prohibiting payment of workers in company scrip, saying it was "utterly unconstitutional" and "an insulting attempt to put the laborer under legislative tutelage" by preventing them "from making their own contract decisions." Its counterpart in Illinois overturned a law banning sweatshops and establishing a forty-eight-hour workweek for women and children on similar grounds. The U.S. Supreme Court overturned federal and state laws that forbade employers from making nonmembership in a union a prerequisite for employment, again because they violated the worker's "right of personal liberty"—in this case, the liberty not to be in a union, rather than to be in one; in the opening years of the twentieth century it struck down a New York law limiting bakers to a sixty-hour workweek and a federal prohibition on the interstate trade of products made by children under the age of fourteen. The former was a breach of the liberty of the bakers, the latter an indefensible encroachment on the power of the states, because the Court believed that child labor, unlike already regulated liquor and gambling, was not inherently immoral. As union leader John L. Mitchell would put it, the Court decisions left workers feeling that "they are being guaranteed the liberties they do not want and denied the liberty that is of real value to them."[5]

Oligarchic interests also succeeded in blocking early consumer safety regulations. In the 1870s, the city of Chicago passed meat inspection ordinances that required inspectors to seize any diseased meats and destroy them; meatpackers succeeded in having the law changed to allow them to sell the diseased meat at auction to unsuspecting buyers. In the mid-1880s, public officials discovered that large amounts of lard, margarine, and other products were being made from the carcasses of animals that had died of disease or had been found trampled to death in railway stock cars, but they were unable to overcome vigorous industry opposition to the establishment of a federal inspection system to prevent such abuse. Meaningful regulations weren't imposed until 1906, after Upton Sinclair, in his novel *The Jungle,* exposed the conditions in the Chicago meatpacking plants: meat tainted with sawdust, rat droppings, spit, and foul-smelling cattle boils. Federal investigators not only found his depiction to be accurate but also revealed that many food products were laced with borax (to hide the smell of rotting ingredients, though the chemical caused headaches and stomach pains), copper sulfates (which kept peas green but caused liver and kidney failure), and sulfuric acid and formaldehyde (both highly toxic preservatives). Unscrupulous drug makers sold soothing infants' syrups laced with opiates (which harmed and often killed the babies), headache powders that caused heart attacks, and cocaine-based cough syrups. After the federal government finally stepped in to require truthful labeling of medicines in 1906, the Supreme Court ruled that this applied only to ingredients, meaning manufacturers could make any false claims they wished about their products' use and efficacy.[6]

★

The oligarchs and other beneficiaries of this laissez-faire system also embraced social Darwinism, which provided philosophical justifications for the growing structural inequalities of the age, in which a person born poor now had little hope of changing his or her condition. The goal of the American experiment was no longer to create a good society, but to allow a natural "struggle for survival" to carry on without interference. "We never supposed that laissez-faire would give us perfect happiness," its greatest defender, Yale professor William Graham Sumner, wrote. "It is nothing but the doctrine of liberty. . . . If the social doctors will mind their own business, we shall have no troubles but what belong to Nature." The poor, he asserted, "constantly neutralize and destroy the finest efforts of the wise and industrious, and are a dead-weight on the society in all its struggles to realize any better things." By contrast, Sumner declared, "the millionaires are a product of natural selection" so that "wealth—both their own and that entrusted to them—aggregates under their hands."

Sumner's intellectual mentor, the British essayist Herbert Spencer, further argued that the state should do nothing to interfere with this "natural" process, especially to assist the poor in any way. "If they are not sufficiently complete to live, they die, and it is best that they should die," he argued. "The whole effort of nature is to get rid of such, to clear the world of them, to make room for the better." Spencer also opposed public education, sanitation inspection and enforcement, and the regulation of housing. It was he, not Charles Darwin, who coined the phrase "survival of the fittest."[7]

Spencer's and Sumner's views were celebrated at the highest levels of society. "The growth of large business is merely a survival of the fittest," John D. Rockefeller proclaimed in a Sunday school address. "The American Beauty rose can be produced in the splendor and fragrance which ring cheer to its beholder only by sacrificing the early buds which grow upon it." Andrew Carnegie was so taken with Spencer's work that he sought out the Englishman and became one of his closest friends. When Spencer visited the United States in the fall of 1882, he was thronged by the press and honored at a gala banquet at Delmonico's in New York attended by Sumner, Henry Ward Beecher, the acting president of the National Academy of Sciences, and over 140 other luminaries. ("May he live to place the cap-stone on that pyramid of achievements which is already one of the wonders of the modern intellectual world," poet and author Oliver Wendell Holmes, who was unable to attend, wrote from Boston.) Spencer's work was eulogized by congressmen, senators, and university presidents. Sumner was an influential public intellectual, the founder of American sociology, and gave lectures that influenced the thinking of thousands of Yale students, including the neoclassical economist Irving Fisher; Yale has an endowed political science chair in his name. He coined the term "the Forgotten Man" for the unsung productive citizen whose hard-earned wealth was sapped to provide for the unworthy poor, a rhetorical figure who, by one name or another, has remained at the heart of libertarian populism ever since.[8]

★

The social Darwinists were right about one thing: The rising tide was not lifting all boats. The libertarian philosophy that served the elite so well was creating a dystopia for their wage employees. In the widespread absence of wage controls, most workers were not paid enough to support their families. In 1900, when a middle-class railroad clerk made over $1,000 a year, a coal miner averaged just $340, domestic servants $240, and farm laborers $178, despite the fact most worked seventy to eighty hours a week. Ten years later, the typical Chicago meatpacker made only a third of the income necessary to support a family of four. As a result, wives had to work and sometimes brought their infants to work with them, and children had to enter the labor force instead of attending school. With few occupational safety regulations, the workplace was usually unhealthy and often unnecessarily deadly. In the mines, children were employed to sit on ladders next to the ends of coal chutes to pick out impurities as deadly coal dust poured over them for hours on end; in textile mills, women and children worked ten- and twelve-hour days in hot, damp rooms filled with clouds of lint (which caused lung disease) and whirling, exposed machinery (which claimed fingers, limbs, and lives, particularly of the exhausted children who often fell into them). There being no workers' compensation laws, anyone who became sick or was maimed or injured simply lost his or her job. There was no unemployment insurance for those laid off, no Social Security for those too old to work, and no protections against discrimination or sexual harassment. In most states, and from a federal perspective, only the fittest were to survive.[9]

The poor also bore the brunt of the tax burden, which was intentionally exacted in the form of taxes on purchased products or physical property, rather than on income, securities, or corporate profits. (During the Civil War, the Yankee-dominated Congress had enacted a 3 percent income tax on the wealthy, but abolished it after the war.) Tax assessors went out into the countryside to count each farmer's cows, pigs, and sheep, but the billions in stocks and bonds held by plutocrats went entirely unassessed. By the late nineteenth century, working-class families were surrendering 70 to 90 percent of their annual savings to the taxman, while the richest 250,000 people in the country paid only 3 to 10 percent. "We tax the tea, the coffee, the sugar, the spices the poor man uses," Senator John Sherman, an ex-Whig from Ohio, said on the chamber floor in 1872. "Everything he consumes we call a luxury; and yet we are afraid to touch the income of Mr. Astor. Is there any justice in that?" When Congress finally passed a modest 2 percent tax on the incomes of upper-class earners—including dividends and rents—in 1894, the Supreme Court declared the law unconstitutional. "The decision involves nothing less than the surrender of the taxing power to the moneyed class," one of the dissenting justices, Henry Brown, wrote. "Even the spectre of socialism is conjured up to frighten Congress from laying taxes upon the people in proportion to their ability to pay them."[10]

An unregulated industrial economy turned out to be extremely unstable. The premier investment bank in the country, Jay Cooke & Co., sold bonds to small investors and loaned millions to the Northern Pacific Railroad to enable it to begin building a second transcontinental line far ahead of demand. The bank had assured investors that the railroad would make money by reselling the arid land it had been given on both sides of its track, but sales didn't materialize. When rural banks began withdrawing funds from Jay Cooke to loan to farmers ahead of the 1873 harvest, the bank collapsed, shocking the country. As depositors began withdrawing their money from banks, which had no insurance to protect them if they failed, they set off a chain of collapses. The New York Stock Exchange closed for ten straight days. Fifty-five railroad companies failed in less than two months, and the stocks of others plummeted; half would be bankrupt by 1876. In the South, cotton rotted in the fields, and on the northern plains farmers burned wheat for heat. Some eighteen thousand businesses collapsed in the next two years while unemployment soared and wages were slashed. The economy shrank every month for five and a half years. The period became known, until the 1930s, as the Great Depression. The federal government did nothing to address the crisis except to cut back spending and return the country to the gold standard, which advantaged creditors over debtors.[11]

The collapse brought unprecedented social unrest, as working people revolted against a system they believed to be rigged for the wealthy. In 1877, unorganized workers in West Virginia struck against the Baltimore & Ohio Railroad, which had announced it would cut their wages for a third time, and the strike quickly spread to Maryland and Pennsylvania. Governors in those states sent in the state militia or National Guard in response. Marching to their trains in Baltimore, Maryland Guard units soon found themselves in pitched battles with thousands of workers; by the time they retreated into Camden Yards, three militiamen and twenty-five workers had been wounded, and ten workers were dead. Federal troops had to be sent in to rescue the Guard. In Pittsburgh, militiamen were set upon by rock-throwing workers and responded with bayonets and rifle fire that killed twenty-five and injured twenty-nine; they were then forced into a roundhouse and watched as workers set fire to trains in the surrounding yards. The next day the militia fought their way out of the city, killing another twenty civilians in the process. A vice president of the Pennsylvania Railroad lobbied authorities to use artillery on the demonstrators.

In sympathy, thousands of workers in Chicago and other Illinois rail centers took over depots, paralyzing rail traffic. Coal workers walked off their jobs, and tens of thousands took to the streets in Chicago itself. The governor of Illinois deployed the National Guard, which killed twenty men and boys while restoring order. *Railway World*, the industry's magazine, editorialized that the strikers should be wiped out for promoting the reintroduction of "slavery," because "it is the inherent right of every man to sell his labor for the best price he can obtain" and of "every corporation . . . to buy labor and every commodity on the best attainable terms." Stopping this enslavement of capitalists was an "imperative duty of all governments," even if it required that "the Gatling guns mow down crowds of the new champions of slavery, and if heavy artillery must batter down whole towns that become citadels of folly and crime." Here was one form of government intervention of which the oligarchs heartily approved.[12]

Fearing an antilibertarian revolution, the oligarchs financed the construction of fortified National Guard armories in Chicago, Cleveland, New York, and other cities. The central Chicago armory was built on land donated by department store magnate Marshall Field amid "the most aristocratic portion of the South Side," its construction and furnishings paid for by Field and his neighbors on Millionaire's Row. Completed in 1890, it resembled a prison, a granite fortress with "great bastions, from which an enfilade fire may be directed against any side of the walls." Field and his associates also bought the Chicago police four twelve-pound cannons, a Gatling gun, and 296 rifles. William Astor headed fund-raising for a castle-like armory in Manhattan, complete with "loop-holes for muskets," a library "in old mahogany," and reception rooms designed by Louis C. Tiffany. The opening ball in 1880, catered by Delmonico's, was attended by Jay Gould, J. P. Morgan, and the Vanderbilts, who danced late into the night. This so-called armory movement led to the construction of similar installations to put down unrest in cities across the country.[13]

Ironically, laissez-faire policies ultimately destroyed rather than enhanced the free market. The railroads used their nearly monopolistic control over the transportation of raw materials, grains, livestock, and finished products to foster the creation of large oligopolies in other sectors or to smother their competitors. This was usually accomplished through preferential pricing. John D. Rockefeller was able to assemble the Standard Oil monopoly because he was charged substantially less to ship oil products to and from his refineries than his competitors were to and from theirs, not least because the Vanderbilts and other rail barons were stockholders in his company. In 1879, a congressional investigation found that Standard had received steep discounts on its shipments—sometimes paying one-sixteenth what its competitors did—plus exclusive use of all of the main lines' tanker cars (to deny them to competitors) and exclusive leases of the railroads' own oil terminals. "The trunk lines have hauled [Standard's] oil 300 miles for nothing to enable it to undersell seaboard refineries not then under its control," the investigators reported. It "has frozen out and gathered in refineries of oil all over the country" as competitors were squeezed into selling out. When Rockefeller's trust grew large enough, he began dictating prices to the railroads, not only of what he would be charged, but what his rivals would be as well. After Standard turned its eyes on eastern Ohio, George Rice, an independent oil refiner in Marietta, saw his per barrel shipping fees jump from seventeen to thirty-five cents, with twenty-five cents of that going back to Standard as a special refund. Rice successfully challenged the arrangement in court, but others weren't so lucky and were unable to survive the unfair competition. The "big four" meatpackers—Armour, Hammond, Morris, and Swift—grew from similar relationships with four rival railroad lines, but eventually colluded to form a single Beef Trust. Eventually, the implied threat of moving their business elsewhere enabled them too to dictate the prices paid by rivals and various livestock farmers, who had no other way to get their animals to market. "This control over the railways enables the Trust to drive its competitors from the markets of the country," Boston University law professor Frank Parsons explained.

> It has acquired a practical monopoly of the trade in dressed meats, fertilizers, hides, bristles, and horn and bone products. It has been able to ruin almost every rival slaughter house and absorb all those it cared to buy. Through its private car lines, with exclusive contracts with the railroads, it has laid hands upon the fruit business of California, Michigan, Georgia, and Florida. It directs what the farmers in the West shall receive for their cattle and hogs, and what the workers of the East shall pay for their meat. They can go far toward fixing the price of wheat, corn, and oats. It bullies the railroads on one hand and the merchants on the other.[14]

The fate of entire regions of the country was decided by these and other trusts, via railroad boardrooms. Thus the interior of the West was not allowed to industrialize, with punitive rates for moving finished goods out of the region or raw materials into it; it was substantially cheaper to send freight from Chicago to Seattle—roughly half as much for most goods—than to drop it off at Spokane or other inland cities en route on the very same train. Similarly, railroads decided that eastern Nebraska farmers would pay about half as much per ton to ship their corn to New York as those in Iowa, who were often hundreds of miles closer. Iowans, who also raised cattle and hogs in abundance, wanted to build their own packing plants rather than ship them to Chicago, but were vetoed by the railroads and their Beef Trust puppeteers, which introduced punitive rates on the export of processed meats, as well as shoes, iron, and steel. "The railroads have decreed that Iowa shall not be a manufacturing state," Iowa governor Albert B. Cummings told a U.S. Senate panel in 1905. "All our manufacturers, when they attempt to reach beyond our own state, meet rates that so discriminate against them they cannot compete with manufacturers elsewhere."[15]

In other words, the unregulated marketplace had stifled innovation, destroyed the possibility of meaningful competition, artificially depressed economic development and market pricing in entire regions of the country, and resulted in higher prices for consumers. Total economic freedom was destroying the free market itself.

⭐

Laissez-faire policies did not create a more free society, but rather one in which freedom itself soon became endangered. In the absence of effective governmental checks on their power, corporate oligarchs not only established monopolies that destroyed the freedom of the market but also effectively assumed control over much of government itself, turning it to do its bidding. Railroad baron Jay Gould's agents practically ran the executive branch; of the seventy-three cabinet members who served between 1868 and 1890, forty-eight were railroad company lobbyists, board members, or relatives of the owners. Grover Cleveland's attorney general, Richard Orley, sat on the boards of two major railroads, which paid him more than his government salary. Five out of six of the major cabinet appointees in both James Garfield's and Chester Arthur's administrations were closely linked to the railroads.

Many state governments became little more than annexes for industrial monopolies. At the turn of the century, Frank Parsons surveyed state legislatures and determined that between 35 and 75 percent of their members were connected to railroad interests and would vote to support them under any ordinary circumstance. The railroads infiltrated their men into the leadership of state parties, the legislatures, gubernatorial administrations, and even the courts. "No lackey was ever more subservient to his master than Pennsylvania to its railroads, or than the State of California to the Southern Pacific. These corporations have owned these states, as the landlords in England owned the rotten borough before the reform," John Graham Brooks, president of the American Social Science Association, wrote in 1903. "The great business not only sets its stamp on politics, it is to a large extent its creator and controller." Cornell University economist Jeremiah Jenks agreed: "It is a matter of rumor and almost common belief that the railroads and the large industrial corporations are able to influence to a material extent the acts of our legislatures and even the decisions of our courts," he noted in 1900. "This influence is thought by many to constitute the chief menace to the integrity of our institutions and the welfare of the country."[16]

The situation was perhaps starkest in the Far Western interior, which was not colonized until the height of the Gilded Age and thus lacked the preexisting social, political, and economic institutions that mitigated corporate control in other regions of the country. When Nevadans met in 1864 to write their first constitution, mining interests introduced a measure that effectively exempted their businesses from taxation, even though they represented almost the entirety of the newborn state's economic activity; delegates passed it in the face of the mining companies' threats to leave the area altogether if they did not get their way. By 1870, two massive cartels—the Bank of California and the Central Pacific Railroad—between them controlled Nevada's mines and railroads and had bought off the state's legislators and congressional delegation; between 1865 and 1900, every U.S. senator from Nevada save one was closely associated with one of these cartels, which cooperated to control state politics.[17]

Similarly, in the late nineteenth and early twentieth century, Anaconda Copper literally ran the state of Montana, buying off judges, local officials, and politicians and controlling elections via "the cemetery vote," a fraud by which the deceased managed to cast large numbers of ballots. Legislators in turn delivered the rules, regulations, and tax policies that enriched Anaconda's executives, and if they did not, they found themselves vetoed by Anaconda-backed governors. Founded by Marcus Daly, a veteran of the Nevada silver boom, and supported by California mining magnate George Hearst, Anaconda owned the mines, the smelters that processed their copper ore, the coal mines that fueled the smelters, the forests that supplied the timber needed in the mines, the power plants that drove the machinery, the railroads that connected the parts, and even the banks that financed them. By 1900 the company employed three-quarters of all wage earners in Montana and as late as 1959 owned five of the state's six daily newspapers, ensuring that its operations received little scrutiny and denying advertising space to candidates who opposed it.[18]

In this era, control of state legislatures also fostered control of the U.S. Senate, whose members were chosen by state legislators, not the voters. Many legislators were attorneys who already represented the railroads and other trusts and could be relied on to do their clients' bidding. Others sold their votes to the trusts, a fact exposed repeatedly by whistleblowers and legislative investigators. In New York, a legislator was given $2,000—more than his annual salary— to vote for a railroad candidate for the U.S. Senate, while in Ohio railroads paid out $5,000 per vote to elect Senator Henry B. Payne. (The legislature subsequently determined that Payne's election was void by bribery, but the Senate refused to unseat him.) In Montana, legislators sold a U.S. Senate seat to copper magnate William Clark in 1899, but he was forced to resign because his election displeased Standard Oil; he was reelected all the same in the next election cycle. "He is a shame to the American nation," Mark Twain said of Clark near the end of his term, "and no one has helped send him to the Senate who did not know that his proper place was the penitentiary, with a ball and chain on his legs." In 1905, Professor Parsons found that two-thirds of the Senate was under railroad control, plus a majority of the House. "There was a time when senators represented the states; but too often now they represent giant corporations," he concluded. "The Pennsylvania Railroad is represented in the Senate, and the Steel Trust, Oil Trust, etc., but not the State of Pennsylvania. . . . So with New Jersey, New York, Connecticut and Rhode Island. . . . The railroads and the Standard Oil and other allied interests *use* these States to send *their* representatives to the Senate, but the people are not represented at all."[19]

By the turn of the century, pro-industry judges were issuing injunctions to prevent strikers from engaging in constitutionally protected activities like parading, picketing, or trying to persuade other workers to join a strike. A West Virginia court forced labor organizer Mary Harris "Mother" Jones out of that state after she refused to respect its injunction preventing her from speaking to striking workers near company property. The U.S. Supreme Court ruled that a millinery union's boycott of a hat company's products amounted to an illegal conspiracy and put foreclosures on union members' homes to force payment of a quarter million dollars in damages. A Missouri court issued a blanket injunction against speaking or writing about a metal polishers' strike against a stove manufacturer, and the Supreme Court upheld a one-year prison sentence against American Federation of Labor president Samuel Gompers for ignoring it. When hundreds of thousands of railroad workers refused to handle the sleeping cars manufactured by George Pullman—who had cut wages by 28 percent amid a renewed depression, but left rents at his company town unchanged—President Grover Cleveland secured an injunction against them (for interfering with the mails carried by the cars) and sent in twelve thousand federal troops to enforce it; thirty strikers were killed, and their leader, Eugene Debs, was sent to prison for six months after losing an appeal to the Supreme Court.[20]

★

It was a libertarian era across the country, but there were marked regional differences in how it was expressed.

In the most individualistic regions—the Deep South, Tidewater, and Greater Appalachia—there was a sustained and successful effort to roll back many of the constraints imposed by Yankeedom and its allies in the aftermath of the Civil War. In keeping with their traditions of aristocratic liberty, leaders of the Tidewater and Deep Southern sections worked to maximize their own freedom by severely limiting the freedom of poor people, and especially people of African descent, who constituted the majority of the population of Mississippi, Louisiana, and South Carolina. In 1872, a white crowd in Colfax, Louisiana, murdered between 70 and 150 blacks, dumping many of the bodies in a mass grave, during a disputed election. When state authorities refused to take action against the killers, the federal government, then still controlled by Yankees, moved to prosecute them under the Force Acts, which tasked the federal government with enforcing the constitutional amendments providing for full citizenship, equal protection, and due process for all Americans, regardless of race. The Supreme Court intervened, ruling that these constitutional amendments applied only to the actions of states, not individuals, and therefore the federal government was not allowed to become involved. The practical effect of this ruling was to permit mass vigilante violence against African Americans across the former Confederacy. In 1874 and 1875, white paramilitaries killed hundreds of blacks and their political allies in Mississippi in a successful effort to intimidate the state's black majority from voting and restore "Anglo-Saxon supremacy"; the Democrats, then the party of white supremacy, won control of the governorship and both houses of the legislature. All the other Deep Southern– and Tidewater-controlled states followed a similar pattern, as did many of the Appalachian ones. By 1877, blacks had effectively been eliminated from political life in these regions, returning control to the oligarchies.

By the end of the century, Tidewater and the Deep South had built a racially based caste system, which made a majority or near majority of the population of the states they controlled into second- or third-class citizens. The watershed moment came in 1892, when a group of leading black citizens in New Orleans challenged a new law requiring racially segregated seating on the state's trains. In a carefully organized test, Henry Plessy, who was one-eighth black, was arrested for refusing to leave a whites-only car. He argued in court that segregation violated the Fourteenth Amendment's guarantee of equal protection under the law. Louisiana and the U.S. Supreme Court disagreed, the latter proclaiming, in effect, that a racial caste system did not imply the superiority of one race over the other.

In the twenty years that followed passage of Louisiana's segregated-train law, all of the states controlled by the Deep South, Tidewater, and the Confederate parts of Greater Appalachia instituted new constitutions or amended existing ones to legally disenfranchise black and poor white voters through poll taxes, record-keeping requirements, and literacy tests administered and judged by white local officials. Voter turnout in these regions collapsed, with black turnout in Louisiana falling to 0.5 percent. Overall voter participation in Mississippi fell from 70 percent in 1877 to under 10 percent in 1910.

African Americans, who had represented Deep Southern states in the U.S. House and Senate in the 1870s, vanished from all elected offices. "The results were everywhere the same," historian Richard Franklin Bensel concluded. "Almost all blacks and poor whites were disenfranchised and the plantation elite achieved hegemonic control over the region." Across these regions, blacks were also prohibited from attending white schools and movie theaters, from using white water fountains and train cars, and from marrying a white person. Restaurant, hotel, and store owners were given the liberty to ban patrons based on race.[21]

Despite their defeat in the Civil War, these regions had restored their traditional system of liberty, one that maximized the freedoms of a privileged minority and suppressed those of millions deemed unfit to enjoy the same. It was a system that would remain in place for the better part of a century.

★

As the Supreme Court and the Senate successfully hobbled federal action in the 1870s, 1880s, and 1890s, states in the more communitarian regions of the country began passing laws and regulations to protect their own "moral communities" from the worst excesses of the age.

Massachusetts, that most Yankee of states, was decades ahead of the pack. It passed the first child labor laws in the nation (1836), introduced the first factory inspection system (1866), the first full-time and investigatory railroad safety commission (1869), the first ten-hour workday limits for women and children (1874), and the first use of secret ballots in elections (1888). It was the first state to forbid employers from paying wages in company-supplied merchandise (instead of cash), to require employers to pay wages weekly, to require disclosure of lobbying activities, and to create a proactive utilities commission, armed with "summary powers as to rates and service." In the 1870s, when laissez-faire was on the rise in much of the country, the Bay State was carefully monitoring and regulating the issuance of railroad stocks, bonds, and fare changes. In the first decade of the twentieth century, the Massachusetts legislature enacted a record of progressive legislation unmatched in the country: a state inheritance tax, a ban on corporate donations to political campaigns and on night work for women and children, savings bank insurance, telephone and telegraph commissions, and the first compulsory medical inspections of children in the United States.[22]

"When the Progressive Era began, Massachusetts already enjoyed most of the institutions and laws for which progressives elsewhere were just beginning to wage strenuous campaigns," Berkeley historian Richard Abrams, who studied this period, later observed. "It owed most of these achievements, however, not to any reform movement, but rather to the character of its tradition, rooted in the Puritan-colonial experience. . . . What was 'new' to reformers elsewhere was often 'old' to Massachusetts." Indeed, virtually all of the aforementioned measures were put forward not by insurgent reformers, but by the state's social and corporate leadership. Using public institutions to enhance and further the public good was established practice in New England, a tradition conservatives sought to conserve. Its Boston Brahmin elite had inherited the Puritan distrust of human instincts and the concomitant desire to order society, uphold community standards, and restrain the worst impulses of the individual. The Brahmins could be xenophobic, regarding foreign immigrants as at least as great a threat to community standards and republican virtue as the railroad barons or southern slave lords. They believed wholeheartedly in capitalism, individual initiative, and the Calvinist work ethic, but not in the genius of unrestrained capitalism or in the promised harvest of "enlightened self-interest."[23]

When another terrible depression shook the country in 1893, reform movements sprang up across its northern tiers. Like the Massachusetts Brahmins, these turn-of-the-century Progressives weren't opposed to free-market capitalism or Lockean individualism, but they did believe that laissez-faire was destroying both. Their philosophical mentor was the sociologist Lester Ward, the son of old New Englanders who had settled in the Yankee north of Illinois, and who became the greatest foe of Herbert Spencer and the social Darwinists. "How can . . . true individualism be secured and complete freedom of individual action be vouchsafed?" Ward asked in 1893. "Herein lies a social paradox . . . that *individual freedom can only come through social regulation*." He elaborated a theory of collective action to maintain the conditions required to keep individuals free:

> Such a powerful weapon as reason is unsafe in the hands of one individual when wielded against another. It is still more dangerous in the hands of corporations, which proverbially have no souls. It is most baneful of all in the hands of compound corporations which seek to control the wealth of the world. It is only safe when employed by the social ego, emanating from the collective brain of society, and directed toward securing the common interests of the social organism.[24]

It was in essence the approach Massachusetts had been taking for decades, which would now be adopted by insurgents in other parts of Yankeedom (Jane Addams in northern Illinois, Charles Evans Hughes in upstate New York, and Robert LaFollette in Wisconsin), the Midlands (William Jennings Bryan in eastern Nebraska), and New Netherland (where Herbert Croly helped found the *New Republic* in 1914 and from whence came the movement's greatest figures, Al Smith and Theodore Roosevelt).

Teddy Roosevelt, who served as president from 1901 to 1909,

broke up Standard Oil, Northern Securities (which controlled both the Great Northern and Northern Pacific railways), the American Tobacco Company, and other great corporate trusts; intervened in a major mining strike to secure a solution beneficial to workers; and founded the National Park Service, national wildlife refuges, and the U.S. Forest Service. He presided over the passage of the Pure Food and Drug Act of 1906, the Federal Meat Inspection Act of 1906, and the Hepburn Act, which regulated railroad fares. His goal, he told a rapt audience at the laying of the cornerstone of the Pilgrim Monument in Provincetown, Massachusetts, in 1907, was to restore the spirit of the early Puritans, who yoked the individualistic Protestant work ethic to communitarian goals and institutions. "The Puritan owed his extraordinary success in subduing this continent and making it the foundation for a social life of ordered liberty primarily to the fact that he combined in a very remarkable degree both the power of individual initiative, of individual self-help, and the power of acting in combination with his fellows," he said. "He could combine with others whenever it became necessary to do a job which could not be as well done by any one man individually. . . . The spirit of the Puritan . . . never shrank from regulation of conduct if such regulation was necessary for the public weal; and it is this spirit which we must show today whenever it is necessary."[25]

★

Frustrated with the pace of reform after he left office, Roosevelt created the Progressive Party and ran as a third-party presidential candidate in 1912. He called for women's suffrage, an end to child labor, unemployment insurance, increased regulation of the trusts, and a "New Nationalism" that would make the protection of human welfare, rather than property, its top priority. "The true friend of property, the true conservative, is he who insists that property shall be the servant and not the master of the commonwealth," he said. "The object of government is the welfare of the people."[26]

But Roosevelt split the northern vote that year, enabling Woodrow Wilson to win the presidency, the one and only southerner to do so between 1897 and 1932. Of the five other men to hold the office in this period, three were Yankees (William McKinley, William Taft, and Calvin Coolidge) and two were Midlanders (Warren Harding and Herbert Hoover). Although identified with laissez-faire capitalism, all of these presidents supported civil rights for African Americans (save Hoover) and expanded federal powers and checks on corporate and oligarchic power (save Coolidge). Taft, the Yale-educated child of Massachusetts Puritans who moved to Ohio, furthered Roosevelt's antitrust investigations and supported constitutional amendments instituting the federal income tax (to shift more of the tax burden to those most able to pay) and the direct popular election of U.S. senators (to disrupt corporate control of that congressional chamber via compliant state legislatures). Harding lowered taxes on the wealthy, but he also sought to make the government more effective through the creation of the Office of Management and Budget, the General Accounting Office, and the Veterans Administration. Coolidge was a laissez-faire president, but while governor of Massachusetts he had supported labor, wage, and workplace safety measures. Hoover, from the Iowa Midlands, founded the Veterans Administration and the antitrust division at the Department of Justice, expanded the national park system, and fought (unsuccessfully) for a federal Department of Education and universal pensions for senior citizens.[27]

Many Progressives also saw alcohol as an insidious force, damaging to the economic security and social tranquility of both the family and community. The temperance and prohibition movements were driven almost entirely by Yankees and Midlanders. The lobbying group that won a constitutional amendment criminalizing alcohol, the Anti-Saloon League, was founded in the Yankee-settled Western Reserve of Ohio in 1893 by a Congregational minister and led by William Wheeler, an Oberlin-educated descendant of Massachusetts Puritans. The Woman's Christian Temperance Union was founded in Yankee-settled Cleveland Ohio, and long led by feminist Frances Willard, daughter of a Congregational schoolteacher from upstate New York. Similarly, Yankees, Midlanders, and New Netherlanders dominated the fight for women's suffrage, staging all their major conventions and drawing their principal leaders—Susan B. Anthony, Lucy Stone, Elizabeth Cady Stanton, and Carrie Chapman Catt—from within these regions.[28]

The Deep South and Tidewater were conspicuously absent from much of the Progressive movement, and Greater Appalachia was only marginally involved. These regions generally fought changes to their libertarian social and economic order and to most efforts to strengthen the federal government's ability to act as a moral agent. The lowland southern regions were locked out of the White House until the late twentieth century. Greater Appalachia, however, had President Woodrow Wilson.

Wilson, born in the Appalachian section of Virginia to slaveholding Scots-Irish parents, exhibited the strengths and weaknesses of his region at the time. He was a white supremacist who oversaw the purging of black administrators at federal agencies and the introduction of racially segregated bathrooms and offices in government buildings and camps for the training of U.S. Army officers. Wilson also had no interest in social reforms, and was an opponent of women's suffrage. In other matters he was more progressive, sensitive to the corporate challenge to individual freedom, but approaching the problem from a libertarian mind-set. "The Wilsonian Progressives opposed trusts on laissez-faire grounds, because they closed the market to individual competitors," historian Garry Wills has noted, while Roosevelt's

"New Nationalism" aimed to "use government power for regulating big companies, not for breaking them up." Wilson created the Federal Reserve system (making the financial system a public concern) and the Federal Trade Commission. He supported passage of the Clayton Antitrust Act, which criminalized a range of business practices that fostered monopolies and specifically exempted labor unions from antitrust actions, a clause sometimes called "the Magna Carta of labor." Philosophically, however, Wilson took these measures in an effort to restore the libertarian vision of Jefferson and Jackson by dismantling the power of banks and monopolies over self-governing individuals, not because he favored enhancing the administrative powers of the state. "If the government is to tell big business men how to run their business," Wilson once warned, "then don't you see that big business men have to get closer to the government even than they are now?" Wilson and Roosevelt may have championed similar economic reforms, but they did so in the pursuit of distinct, regionally grounded traditions.[29]

During World War I, however, Wilson abruptly changed course. To mobilize the country to fight an unpopular overseas conflict, the president implemented a collectivist agenda on a scale unprecedented in American history. The economy was placed under intense federal supervision via the War Industries Board (which organized the production of key war materials), the Food Administration (which attempted to set prices and reduce consumption), the Fuel Administration (which monitored and maintained energy supplies), the War Finance Corporation (which channeled funds to war industries), the U.S. Shipping Board (which could commandeer and operate ships), and the U.S. Railway Administration (which nationalized the railroads). Taxes were raised on the wealthy and, in one of the most symbolic assertions of collective interests over individual ones, the military draft was restored for the first time since the Civil War. "We have come to the time when the old individualistic principle must be set aside," fuel administrator Harry Garfield, son of the former president, said in 1917, "and we must boldly embark upon the new principle of cooperation and combination."

The wartime effort went further than merely directing the economy, however, as it extended into the more fraught challenge of "improving" individuals. Wilson's administration sought to coerce and indoctrinate Americans to be unquestioningly loyal to both the government and a war many thought unnecessary. A raft of authoritarian legislation was passed: the Sedition Act, the Espionage Act, the Alien Act, the Alien Enemies Act, and the Trading with the Enemy Act. Together they criminalized criticizing or disagreeing with either the war effort or the government. The Sedition Act forbade "uttering, printing, writing, or publishing any disloyal, profane, scurrilous, or abusive language about the United States government or the military." Opponents of the war—including Socialist Party presidential candidate Eugene Debs—were given long prison terms simply for speaking against the conflict, while postal officials purged the mail of antiwar newspapers and even personal letters. (Such arrests prompted the foundation, in 1917, of what became the American Civil Liberties Union.) German Americans were pressured to stop using or teaching their language and to give English names to their towns and cultural organizations. Federally sponsored propaganda programs were developed for public schools, public and private colleges, and military training camps, where social workers devised programs aimed at suppressing vice, a category that included not only brothels but jazz and drink as well. "The great European war . . . is striking down individualism and building up collectivism," Progressive Party cofounder George Perkins, a partner at J.P. Morgan, proclaimed. Social philosopher Felix Adler agreed, seeing the war effort as an opportunity to create "the perfect man . . . fairer and more beautiful and more righteous than any . . . that has yet existed."[30]

With the end of the war, the backlash against these extreme collectivist policies was severe. Wilson was denounced as an enemy of individual and states' rights. "Of the effects of the war on America, by far the most fundamental was our submission to autocracy in government," wrote conservative journalist Mark Sullivan. "It was the greatest submission by the individual to the state that has occurred in any country at any time . . . an abrupt reversal of the evolution that had been underway for centuries." The administration's loyalty campaign backfired after the Bolshevik Revolution, as conspiracy-minded Americans engaged in a frenzied search for Red Russian agents locally, an event that came to be known as the first Red Scare. Mobs and soldiers broke up Socialist Party meetings, federal authorities deported radicals to the Soviet Union, and the New York legislature refused to seat five duly elected socialists—all in contravention of the law. Laissez-faire business leaders began referring to Progressives as "parlor Bolsheviks." Wilson's fellow Democrats lost both houses of Congress in 1918, and months later Progressive lion Teddy Roosevelt died at age sixty.

By using the power of the state to try to remake individuals, the Progressives had overreached. Americans of all regional traditions were opposed to such coercion, and even those who had supported the more centrist reforms of the prewar period had grown weary of the constant efforts to improve the country. The pendulum swung wide, inaugurating a decade-long return to laissez-faire individualism, albeit in a more moderate form than that which had reigned in the 1880s.

★

"The group must not endanger the individual," Republican presidential nominee Warren Harding, a laissez-faire conservative, declared, promising a "return to normalcy," a pledge that enabled him to win the 1920 election in a landslide. "The radicalism which had tinged our whole political and economic life from soon after 1900 to the World War period was passed," Harding's running mate, Calvin Coolidge, would later recall. "Its power was gone."[31]

The conservative movement's new leaders, Harding, Coolidge, and Herbert Hoover, recognized that individualism had its limits. When he accepted his party's nomination in 1920, Harding endorsed laissez-faire, but also prohibitions on lynching and child labor; the use of federal aid to solve a national housing shortage; and the collective bargaining rights of workers. Coolidge, who became president after Harding's premature death in 1923, argued that the country "is social as well as individual" and should help empower individuals via "education at public expense, a fair and always a living wage for faithful work, healthful living conditions, childhood and motherhood cherished, honored, and rescued from the grasp of all selfishness." Hoover, who had been head of Wilson's Food Administration and served in Harding's and Coolidge's cabinets, championed what he called "American individualism," which argued that the sole source of human progress was "that each human individual shall be given the chance and stimulation for development of the best with which he has been endowed in heart and mind." During the Harding administration, he wrote:

Individualism cannot be maintained as the foundation of a society if it looks to only legalistic justice based upon contracts, property, and political equality. Such legalistic safeguards are not enough. In our individualism we have long since abandoned the laissez faire of the 18th Century—the notion that it is "every man for himself and the devil take the hindmost." We abandoned that when we adopted the idea of equality of opportunity—the fair chance of Abraham Lincoln. . . . We have also learned that fair division can only be obtained by certain restrictions on the strong and the dominant.

For Hoover, a Quaker-raised Midlander, individualism was a communal enterprise.[32]

Twenty years of Progressive rule had left its mark even on the champions of laissez-faire, who now accepted that naked, completely unchecked individualism led to an unjust, structurally unfair economy and society. Individualists—and Harding and Coolidge were as stalwart in this regard as any political leader of their generation—were no longer opposed to the federal government's setting and enforcing minimum standards of economic and social conduct, nor to its encouraging modest measures that would help the individual reach his or her full potential, be they schools, libraries, public parks, or protection from extreme exploitation.

At the same time, these "new individualists" had what turned out to be excessive faith in the ability of an increasingly modern and fast-paced economy to regulate itself and provide for almost all of the needs of society. "What we need is less government in business and more business in government," said Harding, who later saw several senior cabinet members and agency heads go to prison for their roles in business schemes that transferred taxpayer funds into their own pockets. Harding appointed as treasury secretary one of the nation's leading industrialists, Andrew Mellon, who stayed on in the Coolidge and Hoover administrations and was so influential that he was later said to "have had three presidents serve under him." Mellon, who while in office continued guiding the Mellon Bank, Alcoa, Gulf Oil, and other businesses his family controlled, made dramatic cuts on taxes affecting the corporations and the wealthy, arguing that they would pay for themselves through increased (and taxable) economic activity. As perhaps the first "deficit hawk," he helped defeat efforts to pay certain benefits to World War I veterans ahead of schedule and to forgive some of the wartime debts of America's allies whose countries lay in ruins. Coolidge and Mellon agreed that the economy could get by with minimal interference—nine out of ten problems, Coolidge claimed, "will run into a ditch before they reach you"—and that businessmen would lead the nation. "The chief business of the American people is business," the president famously said. "The man who builds a factory builds a temple; the man who works there worships there."[33]

In the 1920s, the economy boomed, fueled by the spread of new technological innovations: the radio, the telephone, automobiles, airplanes, and, perhaps greatest of all, electricity. The stock market rose steadily, then shot steeply upward as hundreds of thousands of investors speculated on securities on credit. Unemployment fell below 2 percent. The budget deficit shrank. Living standards rose.

Then, with a sudden shock, it all began falling apart.

★

At first it seemed like a run-of-the-mill depression, a downturn like the ones that had occurred in 1873, 1893, or 1907. The stock market crash of October 1929 precipitated a serious but apparently manageable crisis in the banking system and a slowdown in industrial output. Unemployment tripled by the end of that year, from 3 to 9 percent. It was all painful but, as Andrew Mellon argued, an essential, natural adjustment that should be allowed to run its course. "Liquidate labor, liquidate stocks, liquidate the farmers, liquidate real estate," Mellon advised President Hoover, who had succeeded Coolidge in 1928. "It will purge the rottenness out of the system. . . . People will work harder, lead a more moral life."[34]

Much to Mellon's irritation, however, Hoover didn't stand idly by. Within weeks of the crash, he nearly doubled the budget for constructing federal facilities, contacted mayors and governors around the country to encourage them not to cut back infrastructure spending, and held meetings with leaders of banks, railroads, and manufacturing companies to ask them to avoid layoffs and wage cuts—all with the aim of keeping the economy moving. He reached out to state and private actors because it suited his philosophy—volunteerism, not coercion—and because for practical reasons he had to: The federal government was then too small a force to act as an effective countercyclical tool. In 1929 all federal construction expenditures were just $200 million, compared to nearly $2 billion for state governments and $9 billion in the private sector. Hoover also went along with a wrongheaded move by Congress to sharply raise tariffs on a wide range of foreign goods—the Smoot-Hawley Tariff Act of 1930—despite receiving a letter from over a thousand economists urging him to veto the measure, and despite the fact the United States had a $25 billion trade surplus at the time; predictably, other countries retaliated and U.S. exports fell by 40 percent over the following two years. All of Hoover's efforts to buoy the economy were offset by the effects of the tariff and the policies of the Federal Reserve, which tightened the money supply while banks were struggling to maintain liquidity.[35]

By the winter of 1931–32, conditions had turned from bad to catastrophic. Bank failures, which had already reached the disturbing rate of 500 a year during the go-go 1920s, rose to 1,352 in 1931, with some 600 of them taking place in just the final two months of the year. Thousands of businesses failed, driving unemployment in early 1932 to 20 percent nationally and almost 50 percent in Chicago and Detroit. Major employers began cutting wages despite their earlier pledges to the president. In a country lacking unemployment insurance, national medical insurance, or cash assistance to the poor, the human cost was horrific, particularly as charities, churches, and local governments ran out of resources amid the desperate need. There were "men who are the heads of families creeping through the streets of American cities, eating from garbage cans; men turned out of houses and sleeping week after week on park benches, on the ground in parks, in the mud under bridges," the writer Sherwood Anderson reported. "Our streets are filled with beggars, with men new to the art of begging." In Chicago, where fourteen hundred families were evicted in 1931, social worker Louise Armstrong watched "a crowd of some fifty men fighting over a barrel of garbage that had been left behind a restaurant. American citizens fighting for scraps of food like animals." Thousands sought shelter in public bathrooms and bus stations or "Hoovervilles," the sprawling shantytowns that sprang up in cities across the country, where families lived in huts constructed from discarded packing crates, tarpaper, and whatever else could be found. One built on the shore in the port of Seattle housed over six hundred for years on end; another in Oakland consisted entirely of abandoned concrete sewer pipes. Tens of thousands began wandering across the country aimlessly, hitchhiking or riding on railway boxcars. Meanwhile, the 1931 federal budget deficit, originally estimated at $180 million, hit $903 million, and the 1932 budget's shortfall exceeded $2.7 billion, frightening the president and Secretary Mellon.[36]

In the final gasp of small-government thinking, Hoover and Mellon tried to reestablish economic stability by balancing the budget. Even Mellon privately admitted that this amounted to imposing "additional taxes upon industry and commerce that are in no condition to bear additional burdens." New or higher taxes were also placed on items "in wide use but not of first necessity," including radios, record players, telegrams, phone calls, tobacco, automobiles, and gasoline. Hoover vetoed a $2 billion relief bill that would have funded public works projects, loans to farmers, and state unemployment assistance programs. The economy did not respond to this high-minded austerity, and continued to nosedive. Mellon was forced to resign to avoid impeachment hearings over his self-serving business deals while in office.[37]

Even Coolidge expressed despair. "In other periods of depression it has always been possible to see some things which were solid and upon which you could base hope," he told a reporter. "But as I look about, I see nothing to give ground for hope, nothing of man." He died a few days later.[38]

Hoover left office in March 1933, his reputation in tatters, his party's control of Congress lost for a generation. A new figure had taken over the White House, a man who would permanently alter American ideas about individualism and the common good, and who set the country on what would become the greatest and most widely shared economic expansion in human history.

# CHAPTER 6

# The Rise and Fall of
# National Liberalism (1933–1967)

B y the time Franklin Delano Roosevelt was inaugurated on
March 4, 1933, laissez-faire individualism had been completely discredited. The only question was what would replace it.

The stakes were enormous. In the waning months of the Hoover
administration, the banking system had frozen up entirely, and the
governors of thirty-four states had closed their banks indefinitely. The
gross national product had fallen to half the level of 1929, with construction output falling by four-fifths, iron and steel production by 60
percent, and farm incomes by two-thirds. Official unemployment
stood at 25 percent. The Friday before the inauguration, the Chicago
Board of Trade failed to open for the first time in its history, and the
New York Stock Exchange suspended trading indefinitely.[1]

Relief services for the poor were also bankrupt. The Salvation
Army reported that it couldn't distribute funds because the banks
where they were held kept failing. Chicago, which had stopped paying its teachers years earlier for lack of resources, was on the verge of

closing all its relief stations, on which six hundred thousand destitute people depended for survival. Riots had broken out in coal-mining districts of Kentucky, where crowds overwhelmed police guarding a Red Cross warehouse to "help themselves until all the food was gone." Thousands had stormed the Nebraska State Capitol and the county building in Seattle. Food riots were expected across the country as soup kitchens and aid stations shut their doors and there was uncertainty as to whether the atrophied U.S. military had enough soldiers to maintain order in a crisis. "Capitalism itself was at the point of dissolution . . . money was now useless," author and Roosevelt confidant Earle Looker wrote of inauguration day. "Would it be necessary soon to organize our families against the world, to fight, physically, for food, to keep shelter, to hold possessions?"[2]

The economic crisis was not confined to America, and in other parts of the world radical solutions abounded. In Germany, Adolf Hitler had just become chancellor at the head of an extreme collectivist movement that sought not only to nationalize industries, guarantee employment, and expand welfare programs, but also to purify "the race" through the expulsion (and, later, industrialized murder) of Jews, Roma, and others; he was admired by much of the American establishment, including Henry Ford, Joseph Kennedy, publisher William Randolph Hearst, and Charles Lindbergh. In the Soviet Union, Stalin was presiding over a state-engineered famine that would ultimately kill between five and ten million people and had sent two hundred thousand more into forced labor, extracting resources or building infrastructure for the state under horrendous conditions in the remote camps of the newly established Gulag. The USSR did have plenty of jobs available, however, and in 1933 some hundred thousand American workers would apply to work there.

Many feared a violent upheaval in the United States and an end to democracy if the government didn't step in to rescue the situation.

Others called for FDR to suspend democracy himself in order to preempt a fascist or communist revolution. "The situation is critical, Franklin," columnist Walter Lippmann had told the president-elect in February. "You may have no alternative but to assume dictatorial powers." William Randolph Hearst was so taken with Lippmann's proposal that he produced a feature-length propaganda film, *Gabriel over the White House,* in which a laissez-faire president has an epiphany, fires his cabinet, dissolves Congress, declares martial law, allies with an army of the unemployed, lines captured gangsters up against walls and shoots them, and becomes a popular hero; the film was screened for Roosevelt before his swearing in, and he declared it helpful for the country. FDR did contemplate dictatorship, declaring in his inaugural address that if Congress did not act he would seek "broad executive power to wage a war against the emergency, as great a power that would be given me if we were in fact invaded by a foreign foe." A draft of the national radio address he delivered the following day proposed informing the million members of the American Legion that he had "the right to command you in any phase of the situation that now confronts us"—a bid to mobilize his own extraconstitutional militia. FDR dropped the line before the broadcast and quietly passed word to Congress that he was opposed to constitutional dictatorship.[3]

Instead, Roosevelt executed a swift and sweeping program that nonetheless won the overwhelming endorsement of Congress and the vast majority of Americans. It didn't seek to nationalize industries and the banks or to create state-owned farms or to imprison the country's alleged enemies, as extreme collectivists were doing in Europe and imperial Japan. Nor, with minor exceptions, did it seek to directly redistribute the nation's income. What it did do was to vigorously assert the government's role in protecting the common interest against individual avarice to a degree that had never before been seen in the

United States. Roosevelt described his philosophy even before the crash, in his 1929 inaugural address as governor of New York:

> It is the recognition that our civilization cannot endure unless we, as individuals, recognize our responsibility to and dependence on the rest of the world. For it is literally true that the "self-supporting" man or woman has become as extinct as the man of the stone age. Without the help of thousands of others, any one of us would die, naked and starved. Consider the bread upon our table, the clothes upon our backs, the luxuries that make life pleasant; how many men worked in sunlit fields, in dark mines, in the fierce heat of molten metal, and among the looms of countless factories, in order to create them for our use and enjoyment. I am proud that we of this State have grown to realize this dependence and . . . have also come to know that we as individuals, in our turn must give our time and intelligence to help those who have helped us.[4]

The subsequent economic disaster had dramatically demonstrated this interdependence and the bankruptcy of laissez-faire. "Men may differ as to the particular form of governmental activity with respect to industry and business," he told the nation in a 1934 radio address, "but nearly all are agreed that private enterprise in times such as these cannot be left without assistance and without reasonable safeguards lest it destroy not only itself but also our processes of civilization." He sought "greater freedom [and] security for the average man than he has ever known before in this history of America" and rejected "a return to that definition of liberty under which for many years a free people were being gradually regimented into the service of the privileged few."[5]

Roosevelt sought to accomplish this by making the federal government an active agent to increase the security of individuals, markets, banks, and companies. Between March 1933 and August 1935 he enacted a legislative agenda unprecedented in American history, a sweeping set of experimental reforms that transformed the nation's life. Some programs were designed to be temporary measures to relieve suffering and jump-start the economy while expanding public assets. Billions in federal aid were channeled to the states so they could continue to provide for the unemployed. Three million young men were put to work in the new Civilian Conservation Corps building trails, bridges, and campgrounds in national parks and forests. Eight million more constructed parks, schools, libraries, water mains, highways, and stadiums for the Works Progress Administration. Private companies were contracted by the Public Works Administration for $6 billion in projects, including the Grand Coulee Dam in Washington State; the Triborough Bridge, Lincoln Tunnel, and LaGuardia Airport in New York City; the Overseas Highway in the Florida Keys; the San Francisco–Oakland Bay Bridge; and the fleet aircraft carriers *Yorktown* and *Enterprise,* which would later help defeat Japan.

Other initiatives were intended to be permanent structures designed to "civilize" capitalism. The Federal Deposit Insurance Corporation protected depositors' savings from bank failures and the banks from runs. The Securities and Exchange Commission made stock markets more secure by requiring traded companies to release detailed information on their performance, assets, and risks, reducing uncertainty. The Glass-Steagall Act separated commercial and investment banks, stabilizing the financial sector. The Federal Housing Act standardized real estate appraisal methods and insured long-term mortgages, which enabled lenders to reduce interest rates and down payments. Under the Agricultural Adjustment Act, farmers were given subsidies not to plant as many crops, ending a destructive market failure in which a glut in grains caused prices to drop, which led farmers to increase planting in a desperate effort to make enough income to avoid foreclosure. The Social Security Act provided unemployment insurance and old-age pensions to a large proportion of the workforce and was self-financed via payroll taxes. Child labor and discrimination against union members were banned, and a minimum wage and maximum working hours were instituted. Budget deficits were mitigated by new revenues that, unlike those of the laissez-faire era, fell most heavily on the oligarchy. A stiff inheritance tax was imposed because, as FDR put it, "the transmission from generation to generation of vast fortunes . . . is not consistent with the ideals and sentiments of the American people." A new 79 percent tax on incomes over $5 million affected exactly one person: John D. Rockefeller; the base rate of 4 percent affected only the upper 5 percent of the population.[6]

All of the aforementioned initiatives had overwhelming political support. Despite the fact that the nation remained mired in the Depression, FDR's Democratic Party made major gains in the 1934 midterms, leaving it with two-thirds majorities in both chambers of Congress. In the 1936 election, Roosevelt won a second term with a staggering 532–8 electoral college rout over a progressive Republican, Governor Alf Landon of Kansas; Democrats again made gains in both houses, leaving Republicans with just 88 of 435 seats in the House and 16 of 96 in the Senate. The New Deal (as Roosevelt called his program) didn't end the Depression—it took World War II to accomplish that—but Americans endorsed it all the same.

How did FDR achieve this? He did so by making significant compromises to the libertarian-minded conservatives of the Deep South, Tidewater, and Greater Appalachia, without whom no Democratic president could then rule.

★

In negotiations with Dixie's political representatives, FDR had two factors in his favor: the dire state of the economy, and the fact that they were all members of the same political party. The Democrats had a lock on Congress, where all-powerful committee chairman- ships and leadership positions were assigned by seniority. Since the Deep South and Tidewater had autocratic one-party regimes, their representatives rarely faced competitive elections, and thus seniority was nearly a given. When Roosevelt took office in 1933, southerners chaired twelve of the seventeen most important committees in the House and nine of fourteen in the Senate and held the two most powerful positions in Congress: the Senate majority leader and Speaker of the House. They could, if they wished, have blocked their Yankee-born president's communitarian agenda, and they had in fact already been lobbying for austerity, balanced budgets, and fed- eral inaction. To be successful, FDR at a minimum had to avoid offending their cultures' mores, which meant first and foremost ensuring that nothing in the New Deal presented a clear danger to their race-based caste system or the interests of its planter and busi- ness oligarchy.[7]

The three Dixie regions had built their economic development strategy on the availability of a poor, docile, racially stratified labor force. Cotton mills had come to the Appalachian Piedmont not so much as to be near the cotton as to have an abundant supply of low- wage workers willing to toil long hours in bad conditions. The region's all-important agricultural sector was still based on servile labor, though it was now performed mostly by impoverished black sharecroppers and tenant farmers whose grandparents had been slaves. Keeping workers—especially black ones—inexpensive and vulnerable was of paramount importance. If their historic enemies, the northern-controlled banks, railroads, and manufacturers, could be knocked down to size as well, all the better.[8]

Between 1933 and 1935, Roosevelt made every feasible conces- sion to maintain the support of the three southern regions. On the insistence of southern members of Congress, the Social Security Act denied old-age pensions and unemployment insurance benefits to domestic, farm, and agricultural processing plant workers, instantly disqualifying two-thirds of all employed black people. Similarly, southern congressmen insisted that the Aid to Dependent Children program—which provided relief to single-parent families and the elderly—be administered by state rather than federal bureaucrats; as a result, aid was disproportionately distributed to whites across the states controlled by these regions, with eligible Georgian whites ten times more likely to receive assistance than their black counterparts. The NAACP, recognizing the discrimination involved, testified against the bill, likening it to "a sieve with holes just big enough for the majority of Negroes to fall through." The same categories of workers were excluded from the New Deal's minimum wage, maximum working hours, and unionization protection measures. In the Deep South, many New Deal–funded public works projects refused to hire black labor, and landowners were allowed to pocket federal payments not to plant crops that were supposed to have been shared with the sharecroppers and tenant farmers whose livelihoods were being taken away.[9]

Following a spate of gruesome lynchings—including that of a black man who was seized from an Alabama jail and, before a cheering crowd of four thousand, stabbed, burned, castrated, force-fed his own genitals, and finally dragged to death behind a car—two nonsouthern senators introduced a bill that made it a federal crime for state officials to collude with lynch mobs. Southern senators staged a successful six-week filibuster, during which one proposed sending all blacks back to Africa and another declared his commitment "to fight for white supremacy." President Roosevelt had no response. "Southerners by reason of seniority rule in Congress," Roosevelt explained to NAACP secretary Walter White. "If I come out for the anti-lynching bill, they will block every bill I ask Congress to pass to keep America from collapsing. I can't take that risk." Even at its zenith, the New Deal was profoundly shaped by the libertarian regional cultures.[10]

Despite Roosevelt's caution, by 1936 the leaders of the Deep South and Tidewater had belatedly started to realize the challenge the New Deal posed to their oligarchic system. Relief programs, public works jobs, federally funded building projects, Social Security pensions, revitalized union movements, and rising labor standards all reduced poor people's dependency on the so-called county-seat elites, the wealthy landowners, merchants, and bankers who controlled local politics across these regions and, to a lesser extent, Greater Appalachia. The southern elite was further horrified when FDR openly campaigned for the votes of northern blacks in the 1936 election, and even more so when the organizers of the Democratic National Convention welcomed black delegates and journalists to attend. "This mongrel meeting is no place for a white man," U.S. senator Ellison Smith of South Carolina proclaimed before storming from the convention hall. "To any discerning person it is perfectly obvious that the so-called Democratic party at the North is now the negro party, advocating social equity for the races," Senator Carter Glass of Virginia complained, making it a clear "socialistic threat to the South" and "an Autocracy." Roosevelt soon found that his agenda's most dangerous opponents were not northern Republicans but rather the Dixie conservatives within his own party. At a special congressional session that November, southerners rejected his plan to issue a new farm bill and to create "seven little TVAs"—a reference to the Tennessee Valley Authority, a public hydropower-driven regional development project—and instead issued a "Conservative Manifesto" reiterating the small-government orthodoxy of the 1920s.[11]

Chastened, the president worked to remake both Democratic and southern politics in the hopes of building a foundation for a lasting communitarian coalition. He declared the South to be "the nation's number one economic problem" and commissioned a federal study on the region. That report, issued in the spring of 1938, detailed the appalling conditions in the southern states: an average income one-half that of the rest of the country; tenant farmers on cotton plantations earning as little as $38 a year at a time when the average American made $604; Arkansas teachers paid one-fifth what their counterparts in New York earned, while fifteen hundred "schools" in Mississippi had no buildings at all, so children studied in abandoned buildings, churches, or cotton pens; entire counties without medical facilities of any kind; and states with widespread malnutrition, water pollution, and squalid housing. Unmentioned in the fifty-nine-page report, however, was the central and distinguishing feature of the region's economy and society—its racial caste system—for that would have offended the liberal southerners the president sought to empower. The president campaigned in primary elections across the region, touting the need for progressive reforms—a New Deal for the South—and the unseating of anti–New Deal senators like Ellison Smith and Maryland's Millard Tydings. He utterly failed in the effort.[12]

On election day 1938, his southern Democratic opponents were returned to office while some of his key allies were swept away in the first decisive Republican wave of the post-crash era. The GOP doubled its strength in the House and gained seven seats in the Senate, most of them in Yankee-controlled areas. Instead of advancing a communitarian coalition, Roosevelt faced a revived conservative one.[13]

The president now discovered the limits of American toleration for collectivist reform. By late 1938, he had lost considerable support for his agenda across the country. First there had been his unsuccessful experiments not just in regulating the free market, but in trying to actually plan its course. The National Recovery Administration, created during the dark days of 1933, attempted to control production in entire industries through the management of government-fostered cartels, on the questionable theory that the Depression had been caused by excessive competition. An army of forty-five thousand bureaucrats oversaw in excess of seven hundred regulatory codes (nineteen for hardware stores alone), many of which benefited major firms at the expense of smaller ones. "The excessive centralization and dictatorial spirit," the normally sympathetic Walter Lippmann charged, "are producing a revulsion of feeling against bureaucratic control of American economic life."

When the Supreme Court, still a bulwark of laissez-faire orthodoxy, struck down the Agricultural Adjustment Act, the parent legislation of the National Recovery Act, and several state-level minimum wage laws, Roosevelt took a bold and extremely damaging step to head off further reversals of the New Deal. He proposed adding several justices to the nine-seat body, creating a liberal majority. The measure never moved forward, but the Court was sufficiently shaken to begin reversing itself, having been forced to recognize that the era in which liberty could be defined as merely the "freedom of contract" was now over. However, FDR's move was widely condemned as an undemocratic power grab, and his reputation never fully recovered. In 1937 the economy entered a new downturn, drawing attention to the fact that the president had yet to pull the country out of the Depression. When his influence in Congress weakened in the 1938 midterms, Roosevelt's legislative agenda was effectively halted, and proposals for a national health care system came to nothing.[14]

This might have marked the end of what scholars sometimes call "national liberalism," a free-market society overseen by an active, equality-seeking government. A libertarian coalition of laissez-faire capitalists and Dixie conservatives might have undone the reforms of 1933–37, returning the country to the status quo ante of the Harding-Coolidge-Hoover era. A deepening depression might have fueled populist insurrections, a radicalization of labor movements, or a rise in support for the still marginalized socialist movement, which sought to nationalize industries outright.

Then, one morning in December of 1941, bombs began falling on Pearl Harbor, calling forth the greatest collectivist enterprise in American history.

★

World War II ended the Great Depression almost overnight, as the Roosevelt administration transformed the country into a massive, government-run war machine that successfully waged battle on three fronts simultaneously; armed, supplied, and fed our allies; and helped vanquish three major industrial dictatorships, liberating hundreds of millions in occupied Europe and Asia. The United States emerged from the war as the richest and most powerful nation in the world, its key national liberal institutions not only intact, but now ingrained in the country's political culture.

The war effort was centrally organized and guided, with the objective of drowning the Axis powers in a flood of ships, planes, tanks, rifles, bombs, bullets, and materiel. The new War Production Board converted established industries to military production, assigning tasks, priorities, and key resources; setting wages and prices; and banning the manufacture of nonessential consumer products like passenger automobiles, refrigerators, and nylon stockings. Government loans financed new plant construction and the expansion of existing facilities, while military procurement offices awarded contracts on a "cost-plus" basis, guaranteeing profits to private firms while the public absorbed all risk and expenses, including research and development. The Selective Service decided whose skills were needed on the production lines and whose on the front. Government rationing of meat, butter, coffee, and gasoline redistributed goods to the war effort. The Office of Scientific Research and Development drew universities into critical research programs, while the $2 billion Manhattan Project employed 150,000 to create the atomic bomb at huge new facilities powered by the New Deal–built Tennessee Valley Authority and Grand Coulee dams.[15]

Big business, which had formerly clashed with Roosevelt, enthusiastically partnered with the government. Massive privately owned factories and shipyards sprouted up almost overnight, churning out B-24s, jeeps, fighters, and cargo ships. Textile companies made parachutes, car plants built tanks and trucks, and typewriter manufacturers produced machine guns. Henry Ford's Willow Run facility in Michigan, constructed in 1941, built eighty-five hundred medium bombers in three years, while Henry Kaiser's sprawling California shipyard built a 440-foot-long, thirty-five-hundred-ton Liberty Ship in four days and fifteen hours, one of thousands of the cheap, mass-produced freighters assembled at yards on both seaboards. By 1944, the United States was producing 60 percent of the Allies' munitions, and 40 percent of the world's. By war's end, it had produced twice as many tanks as Germany, and more than four times as many airplanes as Japan.

Unemployment ended almost instantly, with cost-plus contracts and round-the-clock operations yielding millions of well-paid jobs with plenty of opportunities for overtime. Competition for labor became intense, and to circumvent the restrictions of wage ceilings, many corporations offered health insurance, retirement benefits, and other perks, establishing an American model of employer-sponsored social welfare. (Henry Kaiser's pioneering health management organization lives on today as Kaiser Permanente.) In the process, big business was rehabilitated in the public eye, its leaders seen as—and seeing themselves as—partners in the collective national project, rather than selfish guardians of privilege. (Even the War Production Board was headed by a business executive, Sears & Roebuck's Donald Nelson.) In guiding this state-directed economic effort and ultimately winning the war, the federal government also demonstrated its competence. "Only the willfully blind can fail to see that the old-style capitalism of a primitive, free-shooting period is gone forever," the president of the orthodox conservative U.S. Chamber of Commerce, Eric Johnson, said in 1943. "The capitalism which thrived on low wages and maximum profits for minimum turnover, which rejected collective bargaining and fought against justified public regulation of the competitive system, is a thing of the past."[16]

But while the economic prosperity of the war years may have put an end to laissez-faire, it also undermined Roosevelt's efforts to push onward from national liberalism to social democracy. In other parts of the industrialized world, governments were assuming a responsibility not just to maintain the individual freedom of ordinary people— an equality of opportunity—but to promote their well-being through "cradle to grave" social programs, redistributive taxes on the wealthy, and robust state-run health, housing, and education systems. Near the end of his life, FDR tried to advance a similar agenda in the United States, proposing a "Second Bill of Rights" in his 1944 State of the Union address, which included the right to a living wage, decent housing, "adequate protection from the economic fears of old age, sickness, accident and unemployment," a "good education," and medical care. "We have come to a clear realization of the fact that true individual freedom cannot exist without economic security and independence," he explained. "'Necessitous men are not free men.' People who are hungry and out of a job are the stuff of which dictatorships are made."[17]

But the ambitious plan was not to be. Roosevelt had lost congressional support in the 1942 midterms, as the public registered a resentment of the growth in government bureaucracy and control. The conservative coalition of Dixie Democrats and old-line Republicans had already repealed the Civilian Conservation Corps, Works Progress Administration, and other programs featuring direct government activity in the labor market. When the first of the new social democratic provisions was introduced—a Full Employment Bill establishing a "right to employment" and requiring the government to attempt to maintain full employment levels through continuous forecasting and investment—Congress gutted it. Returning soldiers were offered health, education, and low-cost mortgage benefits through the GI Bill, but this was a temporary measure to help millions of servicemen reintegrate with the economy and was not extended to the rest of the population. In 1946, the conservative coalition killed a national health insurance bill that would have created a Canadian-style system; the American Medical Association instructed doctors to advise their patients against this "socialized medicine," while southerners worried the system might force them to end the racial segregation of their hospitals. In 1947, they rolled back labor union rights with the Taft-Hartley Act, which banned secondary boycotts, sympathy strikes, and union membership for supervisors, and allowed states to adopt so-called right-to-work laws, which prohibited employers from entering into contracts that require their workers to be union members, a measure that was subsequently used in the South to hobble unionization.[18]

That said, Congress did not attempt to undo the pillars of national liberalism: Social Security, financial regulation, farm price supports, and child labor and minimum wage standards remained in place. Nor did the electorate turn FDR out of office in 1944, or replace his successor, Harry Truman, in 1948. When a Republican finally did win the White House in 1952, he made it clear that he had no intention of dismantling the New Deal order. "Should any political party attempt to abolish social security and eliminate labor laws and farm programs, you would not hear of that party again in our political history," President Dwight D. Eisenhower wrote his brother in 1954. "There is a tiny splinter group, of course, that believes you can do these things. . . . Their number is negligible and they are stupid."[19]

Eisenhower was keenly aware that the United States and the world faced mortal danger. When he took office, Joseph Stalin led the Soviet Union, and both superpowers were preparing to fight what some still thought of as a "winnable" atomic war. The former Allied commander in Europe, Eisenhower saw himself as the captain of a ship entering stormy seas. By his reckoning, a continuation of national liberalism was the best way to ensure a happy crew and a smoothly running and well-maintained vessel.[20]

A Midland centrist, Eisenhower believed in fiscal responsibility, but did not consider that incompatible with making high-return investments in collective projects like education, scientific research, and transportation infrastructure. He signed the law that funded the creation of the Interstate Highway System (which now bears his name) and the 1958 National Defense Education Act, which provided low-cost student loans, offered grants for states to purchase laboratory and teaching equipment for schools and colleges, and funded foreign-language and area studies centers. He presided over an expansion of Social Security; an increase in the minimum wage; the creation of the Department of Health, Education, and Welfare; and the construction, with Canada, of the Saint Lawrence Seaway. Committed to balancing budgets—he did so three times—he raised taxes on the wealthiest Americans to 91 percent to pay for these programs and the Cold War military buildup. He clashed with the laissez-faire old guard of his party, who were furious at his failure to undo the New Deal. "If the right wing wants a fight, they're going to get it," he vowed in 1954. "[B]efore I end up, either this Republican Party will reflect progressivism, or I won't be with them anymore."[21]

The public, however, approved of his approach. Eisenhower was reelected by a wide margin in 1956, sweeping all the regions save the Deep South and Tidewater, where the president's social programs and support of civil rights were unpopular. The laissez-faire wing of his party insisted on adopting an antilabor "right to work" message for the 1958 midterm elections and suffered their worst defeat since the early 1930s, giving Democrats a nearly two-to-one advantage in both chambers; almost all of the Republican losses were in Yankee-dom and the Midlands. Two national liberal moderates, Richard Nixon and John F. Kennedy, faced off in the 1960 presidential contest, and in a tight race, the nation chose the more collectivist of the two. Reporting on the results of a Gallup survey early that year, *Look* magazine summarized the national mood: "Americans today are relaxed, unadventurous, comfortably satisfied with their way of life and blandly optimistic about the future."[22]

Libertarian economists often argue that government regulation, high taxes, and social spending will retard growth and undermine prosperity. The country's experience under the national liberal consensus was quite the opposite, as it was responsible for the greatest and most broadly shared economic boom in American history, an era that saw the creation of a middle-class society in the Yankee and Midlander mold, and the decline of the relative and absolute power of the oligarchy. Nobel Prize–winning economist Paul Krugman has calculated that between 1947 and 1973, the real income of the typical family doubled to the equivalent of $44,000 in 2007 dollars, an annual growth rate of an astounding 2.7 percent. As a result of redistributive tax policies, Krugman estimates the richest 1 percent of Americans saw their after-tax incomes reduced by 20 to 30 percent in absolute terms. The after-tax incomes of the richest of the rich—the top tenth of 1 percent—were reduced by more than 50 percent, even though their inflation-adjusted pretax incomes were essentially unchanged; their overall share of the nation's wealth fell from over 20 percent in 1929 to about 10 percent during the Eisenhower administration. Blue-collar workers, benefiting from FDR-era unionization, the collapse of foreign competition for U.S. manufacturers, and severe restrictions on immigration imposed in 1924, saw their incomes soar, enabling them to afford a car, a home in the new suburbs, and a middle-class upbringing for their children. Between 1949 and 1979 the bottom 60 percent of households more than doubled their pretax incomes. National liberal policies had engineered a more equitable distribution of income, and the result was a prosperous and self-confident society that was envied the world over.[23]

★

During this apogee of national liberal power, the forces of libertarian reaction were retooling and reorganizing.

They started with a losing proposition: a return to the glory days of the Coolidge administration, or better yet, the 1880s, when government did little more than act as a night watchman, protecting the property of the worthy from threats foreign and domestic. In 1945, their leading figures were corporate agents rather than political figures. Leonard Read was a former U.S. Chamber of Commerce official, Ayn Rand devotee, and founder of the Foundation for Economic Education, a corporate-funded think tank tasked with promoting a return to laissez-faire. In 1948, its major funders were U.S. Steel, General Motors, Chrysler, and Consolidated Edison, the same firms that were the primary patrons of another anti–New Deal think tank, the American Enterprise Institute, founded in 1943. AEI—originally the American Enterprise Association—was founded by asbestos tycoon Lewis H. Brown, who was hiding from his employees that they had asbestosis so they would continue working. ("We save a lot of money that way," he told his firm's attorney.) While their papers and conferences helped block any expansion of the New Deal in the late 1940s, the think tanks had no prominent political champion willing to press their case for a restoration of laissez-faire. Even Senator Robert Taft of Ohio, the leading conservative politician of the era, supported the minimum wage, unemployment insurance, pensions for the elderly, public housing, and the tax increases required to pay for them. "The extreme philosophy . . . is to 'let the Devil take the hindmost' and to let those who are unable to keep up suffer poverty and hardship on the theory that in the end the general progress will be faster," Taft told an audience of mortgage bankers in early 1949. "Without arguing the economics of this theory, it is enough to say that it offends every humane sense, and that Americans are humane people."[24]

An important rhetorical advance came with the arrival of two refugees from the former Austro-Hungarian Empire, economist Ludwig von Mises and his onetime Austrian government supervisor Friedrich Hayek, who arrived in the United States in 1940 and 1950, respectively. They had experienced the collapse of the empire and subsequently the fall of Austria's liberal democracy to the extreme collectivist regime of another native son, Adolf Hitler, from whose dictatorship both economists had fled westward in the 1930s. In exile, they pondered why the Austrian republic had failed and came to essentially the same conclusion: Social democracy was to blame. Ruling for the first year and a half of the Austrian republic's existence in 1918–20, the Social Democrats had introduced a comprehensive set of social reforms presaging those of the New Deal: unemployment insurance; paid holidays; an eight-hour workday; regulations on child, female, and mining industry labor conditions; legal protections for collective bargaining; and government aid to the disabled. The Social Democrats subsequently lost power to the party of traditional Catholic conservatives, who in turn were swept away by the fascists. Hayek and Mises concluded that social democracy had undermined free society, serving as the nose of some collectivist camel whose fascistic body inevitably followed, bringing down the tent. Hayek predicted that if the British Labour Party took power and succeeded in enacting its social democratic agenda, the United Kingdom would enter "a state of mind in which naziism could become successful." Instead, Labour's coming to power stabilized the country, while social democrats in Sweden, Norway, Iceland, and Denmark built some of the richest, happiest, and most economically free nations on the planet. By the early 1950s, as social democratic regimes thrived across the West, few in Western Europe took either Hayek or Mises seriously.[25]

In America, however, the Austrians' theories were embraced by the beleaguered laissez-faire movement. Mises was hired by the Foundation for Economic Education (FEE), which vigorously promoted his ideas, while the home furnishings magnate Harold Luhnow paid Hayek's salary at the University of Chicago via his family's foundation. Luhnow, who also supported FEE and underwrote Mises's salary at New York University, distributed both Austrians' books and introduced them to other businessmen. Although some were disturbed by Hayek's acceptance of consumer product safety and working hours regulations and the possibility of "an extensive system of social services," they immediately recognized the rhetorical breakthrough the two Austrians had made. Free markets should be championed not because of their alleged efficiency or because they rewarded the worthy, but rather because they—and only they—could make a people free. "What our generation has forgotten is that the system of private property is the most important guarantee of freedom, not only for those who own property, but scarcely less for those who do not," Hayek wrote in his most famous work, *The Road to Serfdom*. "It is only because the control of the means of production is divided among many people acting independently that nobody has complete power over us, that we as individuals can decide what to do with ourselves." The road to freedom lay not in the political realm, but within the economic one. There, economic libertarians recognized, was a message that might gain popular traction.[26]

Then, in the early 1950s, an additional stimulus was added to the laissez-faire cause: the struggle against Soviet communism. As the relationship with the USSR deteriorated into the Cold War with its attendant arms race and proxy conflicts, Americans found themselves locked in an existential battle with one of the most extreme and powerful collectivist regimes in history. It was a Manichean conflict of the free against the totalitarian, of the godly against the godless, of the righteous against the amoral. As such, anything that could be made to seem akin to Soviet communism was suspect and un-American, and possibly traitorous. The laissez-faire right had long denounced national liberalism as "socialist"; now that charge not only gained credibility but also bore the taint of treason, and at least some on the right were willing to prosecute individuals they judged guilty of that crime.

Senator Joseph McCarthy led the charge, claiming in early 1950 that he had a "list of enemies," communist agents who had purportedly infiltrated the national liberal elite and thus the highest echelons of government and diplomacy. Three years of unsubstantiated allegations, investigations, and purges followed, with Congress hunting down alleged communists and homosexuals in the civil service, the army, industry, and Hollywood, until Maine senator Margaret Chase Smith and other Republican moderates censured the bombastic senator. "The nation sorely needs a Republican victory," Smith told her Senate colleagues. "But I don't want to see the Republican Party ride to political victory on the Four Horsemen of Calumny—Fear, Ignorance, Bigotry, and Smear." Conservative Taft loyalist Representative

George Bender of Ohio put it this way: "McCarthyism has become a synonym for witch-hunting, Star Chamber methods, and the denial of . . . civil liberties."

Others carried on the McCarthyite struggle, including a former vice president of the National Association of Manufacturers, Robert Welch, who founded the John Birch Society in 1958, which was dedicated to stopping the alleged collectivist conspiracy of national liberals secretly plotting to create a Soviet-style one-world government. "There are many stages of welfarism, socialism, and collectivism in general," insisted Welch, who infamously suggested that Eisenhower himself was a communist agent, "but Communism is the ultimate state of them all, and they all lead inevitably in that direction." Despite condemnation by influential laissez-faire conservatives like William F. Buckley and Ayn Rand, by 1961 the John Birch Society claimed a hundred thousand members.[27]

However, the lasting and effective intellectual and rhetorical legacy of Cold War anticommunism wasn't institutionalizing the fear of a one-world government or communist agents, but rather solidly establishing the notion that American freedom and vitality were being weakened by a tyranny of experts and administrators. The argument was no longer that national liberalism was a communist plot, but rather that it was a close cousin of the Soviet-style despotisms, with corrosive effects on the nation. The argument was informed by the writings of Milovan Djilas, whose *The New Class* was published in 1957 while the dissident was serving a ten-year sentence in a Belgrade prison for his dissenting view that communism had brought not equality and freedom but hierarchy and oppression. Communism had turned authoritarian, he argued, because of the necessity, in a society where all economic and civic institutions are state-owned, of all planning and resource allocation decisions being made by an expert and ultimately exploitative administrative class.

Although Djilas emphasized that this communist "New Class" was distinct from its social democratic and national liberal analogs in the West, American laissez-faire circles transposed the concept to postwar America nonetheless.[28]

Since the days of Teddy Roosevelt, progressives had sought to create a government of experts guided by rational inquiry, sound science, and statistical analysis rather than by the political objectives of one or another interest group. Impartial guardians of the public good, they manned the SEC and FDA, the USDA, Forest Service and Federal Reserve, the research labs of Los Alamos and U.S. embassies from London to Lima. By the early 1960s, the individualist right was painting these experts as enemies of freedom and oppressors of the masses and business leaders alike. Entire professions were in on the plot: university professors, scientists, lawyers, journalists, public health workers, urban planners, social workers, and Hollywood studio directors. They populated the faculties of Harvard and Yale, the newsrooms of the *New York Times* and *Washington Post*, and the "silk stocking districts" of the great cities of the Northeast. They didn't make anything useful, like real workers and their entrepreneurial employers. They claimed to know what was good for you, your city, your state, and the world. They were arrogant, out of touch, and elitist. Most important, they were un-American, and had what neoconservative intellectual Irving Kristol would later call "a hidden agenda: to propel the nation . . . toward an economic system so stringently regulated in detail as to fulfill many of the traditional anti-capitalist aspirations of the Left."[29]

It was a powerful argument because it solved the perennial problem of the laissez-faire effort: how to convince working- and lower-middle-class voters to ally themselves with and champion the causes of wealthy industrialists. It substituted cultural resentments for economic arguments. It would ultimately split the national liberals from their historic blue-collar constituents. Its proponents waited in the wings for an opening, and when it came, deployed it to seize the center stage of American political discourse for more than half a century.

★

At the outset, the 1960s promised to witness the triumph of national liberalism. The economy was booming. Millions of working families had joined the middle class, and they were earning more while working less. Big business and government were cooperating to keep the Soviet Union at bay. Public-sector economists had apparently mastered the business cycle. The problems that had confronted the nation in the late nineteenth and early twentieth centuries had been solved. The greatest internal danger appeared to be that Americans, their actual needs having been met, would wallow in mindless consumption and conformity. A book titled *The Affluent Society* appeared on bestseller lists, its author, John Kenneth Galbraith—who was about to join the new presidential administration—arguing that people should be more heavily taxed to divert resources from vapid consumer purchasing and into schools, hospitals, parks, scientific research, and urban renewal projects. The nation, in short, appeared ready to renew and extend its commitment to the common good, to stamp out poverty, end Jim Crow, build up its infrastructure and health care commitments, and send men to the Moon.[30]

John F. Kennedy promised to do all that. He called on Americans to renew their sense of national purpose, "to ask not what your country can do for you, but what you can do for your country." In his brief presidency, he secured passage of a wide range of social and economic reforms: the creation of the food stamp program, the Peace Corps, and the Clean Air Act; and expansions of school lunch programs, food aid for the poor, unemployment and Social Security pension benefits and eligibility, the national park system, and funding to build interstate highways. He also proposed government health care for the elderly—Medicare—but Congress did not pass it.

He was also the first Democrat to take a stand for the civil rights of African Americans, who, as we have seen, were consciously excluded from many of the benefits of the New Deal. Eisenhower had taken steps in that direction, creating the civil rights division at the Department of Justice and federalizing Arkansas National Guard troops to force the racist governor of that state to allow black children to attend Little Rock High School. Despite his party's continued reliance on whites in the Deep South and Tidewater, Kennedy furthered his predecessor's efforts, issuing executive orders forbidding discrimination by federal contractors and assigning federal soldiers and marshals to protect civil rights workers and black students trying to assert their right to enroll at the state universities of Mississippi and Alabama. "Are we to say to the world, and, much more importantly, to each other, that this is a land of the free except for the Negroes; that we have no second-class citizens except Negroes; that we have no class or caste system, no ghettos, no master race, except with respect to Negroes?" Kennedy asked in an address shortly before his death, in which he proposed a sweeping civil rights bill. "This nation, for all its hopes and all its boasts, will not be fully free until all its citizens are free." The bill had bipartisan support in the North and Far West but was blocked in committee by the powerful Tidewater Virginia segregationist representative Howard W. Smith.

Days after Kennedy's assassination, Lyndon Johnson demanded Congress pass the bill, now known as the Civil Rights Act of 1964, as a testament to the slain president. Deep Southern and Tidewater senators and congressmen pulled out all the stops to defeat the legislation, including a nearly two-month-long Senate filibuster. "We will resist to the bitter end any measure or any movement which would have a tendency to bring about social equality and intermingling and amalgamation of the races in our [Southern] states," Senator Richard Russell, Democrat of Georgia, explained. The bill, which barred discrimination in public accommodations and municipal and state facilities, ultimately passed with roughly 80 percent of Republican House and Senate members in favor, and virtually the entire Democratic delegation from Jim Crow regions opposed. The price, Johnson knew, would be steep. A few hours after signing the bill into law he told aide Bill Moyers, "I think we just delivered the South to the Republican Party for a long time to come."[31]

Indeed, the Civil Rights Act shook the nation's political alliances. Most whites in the Deep South and Tidewater, long disturbed by the Democratic Party's turn to national liberalism, were completely alienated by its embrace of the African American cause, a direct violation of the early 1930s bargain that had enabled the New Deal to go forward. And in 1964, unlike thirty years earlier, the laissez-faire faction of the Republican Party was willing and eager to abandon its party's historic embrace of civil rights in exchange for the possibility of political power. Its mouthpiece, the *National Review*, promoted white supremacy, with editor William F. Buckley asking "whether the White community in the South is entitled to take such measures as are necessary to prevail, politically and culturally, in areas in which it does not predominate numerically? The sobering answer is Yes—the White community is so entitled because, for the time being, it is the advanced race." Its standard-bearer was Barry Goldwater, and he would split his party and the old New Deal coalition asunder.[32]

Goldwater, who inherited Phoenix's premier department store and represented Arizona in the U.S. Senate, horrified the progressive Republicans who had backed the New Deal and national liberal order and thrilled the Deep Southern libertarians. He voted against the Civil Rights Act, insisting that it amounted to an unconstitutional infringement of private property rights that would require "the creation of a federal police state of mammoth proportions" to enforce. He argued that "race relations" were "best handled by the people directly concerned," who in the Jim Crow South had already settled on apartheid enforced by vigilante terror. He had denounced Eisenhower from the Senate floor as presiding over a "dime store New Deal" and wrote that "the foundations of my political philosophy were rooted in my resentment of the New Deal." He campaigned for the Republican presidential nomination in 1964, arguing that the federal government should "withdraw from a whole series of programs that are beyond its constitutional mandate—from social welfare programs, education, public power, agriculture, public housing, urban renewal and all other activities" better overseen by the states, individuals, or the private sector. "The collectivists have not abandoned their ultimate goal—to subordinate the individual to the state—but their strategy has changed," he warned. "They have learned that Socialism can be achieved through Welfarism quite as well as through Nationalization." He claimed that "extremism in the defense of liberty is no vice" and promised to abolish Social Security and sell off the Tennessee Valley Authority. To the shock of the party establishment, he defeated progressive Republican stalwart Nelson Rockefeller, governor of New York and heir of John D., and became the party's nominee in the 1964 presidential election.[33]

Goldwater, however, proved to be an electoral disaster. The conservative *Kansas City Star,* which had supported Republicans since 1892, endorsed Lyndon Johnson, as did the mouthpiece of the progressive Republican establishment, the *New York Herald Tribune.* The latter, which had never before supported a Democrat, denounced Goldwater's reliance on "ugly racial passions." Republican candidates avoided appearing with him. On election day, he lost by a landslide, winning only his home state of Arizona and the five states dominated by the Deep South: Louisiana, Mississippi, Alabama, Georgia, and South Carolina. His party lost two seats in the Senate and thirty-eight in the House, leaving it with the smallest delegation since 1936. The question before the voters, the *Washington Post* said, had been, "Do you wish the government to continue its intervention in affairs which before 1932 were largely left to private decision? To that question, the voters have answered 'yes.'"[34]

Indeed, the 1964 elections had given the national liberal project a supermajority of support in Congress such as it had not had since FDR's first term. Moderate Republicans—the ones who supported the Eisenhower consensus—believed themselves to be back in control of their party at a time when laissez-faire Democrats were disappearing from theirs. Johnson realized he had been given the opportunity to complete and further the national liberal enterprise, to enact a "second New Deal" that would make a great society out of one that was simply prosperous. That effort would prove the undoing of the communitarian cause in America for nearly half a century.

★

In his State of the Union address two months after his election victory, Lyndon Johnson proposed a sweeping plan to improve American life. "We worked for two centuries to climb this peak of prosperity. But we are only at the beginning of the road to the Great Society," he told Congress and the nation. "Ahead now is a summit where freedom from the wants of the body can help fulfill the needs of the spirit." He then detailed the steps in a staircase to utopia:

I propose that we begin a program in education to ensure every American child the fullest development of his mind and skills . . . a massive attack on crippling and killing diseases . . . a national effort to make the American city a better and a more stimulating place to live . . . that we increase the beauty of America and end the poisoning of our rivers and the air that we breathe . . . a new program to develop regions of our country that are now suffering from distress and depression . . . new efforts to control and prevent crime and delinquency . . . that we eliminate every remaining obstacle to the right and the opportunity to vote . . . that we honor and support the achievements of thought and the creations of art [and] . . . make an all-out campaign against waste and inefficiency.

And then, amazingly, he and Congress quickly enacted laws aiming to achieve all of that and more.[35]

In its breadth and long-term effect on society, the legislative flood of 1965–66 was matched only by that put forward by FDR in 1932–33. Congress created the Medicare program to provide health insurance to senior citizens, Medicaid to do so for the poor; the Department of Transportation to improve infrastructure and the Department of Housing and Urban Development to address squalor; and the National Endowment for the Arts and the National Endowment for the Humanities to support culture. It passed the Voting Rights Act to do away with race-based barriers to voting; a Water Pollution Control Act and Motor Vehicle Pollution Control Act to reduce environmental damage; the Fair Packaging and Labeling Act to ensure the safety of consumers; the Highway Beautification Act to eradicate ugly billboard signs; and a Higher Education Act to help students attend college. It sent over $1 billion to the long-blighted uplands of Greater Appalachia under the Appalachian Regional Development Act and the Appalachian Regional Commission.

The Great Society's signature campaign, however, was launched during Johnson's caretaker administration of 1964, an "unconditional war on poverty." This war was substantively conducted through the Economic Opportunity Act, which sought to end poverty completely, and while its ambitions were unprecedented, its means were tellingly conservative. Johnson was a Greater Appalachia progressive and a political realist, and in keeping with both he built his war around the traditional libertarian theories about the causes of poverty: that it was not a social problem, but the result of shortcomings in the individual. His tactic, therefore, was to provide the skills and opportunities to "break the cycle of poverty": job training, vocational education, work experience programs for welfare recipients, early childhood education via the Head Start program, and political empowerment through "Community Action Organizations" comprised of the poor themselves. The goal, in Johnson's words, was "making taxpayers out of taxeaters" by offering them "opportunity and not doles." Politically, this enabled the president to sell his policies as an antiwelfare program, which would be appealing to libertarian-minded members of Congress. When Secretary of Labor Willard Wirtz had suggested in a cabinet meeting that a massive jobs program similar to the New Deal–era Works Progress Administration might be more effective, Johnson just glared at him menacingly before moving on. The war would be conducted in individualistic terms, or not at all.[36]

The Kennedy and Johnson administrations both embraced the national liberal faith in the abilities of a technocratic "government of experts." "The central domestic issues of our time are more subtle and less simple" than in the Jacksonian era and Gilded Age, Kennedy declared in 1962. "They relate not to basic clashes of philosophy or ideology but to ways and means of reaching common goals—to research for sophisticated solutions to complex and obstinate issues. . . . [T]he problems . . . in the sixties as opposed to the kinds of problems we faced in the thirties demand subtle challenges for which technical answers, not political answers, must be provided." Both presidents gathered a range of experts—social scientists, economists, scientific planners, psychologists, political scientists, and management gurus—to develop and execute programs and policies they believed could end poverty and racism, sickness and ignorance, pollution, and even the global menace of Soviet communism. For a few short years these technocrats were celebrated in the public square. A breathless 1967 *Life* magazine profile paid tribute to the "priesthood of action-intellectuals—the men who believe they . . . can chart the future" in Johnson's cabinet:

> Over the past 10 years, theories incubated by such action-intellectuals have reshaped the basing and strike patterns that deploy SAC's bombers around the globe; led to the great nuclear test ban treaty of 1963; cut our taxes, reshaped our economy, lifted national income by 50% in the last seven years, made us rich. In the *next* ten years, their theories will change us even more: changing how we travel, how we live, how our medicine is given us, how we make war, how we seek peace, the air we breathe, the water we drink.[37]

Of course, the "action-intellectuals" didn't know as much as they thought, as demonstrated by the failures of the wars against poverty and the Vietcong. The former, always underfunded, did improve conditions for the poor, but largely failed to erect a serviceable ladder to the middle class. The latter, based on a misreading of the nature of the conflict in Vietnam, ultimately killed fifty-eight thousand Americans and some two million Vietnamese soldiers and civilians without achieving the intended geopolitical result. "We failed to recognize that in international affairs, as in other aspects of life, there may be problems for which there are no immediate solutions," recalled Defense Secretary Robert McNamara, the Harvard-educated systems analyst who guided the Vietnam War and, later, the World

Bank as it underwrote the road-and-colonization programs that were behind the destruction of the Amazon and Indonesian rain forests. "For one whose life has been devoted to the belief and practice of problem solving, this is particularly hard to admit. But at times, we may have to live with an imperfect, untidy world."[38]

For the Great Society, the imperfections of the world revealed themselves in August 1965, when a horrific riot broke out in the Watts section of Los Angeles, home to two-thirds of the city's 650,000 African Americans, many of them transplants from the Deep South and Tidewater. Up to 10,000 of the neighborhood's residents took to the streets for several days, looting and burning stores, and pulling white passersby out of cars and beating them. Some shot at police and firefighters. By the time soldiers were deployed to restore order, 34 were dead, over 1,000 wounded, and more than six hundred buildings were destroyed. The violence was all the more shocking to whites because, despite poverty and segregation, conditions for African Americans in Los Angeles were measurably among the best in the country, the city only one year earlier having placed first among the sixty-eight cities evaluated by the Urban League in housing, income, employment, and other opportunities for blacks. A gubernatorial commission tasked with determining the reasons for the unrest emphasized that when Federal poverty programs had arrived "they had not lived up to" the "the glowing promise . . . of their press notices." More disturbances followed from coast to coast in the summer of 1966. In 1967, intense unrest also struck Detroit and Newark, resulting in dozens of deaths, widespread destruction of property, and the use of soldiers to restore order.[39]

While heavy-handed police actions against black civilians prompted the three largest riots, in the public eye such unrest tainted the War on Poverty, with many whites asking why their taxes should go to helping "them" when "they" were burning their neighborhoods down. Whites "can make this one nation only by economic and social processes of agonizing slowness, uncertain efficiency, limited popularity—processes like the 'war on poverty' that are in any case subject to all the pettiness and blindness of human nature," lamented *New York Times* columnist Tom Wicker after the Watts events. "It is easier to lump Negroes together as lawless brutes who have done nothing to deserve the good life in affluent America." House minority leader Gerald Ford of Michigan blamed the Great Society for promising more than it could deliver and creating false expectations, a complaint soon embraced by official Republican organs going into the 1968 presidential campaign.[40]

At least as politically damaging to Johnson's cause was the 1966 Civil Rights Act, a landmark piece of legislation unveiled that January that would have forbidden discrimination in the renting or sale of all forms of housing. Unlike previous civil rights legislation, which had targeted Jim Crow practices in the Deep South, Tidewater, and parts of Greater Appalachia, the new bill prohibited discriminatory practices that were common throughout the country. Coming on the heels of the Watts riots and a chain of lesser disturbances in other non-Dixie cities, the measure was deeply unpopular with many urban whites in Yankeedom, the Midlands, and New Netherland, many of whose parents and grandparents had been core supporters of the New Deal in the 1930s and 1940s. The bill was watered down in the House but was still unable to survive a Dixie filibuster in the Senate that September. For the Great Society, the handwriting was on the wall.[41]

In the midterm elections in the fall of 1966, Johnson's allies were routed. Democrats lost three seats in the Senate and forty-six in the House, most of them freshmen from Yankee, Midland, and Greater Appalachian sections who had swept into office in the anti-Goldwater election of 1964. While he would still manage to pass a few pieces of significant legislation—among them the 1968 act creating the Public Broadcasting System—the president no longer had the votes to push a national liberal agenda forward.

Then the national liberal enterprise was attacked on an entirely unexpected front: the left.

★

The collegiate youth of the mid-1960s were prime beneficiaries of national liberal policies. Many had been born to newly secure middle-class parents and raised in greater affluence and comfort than any generation in American history. They had grown up in a climate where material security was taken for granted and had access to higher education in unprecedented numbers. In the mid-1950s their predecessors—children born during the end of the Great Depression—had sent 2.7 million of their number to college. In 1968, owing to the baby boom and the government-sponsored massification of higher education, the college population exceeded 7 million, with many students the beneficiaries of federal student grants, aid, and subsidized loans.

The children of the 1960s grew up in a world of suburban conformity, and came of age amid the civil rights movement, urban riots, and an increasingly bleak war in Vietnam.[42] The youth movement they initiated started in support of Martin Luther King Jr.'s civil rights campaign in Dixie, but by 1967 it had turned inward, emphasizing not the pursuit of the common good or a collective effort to build a better society, but rather the self-fulfillment and unrestrained freedom of each individual to do his or her "own thing." This New Left rejected the materialistic goals of their fathers and grandfathers—the struggle for economic and social security—and instead vented their wrath on the soullessness and falsity of American society. Their enemies weren't the forces of laissez-faire, but rather "the system," the depersonalized bureaucratic-corporate state that was national liberalism's central operating mechanism. The government they protested against wasn't the libertarian regime of McKinley or Coolidge, but the resurgent New Dealism of Lyndon Johnson, with its misguided war, its arrogant social engineering, its public housing towers and urban renewal projects. Their movement—its famous protests, its major campus sit-ins, its countercultural happenings—was overwhelmingly concentrated not in the libertarian-minded sections of the country, but in the communitarian ones: Yankeedom, the Left Coast, and New Netherland. While their best-known manifesto, the Port Huron Statement, called for the government to promote economic equality by investing in education and universal health care, its broader demand was to dismantle the top-down liberal enterprise and replace it with a participatory democracy on a human scale where private, individual interests were empowered. Bureaucratic planning, scientific objectivity, and faith in the public sector were all held in ill repute in the counterculture, just as they were on the right.[43]

The national liberal effort suddenly found itself stranded between the hedonistic individualism of the New Left and the hierarchical individualism of the laissez-faire right. Its traditional coalition was in tatters, as blue-collar whites in Yankeedom, the Midlands, and New Netherland broke with Johnson over the extension of the civil rights struggle to rectify de facto discrimination in housing and the urban geography of schools. Its allies in the Republican Party— Yankee, Midland, and New Netherland moderates, and progressives like Governor George Romney of Michigan or Nelson Rockefeller of New York—appeared to have vanquished the libertarians, but by no means made up for the growing vacuum left by the departure of the Deep South, Tidewater, and Greater Appalachia from the New Deal coalition.

As the nation lurched toward the 1968 election amid worsening riots, a calamitous situation in Vietnam, and a series of political assassinations at home, it was clear that national liberalism was in free fall. It would take more than a decade to see what would replace it.

CHAPTER 7

# Dixie Takes Over
# (1968–2008)

T he transition from the era of national liberalism to the supply-side consensus of the Reagan Revolution was a long, messy, and debilitating one. From late 1966, when Johnson's Great Society crumbled amid urban rioting and the tumult of Vietnam, to as late as 1979, the country was racked with uncertainty: political, ideological, economic, and cultural. The laissez-faire right had been thoroughly discredited by Goldwater's defeat in 1964, the resurgent national liberals by the devastating Democratic rout in the 1966 midterms. Americans, buffeted by one catastrophe after another, either clung to the old national liberal centrism of the Eisenhower era or manned the barricades of the ongoing culture wars, hoping to topple the center and replace it entirely. As the country lurched toward the 1968 presidential election, few would have predicted the advent of an era, twelve years hence, in which government would simultaneously expand, indebt itself, and cut social programs in order to better serve a plutocracy, and do so with the enthusiastic backing of the electorate in the poorest, most government-dependent regions of the country.

★

If Americans were shocked by the events of 1965 and 1966, they were traumatized by those of 1967 and 1968. While youth—shockingly long-haired and sexually uninhibited—flocked to San Francisco to join the utopian, acid-powered Summer of Love, black sections of Newark and Detroit exploded in flames as thousands of rioters smashed windows, looted stores, shot at firemen, and destroyed buildings. Scores were killed—the majority by police, who fired into crowds, cars, and apartment buildings—federal troops had to restore order, and neither city would ever really recover from the physical and psychological damage. All the while, protestors took to the streets and campuses of Yankeedom, the Left Coast, and New Netherland and marched on the Pentagon to protest the growing war in Vietnam. The Vietcong's Tet Offensive of January 1968—in which even the U.S. embassy in Saigon was attacked—revealed that U.S. officials had been deceiving the public about the actual state of the war. In March, Johnson announced he would not seek reelection. In April, Martin Luther King Jr. was assassinated, and 110 cities exploded in violence; in Washington, D.C., rioters came within two blocks of the White House, machine guns were mounted on the steps of the U.S. Capitol, and nearly fourteen thousand federal troops were deployed to protect the central government. In June, presidential candidate Robert F. Kennedy—brother of the slain president— was gunned down in California. In August, Chicago witnessed a weeklong Democratic Party civil war outside the barbed-wire-ringed hall where they were holding their convention as police under the command of Democratic mayor Richard J. Daley harassed antiwar delegates in the hall and chanted "kill, kill, kill" as they gassed and beat left-wing protestors, journalists, and bystanders outside. The country, it appeared, was tearing itself apart.[1]

The chaos further weakened the forces of national liberalism. The presidential hopes of George Romney, the progressive-minded Republican governor of Michigan, were severely damaged by the Detroit riots, which he argued were due to "horrible conditions which breed frustration, hatred and revolt." ("We must not permit a backlash to weaken the valuable programs and policies designed to bring about first-class status for all our citizens," he said in the riots' aftermath.) His candidacy came to an end over Vietnam, where he said he'd received a pro-war "brainwashing" by U.S. generals and diplomats during his 1965 visit, which had since worn off. "When Romney's candidacy sank," political historian Geoffrey Kabaservice has written, "so did the moderates' likelihood of leaving a lasting imprint on the Republican Party. For moderates, the path ahead would lead continuously downward." The Democrats had lost RFK to an assassin's bullet, and any serious competition in the Deep South and Tidewater to the white supremacist George Wallace, dictatorial governor of Alabama, who ran against the civil rights movement as an independent. In California, Governor Edmund Brown—who had built public school, public university, and high-speed highway systems that were then the envy of the world—was defeated by a former Hollywood actor, Ronald Reagan, who campaigned against the "arson and murder in Watts," the "sexual orgies" at the University of California, Berkeley, the new laws against discrimination in housing that blocked "our basic freedom," and welfare programs that attracted the lazy to the state to "loaf."[2]

In November 1968, Richard Nixon, who promised "we shall have order in the United States," won a tight race for the presidency against Johnson's vice president, Hubert Humphrey. He had adroitly targeted his opponent's weaknesses. He campaigned on behalf of the "silent center"—the "millions of people in the middle of the American political spectrum who do not demonstrate, who do not picket or protest loudly"—and against "forced busing" (to integrate schools), "lawbreakers" (black rioters and antiwar demonstrators), and "domestic violence" (riots). He stumped extensively in the former Confederacy, seeking to capture votes from Wallace. The strategy, according to Nixon special counsel John Ehrlichman, was to "go after the racists. That subliminal appeal to the antiblack voter was always present in Nixon's statements and speeches." This approach—an appeal to the fears and resentments of southern and urban whites against blacks and the "New Class" elite—would soon be codified by Nixon campaign aide Kevin Phillips as the "Southern Strategy" and used to great effect for the next forty years. But in 1968 it was still in its infancy, and was overshadowed by Wallace's expressly racist candidacy, which proved popular in the Deep South. Nixon ultimately won swaths of Greater Appalachia, but lost the Deep South and most of Tidewater to Wallace. He also lost most of Yankeedom and nearly every city outside the Deep South. His real victory was in suburban and rural America; he won nearly every such county in the Far West, the Midlands, and El Norte, including hundreds that had supported Johnson just four years earlier. (Republican gains in Congress, meanwhile, were extremely modest, with both houses remaining under comfortable Democratic control.)[3]

While Nixon capitalized on national liberalism's weaknesses on the campaign trail, he governed within its tradition. During his first term he implemented affirmative action programs for minorities, issuing executive orders requiring that federal agencies establish equal employment opportunities, expand procurement from minority-owned suppliers, and insist that any construction union working on a federally financed project hire and give membership to a fixed number of minority workers. (At the time, many unions were all-white and intended to stay that way.) He proposed a negative income tax—the Family Assistance Plan—and new federal-state revenue sharing to help the working poor. He intervened in the economy with wage and price controls. He signed the Clean Air, Endangered Species, Marine Mammal Protection, and Estuary Protection acts into law, an accomplishment Republican representative Pete McCloskey of California later said constituted "the golden age of environmentalism." Nixon also proposed and created the Environmental Protection Agency and the Occupational Health and Safety Administration, the latter passed with strong bipartisan support everywhere outside of the Deep South and Tidewater, where there was bipartisan opposition. He reinvigorated the old national liberal consensus on containing rather than "rolling back" communism abroad, winding down U.S. involvement in Vietnam, signing nuclear arms control treaties with the Soviets, and opening diplomatic relations with China. With respect to policy, his first term as president wasn't a repudiation of national liberalism, but rather a furthering of its policies.[4]

In the 1972 election, Nixon completely obliterated the candidate of the "New Left," George McGovern, receiving 61 percent of the popular vote and an electoral college tally of 520 to 17, the greatest victory margins of any Republican presidential candidate up to that point. With George Wallace out of the race—he'd been shot and paralyzed on the campaign trail by an attention-craving madman—Nixon had the former Confederacy to himself, enabling him to sweep every state save Massachusetts. His reelection was a rebuke to the New Left—McGovern had promoted amnesty for draft evaders, a 37 percent cut in defense spending, and a $1,000 payment to every U.S. citizen—but also to the laissez-faire right, whose leading luminaries had refused to endorse the president. Tellingly, voters left Democrats with a large House majority and three extra seats in the

Senate, while returning progressive Republicans to office and cast-
ing out twenty-five conservative congressmen. The president, the
*New York Times* editorialized, had "moved the G.O.P. closer to a
party of government rather than a chronic opposition which occasionally holds office by accident."[5]

Having successfully identified the middle ground of American
opinion in 1972, Nixon then proceeded to drive himself off a cliff.

His paranoid, bigoted ramblings can be heard on thousands of
hours of secret recordings he made of his intimate White House conversations and phone calls. They were all out to get him. "Never
forget, the press is the enemy, the press is the enemy," he told his
national security adviser a few weeks after the election. "The establishment is the enemy, the professors are the enemy, the professors
are the enemy. Write that on a blackboard 100 times." He drew up a
vast "enemies list" including everyone from football star Joe Namath
to conductor Leonard Bernstein and asked, "How can we use the
available federal machinery to screw [them]?" He ordered his chief
of staff to break into the Brookings Institution—and discussed fire-
bombing the building as well—in an effort to procure any documents
that might impugn the reputations of Kennedy and Johnson, and
ordered the White House purged of any pictures of past presidents.
Before the election, one of his senior advisers ordered a group of
White House operatives to plan the assassination of newspaper columnist Jack Anderson, but later reassigned them to break into the
Democratic National Committee headquarters at the Watergate
Hotel to steal documents and replace faulty (and illegal) phone taps.
When the break-in came to light, Nixon ordered the CIA to inter-
fere with the FBI's investigation of the incident, and later provoked a
constitutional crisis by refusing to cooperate with congressional
investigators and then not immediately complying with a Supreme
Court order to turn over White House tapes that later proved his

involvement in the cover-up. In the final weeks of Nixon's presidency, Secretary of Defense James Schlesinger instructed military personnel to only follow orders that had passed through the chain of command, suggesting he may have shared concerns in Congress and the press that an increasingly erratic president might go behind his back to use military force or launch nuclear weapons. Minutes after a House committee voted to impeach the president on July 27, 1974, the chairman ordered the Rayburn Office Building evacuated on account of a reported "kamikaze flight" that had taken off from National Airport intending to "crash into" the structure. The plane never materialized, but the belief that anything could happen—even a pro-Nixon military coup—persisted until the president's televised resignation twelve days later.[6]

All the while, the nation's once invincible-seeming economy was in trouble. The trade deficit was soaring as new manufacturing rivals—Germany, Japan, Taiwan—ate into U.S. car, steel, and consumer products markets, foreign and domestic. Meat prices mysteriously doubled in a single year, prompting Nixon's consumer adviser to encourage Americans to eat more offal. In the fall of 1973, a coalition of developing-world oil producers launched an embargo against the United States to compel it to abandon military aid to Israel. Oil prices quintupled over the next nine months, gas stations ran out of fuel, and the secretary of the interior warned there might be heating energy shortages that winter. Cities banned outdoor store lighting and held council meetings by candlelight. Los Angeles banned Christmas lights. By the time Nixon resigned, inflation had hit 12 percent, even as unemployment rose and the economy stagnated—a combination that was supposed to be impossible under the Keynesian theories that had long underpinned national liberalism. Half of the country thought it was on the verge of another depression.[7]

In the end, Nixon's lasting legacy was to destroy Americans' faith

in government, the nation, and themselves. In 1964, Americans believed their country, their military, and their government could accomplish anything. Ten years later—with inner-city neighborhoods
burned out, their president ousted, their armies defeated by one third
world country, the economy held hostage by several others—most felt
the nation could accomplish nothing. The percentage of the population that retained "a great deal of confidence" in the executive branch
stood at just 19 percent in 1973, down from 41 percent in 1966, and
confidence in Congress wasn't much better. For national liberals—be
they moderate Republicans or middle-of-the-road Democrats—this
loss of public trust in the institutions of common enterprise would
spell disaster.

★

When Nixon's helicopter lifted off the White House lawn, leaving
Gerald Ford behind as president, the nation wasn't eager for a return
to the principles of Calvin Coolidge. Ford, who had represented the
conservative (Dutch separatist–founded) enclave of Grand Rapids,
Michigan, for many years in Congress, was an old-school economic
conservative. Like Hoover, he believed in balanced budgets and in
raising taxes to achieve them, and in government taking a role in
regulating business and promoting the common good—but a frugal
and limited one. Faced with an economic crisis, Ford first championed austerity, placing an excise tax on the wealthy and vetoing
numerous Democratic appropriations bills. Three months after he
took office, voters replaced almost fifty GOP congressmen and four
senators, giving Democrats a more than two-thirds majority in both
houses.[8]

After this congressional defeat, as the economy sank into the
worst recession since the Great Depression, Ford changed course,

agreeing to tax rebates (and a deeper deficit) aimed at stimulating the economy. Laissez-faire proponents were appalled, with Ronald Reagan privately dismissing the president as a "caretaker" who'd "been in Congress for too long." Ford's naming of Nelson Rockefeller, standard-bearer of Republican moderates, as his vice president had further alienated the right, while his pardoning of Nixon had upset most everyone else. Reagan challenged Ford from the right for the 1976 presidential nomination, arguing that government itself was the problem and that "Fascism was really the basis for the New Deal." Although even Goldwater himself campaigned against him, Reagan nearly won, shocking the GOP establishment. Wealthy far-right groups had been raising huge amounts of money and organizing giant turnouts of new caucusgoers, an internal Ford campaign memo had warned late in the primary battle. "We are in real danger of being out-organized by a small number of highly motivated *right wing nuts*," the memo concluded. Those "nuts" managed to seize control of the party convention, passing a platform supporting gun rights and school prayer and opposing détente, abortion, and busing. Reagan himself stole the show with a speech denouncing "the erosion of freedom under Democrat rule in this country."[9]

In November, Ford was swept aside by the Democrats' unlikely nominee, former Georgia governor Jimmy Carter, who would also preside over an ideologically ambiguous administration. A peanut farmer and born-again Baptist, Carter was an accomplished straddler of the hot-button issues of the day. He opposed racial discrimination, but had no problem with neighborhoods wanting to maintain their "ethnic purity." He supported the biblical injunctions against homosexuality *and* a bill protecting gay rights. He would never give up U.S. control of the Panama Canal Zone, but would renegotiate the treaty, even though Panama's precondition was for the United States to give up control. He was against amnesty for Vietnam draft evaders but for pardoning them—and insisted there was a meaningful difference between those positions. Few in the national liberal establishment took him seriously. "How can he be nominated?" Averell Harriman, a senior adviser to Roosevelt, Truman, Kennedy, and Johnson, had sniffed. "I don't know him, and neither do any of my friends." Yet with the national liberal coalition shattered, Carter defeated four senatorial lions, a senior Kennedy aide, the demagogic George Wallace, and even Hubert Humphrey to become his party's nominee. In the general election, Carter lost Yankeedom and the Midlands but swept the Deep South, Tidewater, and Greater Appalachia, further confirming the rise of Dixie.[10]

In both parties, the establishment was on the ropes. In one, however, a new force was rapidly consolidating control.

★

Since Goldwater's catastrophic defeat in the 1964 presidential election, few in the country had paid the laissez-faire right much attention. Had they done so, they would have seen it steadily building its political and intellectual resources, capitalizing on the discrediting of national liberalism and the growing social turmoil. And it started with a few wealthy businessmen, heads of family-held companies based in the libertarian regions of the country—the Far West and Deep South—who championed individualism, loathed government intervention in social or economic matters, and sought to return America to the halcyon days of Coolidge's administration, if not McKinley's.

Joseph Coors, the Colorado beer magnate, was one of the movement's greatest benefactors. Coors, whose company was twice found guilty of discriminating against blacks and faced boycotts by civil rights activists, was a donor to the John Birch Society, a committed union buster, and deeply opposed to the ongoing student protests at the University of Colorado and elsewhere. In 1973, he put up $250,000 to found a new, more aggressive and ideological alternative to the American Enterprise Institute, which he felt had become too timid. The Heritage Foundation saw itself not as a sober scientific enterprise, as AEI and Brookings did, but as a political weapon, churning out intellectual ammunition for like-minded lawmakers and opinion leaders. "We don't stress credibility," its longtime president, Edwin Feulner, once explained, "we stress timeliness." Burton Yale Pines, Heritage's vice president for research in the late 1980s, described the Heritage Foundation's distinctiveness thusly: "AEI is like the big gun on an offshore battleship. We are the landing party. If they hadn't softened it up, we wouldn't have landed." It quickly attracted funding from the corporate goliaths of its day—General Motors, Dow, Pfizer, Chase Manhattan Bank, Mobil, and Sears— as well as from South Carolina textile magnate Roger Milliken and Richard Mellon Scaife, heir to Andrew Mellon's fortune and an important donor to the Nixon slush fund that paid for the Watergate burglaries. Within a decade, Heritage would have a staff of over a hundred, and would serve as an informal recruitment agency for the Reagan administration.[11]

It wasn't alone for long. In 1974, Charles Koch established an eponymous foundation devoted to libertarian principles, which was renamed the Cato Institute two years later. In 1978, Nixon's Securities and Exchange Commission chair, William Casey, teamed up with British philanthropist and Hayek disciple Sir Antony Fisher to found the Manhattan Institute, dedicated to "fostering greater economic choice and individual responsibility." The Hoover Institution at Stanford University, founded as a library collection by Herbert Hoover in 1919, transformed into a think tank in 1959 and grew rapidly during the 1960s and 1970s; it confirmed its ideological drift during the 1976 Republican primaries, when its president, W. Glenn Campbell, denounced Gerald Ford—the most Hoover-like president since Hoover—as a "leftist." (Ronald Reagan, then an ex-governor with a reputation as an intellectual lightweight, had been named an honorary fellow the year before.) By 1985 it had a staff of two hundred and was generating controversy at Stanford, from which it was autonomous and yet drew a quarter of its funding. With Richard Mellon Scaife's generous donations, the American Legislative Exchange Council, an alliance of Goldwaterite state legislators founded in 1973, was transformed into a political laundering machine through which corporations could draft laws and give them to state legislators to introduce and call their own back home.[12]

With corporate backing, AEI experienced phenomenal growth as well, increasing from just two resident scholars in 1969 to a full-time staff of 176 in 1985. Irving Kristol, one of its resident scholars, made one of its most famous fund-raising pitches in the *Wall Street Journal* in the spring of 1977. Kristol warned corporate leaders on the dangers of the "New Class" who dominated the "idea-germinating and idea-legitimizing institutions of our society" and perpetuated support for advancing national liberalism via "the ideas the children encounter in their textbooks, in their teachers, and on their televisions." Reshaping public opinion, he said, required business "to decide not to give money to support those activities of the New Class which are inimical to corporate survival" and instead support the minority of scholars and intellectuals "who *are* interested in individual liberty and limited government, who *are* worried about the collectivist tendencies in our society. . . . You can only beat an idea with another idea, and the war of ideas and ideologies will be won or lost *within* the New Class, not against it." Since laissez-faire ideas had failed to win support within independent institutions, proponents had set out to build an alternate, corporate-funded network of institutions where these and only these ideas would be promulgated.[13]

Unnoticed, the think tanks went to work. When meat prices jumped in 1973, AEI put together a Center for the Study of Government Regulation financed by food industry executives. John M. Olin, aging head of a family-owned arms manufacturing firm, donated thousands to AEI to fight the estate tax, because he feared his fortune "would be practically liquidated upon my death." In the summer of 1974, thousands of Christian fundamentalists in West Virginia boycotted schools because they opposed new textbooks that included the perspectives of black civil rights leaders, atheists, and Inuit people—a protest that included the bombing of school buildings, firing shotguns at loaded school buses, and the stoning of children who failed to abide by the boycott. The Heritage Foundation sent two staffers to help defend the indicted terrorists, and they appeared onstage alongside some of the most militant fundamentalist leaders. "If you pick the right fight at the right time it can be profitable," one of the staffers later recalled. "You can make your political points, you can help the people involved, and you can become a force in the political community."[14]

The Christian right was itself becoming a powerful force in the political community. Anchored in the Deep South, Tidewater, and Greater Appalachia, southern evangelicals and fundamentalists had been strengthened by the federal government's demands to end school segregation, which prompted the creation of thousands of private, segregated Christian academies providing "faith-based" education, with an emphasis on conservative social values, creationism, and obedience to authority. The financial burden of supporting these schools fell on parents, prompting evangelical leaders to demand that taxpayers support them via the creation of "school vouchers." The federal government's questioning of their tax-exempt status on civil rights grounds drove many into politics. The moral relativism of the 1960s youth and counterculture movements was of course also upsetting to fundamentalists and evangelicals, and in the 1970s some of their leaders began blaming it on national liberalism. The welfare state, Jerry Falwell's newspaper declared in 1978, was "corrupting a whole generation of people" and needed to be replaced with "individual freedom and family responsibility"; the "greatest threat to the average American's liberty does not come from Communistic aggression," it declared, but from "government bureaucrats as they limit the freedom of Americans through distribution of rules and regulations."[15]

Such messages reached ever-wider audiences as Dixie preachers took to the airwaves, building powerful media empires like Pat Robertson's Christian Broadcasting Network and nationally syndicated *700 Club,* Jerry Falwell's Heritage USA, and the Billy Graham Evangelistic Association. Soon the movement wasn't just disseminating ideas; it was creating messengers through its own higher education institutions: Bob Jones University in South Carolina (which banned blacks until 1971, and interracial dating until 2000), Robertson's Christian Broadcasting Network College (now Regent University, founded in Virginia in 1978 with the mandate to train "God's representatives on the face of the Earth"), and Falwell's Liberty College (founded in 1971 in Virginia and still teaching that dinosaur fossils are four thousand years old). Falwell made the final step into political activism when he founded the Moral Majority in 1979, a group that promised to be "lobbying intensively in Congress to defeat left-wing, social-welfare bills that will further erode our precious freedom." The founding ceremony in Lynchburg, Virginia, was attended by the head of the Heritage Foundation, Paul Weyrich.[16]

While the new Dixie religious leaders claimed concern for family and tradition—communal values of the Burkean sort—this did not square with their support for unrestrained capitalism, a dynamic force that tended to undermine both. For the time being, however, that fissure was ignored. The laissez-faire alliance had a government to capture, and a candidate who could lead them to victory.

★

By the late 1970s, many voters felt their taxes were too high and that the government was wasting the funds they generated on failing social programs to help the wayward poor. White working-class voters, meanwhile, were coming to regard the ownership class as their allies against their true opponents, the undeserving poor and the "New Class" elite that coddled them. They continued to support the basic institutions of the New Deal—plus Medicare and Medicaid—but were critical of much of the agenda of the Great Society, especially government interventions to raise the poor and integrate schools, neighborhoods, and factories. In an increasingly globalized economy, environmental regulations and even strong unions seemed to pose a threat to jobs that could up and leave Yankeedom for the "right to work" counties of Greater Appalachia, or abandon the Deep South for Mexico or beyond. As well-paying blue-collar jobs began growing scarce, affirmative action programs threatened to give some of those that were available to minorities. Activist government no longer seemed on the workers' side and no longer had their reliable support.

Such was the situation that confronted President Carter, who, like many Deep Southern Democrats, had never really been a national liberal. His modest regulatory proposals—to increase the powers of the Federal Trade Commission and compel corporate compliance with National Labor Relations Board regulations—were defeated in a Congress theoretically controlled by Democrats. Reacting to pressure from business interests, Congress in 1978 slashed capital gains and corporate tax rates, while raising payroll taxes; as a result, investors and owners of large estates received billions in tax relief while the burden on working- and middle-class taxpayers was increased. Disillusioned Democratic primary voters ousted many liberal senators, whose seats were captured by well-financed Republican challengers, many of them aligned with the laissez-faire movement, tilting Congress further rightward. Carter then raised military spending while cutting Social Security benefits and grants to states and cities. When the Organization of the Petroleum Exporting Countries (OPEC) doubled the price of oil in 1979, creating long lines at the gas pumps, Carter disappeared for days at the presidential retreat at Camp David, Maryland, then emerged to tell Americans they needed to look inward and reassess their values. Government, their leader was telling them, couldn't solve their problems.[17]

Across the country, Americans were ready to elect someone who would.

★

In November 1980, fourteen years to the week after the Great Society had been stopped in its tracks, Republicans captured control of the Senate for the first time since 1954, gained thirty-three seats in the House, and saw Ronald Reagan elected president. The transition period had ended with a result few in either political party would have thought possible in the late 1960s: the return to power of the laissez-faire individualism of the Coolidge era.

Reagan was a true believer. The self-made son of a struggling, alcoholic shoe salesman in rural Illinois, he passionately believed in the virtues and efficacy of self-reliance, hard work, risk taking, and positive thinking. Though originally a New Deal Democrat, in middle age he became increasingly hostile to active government and the taxes assessed on the rich to support it. Government, he famously declared, was itself the problem. It thwarted the virtuous and productive by picking their pocketbooks to support the lazy, the shiftless, the people Herbert Spencer had called "the unfittest" and whom Reagan would shorthand as "welfare queens." The entrepreneurial spirit of business owners and industrialists was being hindered by what he called "whimsical bureaucratic changes in energy, environmental, and safety regulations." Detroit's problem wasn't poor products and increased competition from Japan; it was the federal government. "The U.S. auto industry is virtually being regulated to death," he told the Detroit Economic Club in a campaign speech that painted Carter as a hapless Hoover-like figure, clinging to a discredited order. "There is no crisis of confidence. . . . We are suffering from misguided, thoughtless government policies," he continued. "Our choice is between up and down; up to the ultimate in the individual freedom, consistent with an orderly society, or down through statism and government intervention to a centrally controlled society, authoritarianism, or even totalitarianism."[18]

Sunny, optimistic, a man with a plan: The individualists had finally found their Roosevelt.

The problem was that polls showed that most Americans still supported the central planks of the New Deal, as well as Medicaid and Medicare, even as their faith in government had faltered. Distrust of business was also high, and few working- and middle-class voters were clamoring for cuts to the estate tax and the top income tax brackets. The laissez-faire ascendency had to find ways to focus popular resentment from plutocrats to the welfare and regulatory state. The path forward, as Republican strategist Kevin Phillips had advised Nixon back in 1969, lay in capitalizing on race. "The principal force which broke up the Democratic (New Deal) coalition is the Negro socioeconomic revolution," Phillips wrote in *The Emerging Republican Majority,* which set forth a "Southern Strategy" for the party. "The Democratic party fell victim to the ideological impetus of a liberalism which had carried it beyond programs taxing the few for the benefit of the many (the New Deal) to programs taxing the many on behalf of the few (the Great Society)." William Rusher, publisher of the *National Review*, took things a step further, arguing in 1975 that the political battle was no longer between "the haves and have-nots" but between the producers "at all economic levels of society" and the "New Class" and "their huge welfare constituency." Workers and tycoons alike were apparently ready to rise up against college professors, bureaucrats, and the black urban poor who had been the primary beneficiaries of the War on Poverty.[19]

Reagan deftly tapped on racial resentments, and, unlike Nixon, he was willing to direct public ire not just onto the "New Class" elite who ran government, but onto government itself. If middle Americans were shell-shocked by higher inflation and taxes, the problem wasn't to be traced to the regressive 1978 tax cuts or the soaring trade deficit with Japan. Instead he claimed both were caused by the nation's deficits, which he blamed not on tax cuts and the $111 billion price tag for the Vietnam War, but on "wasteful" social and welfare program spending to help racial minorities. He kicked off his 1980 campaign tour in Philadelphia, Mississippi, a town known across the country for one thing: the brutal 1964 murders of three young civil rights organizers by white supremacists, many of whom were still being sheltered when Reagan gave his speech. "I believe in states' rights," he told the cheering crowd, who knew exactly what this meant when it came to the Deep Southern racial order. "I believe in people doing as much as they can for themselves at the community level and at the private level." Despite facing a native Deep Southerner in the presidential election, Reagan would win all the Deep Southern–controlled states save Carter's home state of Georgia with overwhelming lowland white support. He won forty-four states overall, crushing the incumbent.[20]

In office, Reagan deviated from the Coolidge tradition in one important respect: Whereas Republicans had traditionally placed great emphasis on balancing the nation's budget, considering it a sign of moral fortitude and the cornerstone of economic stability, Reagan blithely accumulated debt at a rate never seen in peacetime. While he criticized the "tax and spend" Democrats, he was a "tax cut and spend" president who mortgaged the future to give the wealthy a big payout. Reagan allowed himself to be convinced that tax cuts would pay for themselves, unleashing such a torrent of new economic activity that federal revenues would actually increase. This theory—called "supply-side economics" by its promoters and, famously, "voodoo economics" by George H. W. Bush—was in fact a cynical hoax. David Stockman, Reagan's libertarian budget director, had run his boss's budget numbers during the 1980 campaign and promptly realized there would be, as he later put it, no surplus "at the end of the supply-side rainbow." Instead, Reagan's plan to dramatically cut taxes while increasing spending (on a military buildup against the USSR) would nearly double the annual deficit, requiring huge cuts in other areas of government. "That should have been cause for second thoughts and reassessment of the whole proposition," Stockman recalled. "But it didn't turn out that way."[21]

It didn't do so because, as Stockman revealed, knowing supply-side economics would actually create huge deficits was seen by Reagan's team as "an opportunity, not a roadblock," a chance to bring down the national liberal legacy, which he called the Second American Republic. Once their budget was enacted "we would have the Second Republic's craven politicians pinned to the wall," Stockman recalled. "They would have to dismantle its bloated, wasteful and unjust spending enterprises—or risk national ruin. The idea of a real fiscal revolution, a frontal attack on the welfare state, was beginning to seem more and more plausible." The incoming president intended to sabotage the government he'd been elected to lead, using deficits as his weapon.[22]

Reagan moved forward with a four-year, $749 billion tax cut conceived, Stockman also later admitted, to help the rich. While slashing the top income tax rates from 70 to 50 percent, cutting estate and capital gains taxes, and enacting unprecedented tax breaks for business, the administration and a compliant Congress cut funding for food stamps, Aid to Families with Dependent Children, and employment, education, and housing measures for the poor by over $100 billion over four years. It was, to paraphrase Phillips, taking from the many to help the few, only with the direction of the flow reversed. Finally, Reagan pushed a massive buildup in military spending: $400 billion over five years. The predictable result was a doubling of the annual budget deficit in year two, and nearly a quadrupling in years three and four. It wouldn't get better from there.[23]

Indeed, the deficits were rising even faster than Reagan's team expected, on track to hit over $200 billion a year, rather than the predicted $100 billion, by 1984. In early 1982, Stockman and Chief of Staff James Baker tried to convince Reagan to raise taxes to check the rapidly expanding national debt; the supply-siders in the administration dissuaded him, leaving Stockman with no good options: "I out and out cooked the books, inventing $15 billion a year of utterly phony tax cuts" to get Reagan's proposed budget deficit out of triple digits. At this point, actual fiscal conservatives—the ones who believe you need to balance the budget before you cut taxes—panicked, sending Senate leader Bob Dole to press the president to see reason. The result was a tactical retreat by Reagan: the promulgation of a three-year, $98.3 billion tax hike, the largest in history, coupled with another $30 billion cut to entitlement programs. "But even that had not been enough," Stockman recalled. "By the end of 1982, the fiscal situation was an utter, mind-numbing catastrophe."[24]

Meanwhile, Congress and the president worked to loosen regulations, opening public lands in the West to development, weakening the oversight powers of the Federal Trade Commission, stopping new automotive safety regulations, delaying environmental rulemaking, and freeing the loosely regulated savings and loan industry to engage in commercial banking while lowering each S and L's capital reserve requirements and raising their federal deposit insurance levels. Reagan called the latter measure "the most important legislation for financial institutions in the last fifty years." It resulted in a flood of risky investments, the collapse of hundreds of banks, and a federal bailout that cost taxpayers $125 billion over the next thirty years.

In 1984, many of the baleful consequences of these policies had yet to be become clear and the Democrats remained in disarray, torn between the McGovernite liberal left, the remnant national liberals, and a growing faction of what would once have been called moderate Republicans, but were now known as New Democrats. Reagan, charming, likable, and optimistic, was reelected in a landslide comparable to Nixon's in 1972: 59 percent of the vote, forty-nine of fifty states, and 525 of 538 electoral college votes, a proportion exceeded only by FDR's 1936 triumph. However, the public endorsement of the Reagan Revolution was not absolute: Even at the apogee of Reagan's popularity, Democrats maintained a seventy-one-seat majority in the House and actually gained two seats in the Senate; they would capture it two years later.

In 1986, Reagan championed another round of tax cuts that lowered the top tax rate from 50 to 28 percent while raising the rate of the lowest bracket from 11 to 15 percent. The New Democrats who sponsored the bill—Senator Bill Bradley of New Jersey and House majority leader Dick Gephardt—demanded that it be paid for by the closure of $30 billion in tax loopholes, including ones favored by the oil and gas and real estate interests, and an 8 percent increase in the capital gains tax. "In the end," Bradley noted, "the tax bill passed because each party got something it wanted." The bill was revenue neutral, but it shifted the tax burden further onto the lower middle class. Economists have found that it substantially increased income inequality and that working-class people would have been better off—and the wealthy worse so—if it had never passed. Compounding the situation were Reagan's cuts, including a 60 percent reduction in federal assistance to municipalities, forcing public schools, libraries, clinics, hospitals, and housing programs to take draconian measures.[25]

Indeed, Reagan's laissez-faire counterrevolution dramatically increased inequality by almost any measure. During his presidency, the number of people living in poverty rose from twenty-nine million to thirty-two million. The number of homeless grew substantially in his first term, then nearly doubled between 1984 and 1987, from an estimated 330,000 to half a million. Between 1983 and 1989 alone, the top 1 percent of households' share of the nation's wealth grew from 33.8 to 37.4 percent, while the bottom 60 percent lost ground. While the rich had seen boom times, the economy hadn't done particularly well, with twice the inflation, half the productivity gains, and higher unemployment than in the postwar national liberal period. Meanwhile the nation's debt had grown from $914 billion when Reagan took office to a staggering $2.6 trillion, diverting more and more of the taxpayers' money to interest payments rather than to productive public investments, social or otherwise.[26]

It was, like the 1920s, a good time to be rich. Gordon Gekko, the self-serving antihero of Oliver Stone's 1987 film *Wall Street*, articulated the spirit of the times in Ayn Randian terms: "Greed, for lack of a better word, is good. Greed is right. Greed works."

★

In 1987, Reagan's approval rating rarely broke 50 percent. Seven in ten Americans said there was too little government spending to help the poor, and over six in ten thought that there was too little spent on education and health care. Ninety percent wanted more regulation of the environment. The following year, Democrats gained seats in both houses of Congress, and Reagan was succeeded in the Oval Office not by supply-side evangelist Jack Kemp or televangelist Pat Robertson, but by a Yankee conservative in the Burkean mold, Vice President George H. W. Bush. The laissez-faire revolution had stalled.[27]

Reagan left an enormous mess for his successors to deal with. Bush, because he saw himself as a statesman, not a revolutionary, felt compelled to renege on a high-profile campaign promise not to raise taxes in order to pay down the savings and loan disaster and confront the nation's multitrillion-dollar debt. Had he not done so, biographer and former Nixon Presidential Library director Timothy Naftali has said, "Ronald Reagan would be associated with an economic collapse in the United States. Instead, because George Bush was willing to give Americans strong medicine, Bush gave Reagan a different legacy."[28]

Bush negotiated a deficit-cutting agreement with congressional Democrats that raised the top income tax rate from 28 to 31 percent in exchange for spending caps and new pay-as-you-go rules that compelled Congress to balance the budget within five years. He supported and signed amendments to the Clean Air Act, which banned the industrial emission of certain toxic chemicals and tightened regulation of smog- and acid rain–causing emissions. Over the objections of business leaders, he championed the Americans with Disabilities Act—which guaranteed disabled people access to businesses and public venues—saying, "In our America, the most generous, optimistic nation on the face of the Earth, we must not and will not rest until every man and woman with a dream has the means to achieve it." Social Darwinism had departed from the White House.[29]

The political cost was considerable. Despite having negotiated a peaceful end to the Cold War and the successful liberation of Kuwait from Iraqi invaders, Bush endured a crippling backlash from laissez-faire conservatives. "I think he betrayed the Reagan revolution in many ways, by new government programs, greatly increased government spending . . . [and] because he didn't raise taxes kicking and screaming; he seemed very comfortable with it," New Right founding father Richard Viguerie once said of him. "It was easy to oppose his nomination." A deep recession—itself largely caused by Reagan's supply-side economics—left Bush looking hapless. He faced a boisterous primary challenge from a demagogic former Nixon aide named Pat Buchanan, and had a large slice of his general election support cut away by third-party candidate Ross Perot, a Texas billionaire running on a populist platform. When another riot in Watts broke out during the 1992 primaries, in which fifty-four were killed, Bush tried to blame it on the failed policies of Johnson's War on Poverty, but this time progressives could credibly assign blame on Republican neglect. "Twelve years of Reagan and Bush has not cured our problems [or] given us morning in America," former Nixon strategist Kevin Phillips said. "It's produced more columns of smoke rising from our inner cities."[30]

The Reagan Revolution was over. A new leader from Greater Appalachia was about to arrive, bearing his own ideas of how to balance individual freedom and the common good.

For the third time in a row, a new Democratic president was from the South. Born in a hamlet in the Appalachian section of Arkansas a few weeks after the death of his father, Bill Clinton had attended Georgetown and Yale Law School, returned home, and been elected governor in 1978 at the age of thirty-two. He had introduced a number of progressive policies, trying to overhaul the state's backward education system, boost teacher pay, reform rural health care, stop clear-cutting, fix the neglected roads with steep increases in automobile registration fees, and implement an aggressive energy conservation program, all in a two-year term. He was soundly defeated for reelection by a born-again Christian who appointed segregationist former governor Orval Faubus to a cabinet post and tried to force creationism into the public school curriculum.

Stung by his loss, Clinton retooled, adopting the rhetoric of the communitarian philosophical movement, which emphasized the individual's responsibilities to the community, rather than simply their rights to be exacted from it. He called for a "constructive partnership between business and government" and joined the ranks of the New Democrats. "He was a Democrat who often sounded like a Republican," wrote biographer Steven Gillon. "He championed welfare reform but argued that government needed to spend more on education and training before it cut benefits. . . . He incurred the wrath of teacher unions by imposing teacher testing, but he also raised taxes to increase salaries and reduce class size." He was reelected twice by nearly 25-point margins, uniting rural Appalachian whites and Deep Southern blacks, and drawing the attention of pro-business Democrats on the national stage. In 1992 he defeated the sitting president in a three-way race, sweeping Yankeedom, the Left Coast, El Norte, and Greater Appalachia, four regions that hadn't aligned in a competitive election since before the passage of the Voting Rights Act of 1965. His supporters believed he'd identified the new American center.[31]

True to promise, Clinton pursued a policy agenda combining communal social investments with deregulatory policies sought by big business and the financial sector. He tried (and failed) to pass comprehensive health care reform, expanded the Earned Income Credit so that people on welfare could take a minimum wage job without going into poverty, mandated (unpaid) family and medical leave, and raised taxes on the wealthy to control the deficit, all of which were popular with liberals. He also spearheaded passage of the North American Free Trade Agreement—a measure so disliked by labor and environmentalists that it passed only via the near-unanimous support of congressional Republicans—and expanded the death penalty to include drug kingpins and certain acts of violence not resulting in death. The deficit was dropping rapidly, with surpluses visible on the horizon. "The joke on Wall Street," London's *Guardian* newspaper reported before the 1994 midterm election, "is that Clinton is the first conservative Republican president in the White House." Barry Goldwater was also impressed. "He's a Democrat, but I do admire him," he wrote a Georgia congressman named Newt Gingrich. "I think he's doing a good job."[32]

Then, two years into his presidency, Clinton's Democratic allies experienced a humiliating electoral rebuke. When Congress reconvened in January 1995, Republicans had seized control of the House and Senate for the first time since 1954. Not a single Republican incumbent senator, representative, or governor had been defeated on election night. Newt Gingrich, their bomb-throwing new leader, stood ready to bring down the president, regardless of the cost to the nation. A destructive new era in federal politics had begun.

★

Newt Gingrich called himself a "transformational figure" and, as Speaker of the House, attempted to set himself up as America's first prime minister, an "executive in parliament" who would rule the country, leaving Clinton a symbolic head of state. He rewrote the House rules to allow himself to appoint all committee chairmen and thus control the agenda; shortened the workweek from five to three days to keep members commuting from their home districts and thus prevent their building social relationships with one another; and slashed the budget of Congress's watchdog agency, the General Accounting Office, thus depriving members of dispassionate analysis of

government programs. "Bills reported out of committee would mysteriously disappear and reappear rewritten," longtime Republican committee staffer Mike Lofgren recalled. "Gingrich turned the institution
upside down." Representative Mickey Edwards, a Republican from
Oklahoma, later said the new Speaker had created a system "demand-
ing uniformity" rather than representing the interests of constituents. "This is a man only interested in his own grandiosity," he later
warned.[33]

Aside from Senate majority leader Bob Dole, the new leadership
team represented the libertarian regions of the country: House whip
Tom DeLay (the Deep Southern section of Texas) and House majority leader Dick Armey (Appalachian Texas), Senate whip Trent Lott
(Deep Southern Mississippi) and Gingrich himself (Deep Southern
Georgia). Indeed, the real significance of the 1994 election wasn't
that laissez-faire conservatism had gained control of the country, but
that the Deep South and its allies had finally taken over their former
nemesis, the Republican Party. The movement had been building
since Johnson had signed the Civil Rights Act, with many champions
of hierarchical libertarianism abandoning the Democrats and a
younger generation of politicians never joining them at all, creating
an ever-deeper bench to run for federal office. "The results were on
display in 1994," wrote Michael Lind, a Texan national liberal who
had run in neoconservative circles until the takeover. "One thing is
certain: The Republican Party now, and for the indefinite future,
speaks with a Southern drawl." Their goal, Lind predicted, was Deep
Southern as well:

> When they were the ruling class of a region, threatened from without
> by the federal government, elite white southerners were "conserva-
> tives" defending the post-Reconstruction status quo. Today, having
> hijacked the Republican party, they are "radicals" seeking, in alliance

with the multinational corporate elite, to dismantle the New Deal and to impose their own peculiar "New South" version of the United States as a low-wage, low-tax, low-regulation economy in which economic segregation replaces formal legal segregation not merely in their native region but in the country as a whole.[34]

Indeed, they made little secret of their aims. Tom DeLay outlined his goals shortly after the election, which represented a rollback of postwar national liberal advances:

> I would like to eliminate the Department of Education, the Department of Energy, HUD, seriously pare down the Environmental Protection Agency and OSHA. . . . The National Endowment for the Arts—we ought to zero them out. The National Endowment for the Humanities—we ought to zero them out. And we will do a lot of that. Looking forward to it. By the time we finish this poker game, there may not be a federal government left, which would suit me just fine.[35]

The Gingrich radicals had a familiar enemy: the "New Class" of professors, schoolteachers, and movie producers who had supposedly spawned the permissive, immoral 1960s counterculture, including Bill and Hillary Clinton. From the founding of Jamestown through 1964, the House Speaker declared shortly after the election, there had been "a core pattern to American history. Here's how we did it until the Great Society messed everything up: don't work, don't eat; your salvation is spiritual; the government by definition can't save you; governments are into maintenance and all good reforms are into transformation." Then, "from 1965 to 1994, we did strange and weird things as a country . . . a momentary aberration in American history that will be looked back upon as a quaint period of Bohemianism brought to the national elite." By then he'd already called for the elimination of the flagship achievements of that era, including Nixon's Corporation for Public Broadcasting (which existed for "a bunch of rich, upper-class people who want their toy to play with"), Johnson's National Endowment for the Arts ("art patronage for an elite"), and the National Endowment for the Humanities (which proposed history standards "that are destructive for American civilization"). In his rhetoric, Gingrich combined two forces whose proponents had actually been at odds with one another throughout the 1960s—LBJ's technocrats and "system"-hating hippies—into a fantastical construct: "the Great Society counterculture model." With it, he redirected public ire against "drugs, sex, and rock and roll" toward public programs and institutions created by the squares. It was bold stuff for a man with a doctorate in American history.[36]

Indeed, Gingrich was a political opportunist par excellence: To rally his electoral coalition, he had no reservations about reframing each and every issue as a struggle of good against evil, even though privately he recognized the matters at hand were more complex and required negotiated solutions. "Unfortunately for him," biographer Gillon notes, "an entire generation of Republicans would come to power adopting his strategy and his message, but failing to appreciate the distinction between means and ends." Gingrich would become the first casualty of his methods, but a decade hence compromise itself would join him in the political graveyard.[37]

★

Taking office in 1995, the Gingrich revolutionaries pushed a phalanx of measures they called a "Contract with America"—a sort of Reagan-redux agenda by which the budget would supposedly be balanced while increasing military spending, building more prisons, and halving capital gains taxes for the wealthy. To make that possible,

critics reckoned, would require steep cuts in everything from Medicare and Medicaid to student loans and aid for the poor. Gingrich
also sought to institute a "loser pays" policy for lawsuits, whereby the
defeated party would have to pay the winner's legal fees as well as his
own, greatly increasing the risks for ordinary individuals seeking to
challenge corporations or the very wealthy in court. "Gingrich," anti-
tax crusader Grover Norquist proclaimed, "is Reaganism at warp
speed."[38]

Convinced the American electorate shared his caucus's laissez-faire
convictions, Gingrich charged forward with his budget plan, which
included $894 billion in spending cuts over seven years, $287 billion
in net tax cuts, and the elimination of the Commerce, Education,
and Energy departments, fourteen federal agencies and 283 federal
programs. "That summer threatened to be the season that swept
away the Great Society," Clinton aide George Stephanopoulos
recalled. "Medicare would be privatized. Medicaid sent to the states,
immigration blocked, and the federal battle against poverty abandoned because, they said, 'poverty won.'" Then Clinton stepped forward with his own plan to balance the budget and give $105 billion
in tax cuts to lower- and middle-income Americans, one that would
cut Medicare by $128 billion (instead of Gingrich's $270 billion), reduce
military spending slightly (instead of increasing it), and cut $38 billion
from poverty programs. His national liberal allies and aides were disheartened; the debate would be not whether to cut back an already
diminished safety net, but by how much.[39]

Gingrich, blinded by arrogance and self-regard, lost the battle in
a spectacular fashion. Refusing to compromise, his caucus declined
to raise the debt ceiling or pass a budget, risking national default and
forcing a weeks-long shutdown of all nonessential federal functions.
They learned the hard way that the vast majority of Americans actually liked and valued federal programs and services, and blamed the

closure of passport offices, the national park system, and veterans affairs offices on Gingrich's revolutionaries, not the president. In a single year, public approval of the Republican House fell from 52 percent to under 30, and Gingrich's own stood at 27 percent, about the same as Nixon's at the end of the Watergate crisis. "We looked at the election of '94 as a mandate to dramatically change government, and it really wasn't," recalled Bob Barr of Georgia, then a freshman GOP congressman.[40]

Clinton had won the battle, but he abandoned any pretense of fighting a war to protect national liberalism. "The era of big government is over," he famously announced in his January 1996 State of the Union address, formally disassociating his party from its New Deal legacy. For liberal Clinton aide George Stephanopoulos "the triumphalist tone of the declaration felt dishonest and vaguely dishonorable, as if we were condemning Democrats from Franklin Roosevelt to Lyndon Johnson to the trash heap of history for the sake of a sound bite." Speechwriter Michael Waldman judged it more harshly as "the death of liberalism at its own hands." But Clinton had in fact left the national liberal camp long before, agreeing in 1989 to take over the chairmanship of the Democratic Leadership Council, a New Democrat organization that argued the party should focus on attracting the support of socially liberal professionals and the corporations for which they worked, rather than the blue-collar voters who had been the chief supporters of the New Deal coalition. This shift, so clearly on display in the Clinton White House after 1995, meant that both parties now effectively represented the economic interests of corporate America, but only one was making a pitch to the often socially conservative white working class: the Republicans. This realignment would bring the Democratic Party new sources of campaign money, but played right into the laissez-faire Republicans' "New Class" playbook even as it shifted the political conversation away from the common good.[41]

What followed were five years of the most libertarian-minded Democratic administration since Woodrow Wilson, with a flurry of deregulation and spending cuts that set the stage for growing inequality and a near meltdown of the global economy. "His highest legislative priorities were to cut back one of our few income transfer programs for the very poor—Aid to Families with Dependent Children or, in the hated word, 'welfare'—and to seek a balanced budget deal with the Republicans that would have mandated cutbacks in other domestic programs as well," Representative Barney Frank, a New Deal Democrat from Massachusetts, recalls of the post-1995 Clinton.

Indeed, Clinton joined the GOP-controlled Congress to "end welfare as we know it," abolishing the $16 billion AFDC program, tightening food stamp eligibility rules, requiring able-bodied adults to go to work within two years (which wasn't easy for single mothers), and establishing a five-year maximum lifetime quota for welfare benefits.

Reelection was behind him, the economy was booming, and the federal budget was suddenly in surplus for the first time since 1969. Clinton and Gingrich held secret meetings in late 1997 aimed at forging a new center-right alliance that, in the words of their joint biographer Gillon, "would rival the New Deal and the Great Society in terms of the significance of legislation enacted." To make Social Security solvent ahead of the retirement of the enormous baby boomer generation, the two agreed to raise the age of eligibility, reduce cost-of-living adjustments, and create some sort of private accounts by which some portion of this pension fund would be invested in the stock market. The Monica Lewinsky scandal killed the plan, with Gingrich leading the theatrical impeachment of the president for lying about an extramarital affair and Clinton having to rely on solid Democratic support to avoid being removed from office.

Clinton would go on to repeal the Glass-Steagall Act, the cornerstone of New Deal financial regulation, which had forbidden (taxpayer-insured) commercial banks from engaging in speculative ventures. He also signed and supported the Commodity Futures Modernization Act, which prevented the regulation of credit default swaps, the "financial weapons of mass destruction" that nearly destroyed the world financial system a decade later. (In 1994 he had cleared the path for "too big to fail" banks by deregulating the industry to allow interstate banks to expand anywhere in the country.) He twice renominated Ayn Rand disciple Alan Greenspan to the chairmanship of the Federal Reserve.[42]

By the end of Clinton's term, voters were having a hard time distinguishing between the two parties on economic policy, which enabled Republicans to capitalize on social "wedge" issues to build support among working- and middle-class whites in key swing states and across Greater Appalachia. Consumer advocate Ralph Nader announced that he too would run for president in 2000, because "the only difference between Al Gore and George W. Bush is the velocity with which their knees hit the floor when corporations knock on their door." His argument was convincing enough to earn him nearly 3 percent of the national vote—enough, it would turn out, to change the course of history.[43]

★

In November 2000, with the help of Nader, an uninspiring Democratic candidate, and five Supreme Court justices, the Deep Southern oligarchy finally got one of their own elevated to the Oval Office for the first time since 1850, albeit without a majority of the vote in either Florida or the nation as a whole. George W. Bush was the son of a Yankee president and spent his early childhood in the Far Western section of Texas, but he was a creature of Deep Southern East Texas, where he spent his late childhood, built a political career, found God, and cultivated his business interests, political alliances, and policy priorities. His domestic policy concerns as president were those of the Deep Southern oligarchy: a cut in taxes for the wealthy and for corporations, privatization of Social Security, deregulation of energy markets, the opening of protected areas for oil exploration, the appointment of industry executives to run the agencies that oversaw their respective industries, the replacement of as much of the federal civil service as possible with corporate contractors, and the sluicing of billions in taxpayer money to corporations in no-bid contracts executed without effective oversight. With Dixie allies controlling Congress, the administration enacted an agenda that wasn't so much laissez-faire as simply mass theft, and its critics soon included many of the most stalwart supply-side warriors of the Reagan administration. "Bush is more like Richard Nixon—a man who used the [political] right to pursue his agenda, but was never really part of it," Reagan aide Bruce Bartlett, author of *Reaganomics,* the bible of the supply-side movement, warned in 2006. "In short, he is an impostor, a pretend conservative . . . incapable of telling the difference between being pro-business and being for the free market."[44]

Bush presided over perhaps the most craven diversion of public resources to the rich and powerful in the nation's history, behavior that is only libertarian in the sense of enhancing and protecting the benefits accruing to the winners of an increasingly Darwinian economic landscape. One of his first actions on taking office was to scuttle the U.S.-led initiative to shut down the offshore tax havens where unscrupulous tycoons hid their money from the IRS. (Dick Armey, the House majority leader, had decried the plan as creating a "global network of tax police.") As a result, dozens of the nation's richest corporations moved their "headquarters" to glorified post office boxes in Bermuda and other tax sanctuaries, allowing them to avoid paying taxes and in some cases even to qualify for new deductions. In 2009, for instance, General Electric made a profit of $14 billion but filed for a $3 billion tax rebate, more than the annual budget of the National Park Service. Bush then delivered a $1.6 trillion tax cut, the majority of which went to the top 1 percent of earners, and was backed by Greenspan, who argued that a budget surplus would be bad for the economy. Representative Tom Allen, a Maine Democrat who later sat on the budget committee, called it "the most fiscally irresponsible act in the history of Congress."[45]

The worst terrorist attack in American history did not prompt a change in course. As the country fell into recession and U.S. forces arrived in Afghanistan to commence what would be the longest war in American history, the Republican-controlled House passed another staggering transfer of wealth to the rich, eliminating a law that forced tax-dodging corporations to pay at least a nominal sum in taxes and even issuing rebate checks for past payments. The bill, which was quashed by the Democrat-controlled Senate, would have resulted in a $1.4 billion payment to IBM, $671 million to GE, and $254 million to Enron, the Houston-based energy firm that collapsed eight weeks later amid a massive criminal accounting fraud. The administration pushed forward with plans for another tax cut, prompting its own treasury secretary, Paul O'Neill, to warn that the measure would lead to a deficit that would undermine "our economic and fiscal soundness." Vice President Dick Cheney cut him off, insisting, "Reagan proved deficits don't matter," before adding, "We won the [2002] midterms. This is our due." (Shortly thereafter, Cheney called O'Neill to inform him he was being fired.) Two moderate Republican senators refused to go along with the proposed $1 trillion cut, which was even more targeted to the wealthy than the previous ones; they boldly agreed to a mere $350 billion plan, 53 percent of it going to the top 1 percent, because it focused on lowering taxes on capital gains and dividends, while leaving taxes on actually working families unchanged. The tax cuts passed, along with authorization for two wars financed entirely by borrowing. As Tom DeLay, now House majority leader, put it, "Nothing is more important in the face of a war than cutting taxes."[46]

Backers of these policies were sometimes candid about their true goal: to return the country to the Gilded Age. "Yes, the McKinley era, absent the protectionism," affirmed Grover Norquist—who had become the top liaison between Bush and DeLay on one hand and far-right activists on the other—in early 2003. "You're looking at the history of the country for the first 120 years, up until Teddy Roosevelt, when the socialists took over. The income tax, the death tax, regulation, all that." In 2001, he pledged, "My goal is to cut government in half in twenty-five years, to get it down to the size where we can drown it in the bathtub." Norquist's acolytes, who pledged to never raise taxes or to close loopholes for the rich, took this "starve the beast" strategy to heart. Pressed on the cost of the first round of tax cuts, Senator Jon Kyl of Arizona made this remarkable statement: "You do need to offset the cost of increased spending. . . . But you should never have to offset [the] cost of a deliberate decision to reduce tax rates on Americans." This fiscally delusional position was endorsed the next day by Senate Republican leader Mitch McConnell of Kentucky, who denied that tax cuts would diminish revenue. "They increased revenue," he said, contradicting the Treasury Department's own figures, "because of the vibrancy of these tax cuts in the economy." There was apparently no stopping place for such measures. "I have never once heard a [post-Gingrich] conservative admit that there is a level of taxation below which it would be unwise to go," Bruce Bartlett lamented. "But of course there is a limit, unless one believes anarchy is the preferred state in which people should live."[47]

Then there were the wars, one of which was undertaken under the false pretense that Iraq's Saddam Hussein possessed weapons of mass destruction. By 2012, the Iraq and Afghan wars had cost taxpayers $1.38 trillion, plus $300 billion in interest, because they were paid for with borrowed money while Bush and his allies dispensed tax cuts. Add the expenses of establishing the new Department of Homeland Security and war-related increases in spending at the State Department and Veterans Affairs, and the total cost amounted to over $4 trillion, more than the entire federal budget. Meanwhile, Cheney's former firm, Halliburton, was given billions in no-bid contracts to supply troops and manage the occupied oil fields. There was little oversight; Pentagon auditors discovered that Halliburton had billed the United States between $20 million and $34 million for meals it had never served the troops and $61 million in bogus fuel charges. House Republicans blocked Democratic efforts to convene oversight hearings on the waste, fraud, and abuse committed by the hordes of American contractors. Nor was there oversight of the $12 billion in cash flown into Baghdad in 2004, funds that had belonged to Hussein's government and were supposed to be used to rebuild the country; an incredible $8.8 billion in Saran-wrapped bricks of cash simply vanished. When Bush administration officials were pressed on the issue, they shrugged it off because it was Iraq's money, not theirs. "Billions of dollars of their money," occupation administration financial adviser David Oliver told the BBC. "I'm saying what difference does it make?"[48]

Worried about reelection, Bush offended what few deficit hawks were left by passing a $121 billion prescription drug benefit for the Medicare program. Once again, his administration put corporate interests ahead of those of the public by forbidding the federal government to use its very large bulk purchasing power to negotiate discounts from drug manufacturers. Instead, the law prevented seniors from buying the same drugs at the much lower prices offered in Canada. Mike Lofgren, then a senior Republican analyst on the House Budget Committee, stated the obvious: "it was overtly planned as a payday for Big Pharma."[49]

A further transfer of taxpayer wealth to the private sector was an unprecedented effort to privatize government services by contracting out work to private-sector companies, often with Iraq levels of oversight. Bush argued that half of all federal positions could be filled by private companies, and proceeded to double spending on contractors by the end of 2006. The *New York Times* reported that "contractors have become a virtual fourth branch of government," with the General Services Administration even contracting out its duty to oversee the contractors (to CACI, a firm whose personnel were alleged to have overseen the torture of prisoners at the notorious Abu Ghraib prison, and which charged GSA the equivalent of $200,000 a year per employee). By 2005, only 48 percent of contract actions were subject to full and open competition, down from 79 percent the year Bush took office, meaning competition was disappearing. Contractors were also far less accountable, their firms being immune from public records laws and, when operating in Iraq, prosecution for serious crimes. By the time Hurricane Katrina damaged much of New Orleans in 2005, killing more than fourteen hundred people, the Federal Emergency Management Agency had been gutted by the loss of experienced personnel via outsourcing. Headed by Michael Brown, a political hack who had previously run an Arabian horse breeders' association, FEMA was able to station only one person in the city before the storm hit. In the aftermath, corporate contractors received over $100 billion in reconstruction contracts, most of them no-bid, yet much of the city's public housing remained uninhabitable. "There's something civil servants have that the private sector doesn't," GSA head David M. Walker told the *New York Times*. "And that is the duty of loyalty to the greater good—the duty of loyalty to the collective best interest of all rather than the interest of a few. Companies have duties of loyalty to their shareholders, not to the country."[50]

By the middle of 2006, the Republican-controlled Congress was refusing to spend $648 million to increase security at U.S. ports to ensure that terrorists or perhaps a crude nuclear weapon could not be smuggled into the country in a shipping container; instead, Senate majority leader Bill Frist, Republican of Tennessee, was attempting to push through the elimination of the estate tax—which only affected estates valued at $2 million or more—at a cost of $355 billion over ten years. As Paul Krugman observed at the time, "Nothing is more important in the face of war than cutting taxes for very, very wealthy people, like the tiny minority of Americans who are heirs to really big estates."[51]

By 2008, the first Deep Southern administration in 150 years had done incalculable damage to the country while greatly enriching its real constituency: the oligarchy. Then the day of reckoning came for the deregulation craze of the Clinton-Gingrich and Bush-DeLay eras, with eerie parallels to the dark days of 1932, when no one could be certain that liberal democracy would survive.

# CHAPTER 8

# Rise of the Radicals
## (2008–)

As in 1929, at first it seemed as if the country were facing a serious but not catastrophic recession. In 2006, a bubble in the housing market—fueled by a deregulated financial sector willing to issue a mortgage to virtually anyone— began to burst, causing home prices to tumble. Millions of Americans found themselves owing considerably more on their mortgages than their homes were worth. The most vulnerable defaulted, many just walking away from their houses. In the old days, the banks that had made foolish loans would have been the ones punished, but in the deregulated environment of the previous decade, the loans had been rolled into securities, stamped "safe" by incompetent or unscrupulous auditors, and sold to other banks and investors, while their future failure or success was bet upon by other investors through arcane new financial products. The "innovative" products had been marketed as hedges against the risk that a mortgage might collapse, when in fact they concentrated the risk and injected it in potentially lethal doses to banks around the world. When the first large investment banks began to face trouble in early 2008, few took the matter seriously.[1]

Then, on a mid-September weekend, the world nearly came to an end. Lehman Brothers, the fourth-largest investment bank in the United States, went bankrupt after both the government and Barclays declined to rescue it. Simultaneously, Merrill Lynch, the nation's largest retail securities brokerage, was absorbed by Bank of America to prevent its immediate failure. On Monday, September 15, the stock market took the largest fall since the September 11 attacks. On Tuesday, AIG, the world's largest insurance group, was taken over by the government and rescued from collapse with an $85 billion emergency loan. The six largest surviving U.S. banks—J.P. Morgan, Bank of America, Citigroup, Wells Fargo, Goldman Sachs, and Morgan Stanley—were so vulnerable the Federal Reserve secretly gave them $460 billion in emergency, below-market-rate loans to ensure their solvency, a fact hidden from the public and Congress until 2011, when a Bloomberg news service lawsuit forced disclosure. Overall, the Fed secretly committed $7.7 trillion over the months that followed to rescue the financial system. This commitment was in addition to the $700 billion taxpayer bailout the public was aware of, and furious about: the Troubled Asset Relief Program (TARP), which also saved the automotive industry. "All these institutions were about to collapse, and they never would have survived but for the trillions of dollars afforded them by the taxpayers," the chair of the Financial Crisis Inquiry Commission, Phil Angelides, later told PBS's *Frontline*. Blythe Masters, a top executive at J.P. Morgan, put it this way: "The Great Depression would have looked like a small event by comparison to what I think would have happened had that process continued unrestricted." Bush administration officials called Democratic presidential nominee Barack Obama and warned him, "Look, we think the world is close to coming to an end, and we really need your support" for the bailout.[2]

The banks had been allowed to grow so big they could not be allowed to fail, meaning they had succeeded in privatizing their profits (when they won their bets) while socializing the risks (when they didn't). Six months after what had become a $170 billion tax-payer rescue, AIG executives gave $165 million in bonuses to executives of the very unit that had driven the company to disaster, an act the chair of Obama's Council of Economic Advisers would later say deserved "the Nobel Prize for evil." No one in Washington felt empowered to stop the bonuses, even though the federal government now owned 80 percent of the company.[3]

The consequences of the collapse were profound, both economically and politically. It triggered the Great Recession, the most severe economic downturn since 1932, wiping out 5.5 million American jobs, $7.4 trillion in stock values, $3.4 trillion in real estate value, and $648 billion in lost economic growth in less than a year. Politically it had several effects. It marked the final verdict on George W. Bush's crony capitalist administration, whose approval ratings matched those of Nixon at the depths of Watergate. Even former Federal Reserve chair Alan Greenspan, whose lax monetary policies had fueled the housing bubble, found himself in "a state of shocked disbelief" that the deregulated bankers hadn't regulated themselves. It propelled a political neophyte, Barack Obama, to the White House bearing a message of hope, change, and bipartisanship. The most significant political effect, however, was the radicalization of the Republican Party's base, a development with lasting and corrosive effects on the Republic.[4]

⭐

Most Americans were infuriated by TARP, which was seen as fundamentally immoral because it rewarded those who had brought about the disaster. "I don't think a single call to my office on this proposal has been positive," Senator Sherrod Brown, Democrat of Ohio, said as Congress hastily debated passage of the measure in the final weeks of the Bush administration. Senator Richard Shelby, Republican of Alabama, noted the administration's plan was "aimed at rescuing the same financial institutions that created this crisis, with the sloppy underwriting and reckless disregard for the risks they were creating, taking or passing on to others. Wall Street bet that the government would rescue them if they got into trouble. It appears that bet may be the one that pays off." Chris Dodd, chair of the Senate Banking Committee, noted TARP "would do nothing to help a single family save a home" or "stop the very authors of this calamity to walk away with bonuses and golden parachutes worth millions of dollars," but voted for it anyway. Fearing the entire global economy could collapse without a prompt government bailout, they had little choice. Government intervention, long derided by the business lobby, was suddenly the only thing that could rescue Wall Street from its self-inflicted destruction.[5]

Ironically, the first significant call to resist government intervention came not from a person who had lost his home or job because of the recklessness of the banks, but from a career commodity trader turned financial journalist in a rant against the banks' victims. Standing before cheering derivatives traders on the floor of the Chicago Mercantile Exchange on February 19, 2009, CNBC's Rick Santelli held forth against the new Obama administration's plan to reduce the mortgage payments of some distressed homeowners. Santelli said he and the traders didn't want to "subsidize the losers' mortgages" and would rather "buy cars and buy houses in foreclosure and give 'em to people that might have a chance to actually prosper down the road and reward people that could carry the water instead of drink the water." He said that he and the traders were going to organize a "Chicago Tea Party" that summer to protest what he characterized as a Cuba-like descent into collectivism. A few hours later, Fox News's popular conservative firebrand Sean Hannity replayed footage of what would soon be called "the rant heard round the world," and the following day his Fox colleague Glenn Beck began promoting the idea of tax revolts. By then, FreedomWorks, a Washington, D.C.–based laissez-faire advocacy organization founded by the Koch brothers and run by former Republican House majority leader Dick Armey, had created a "I Stand with Rick" Web site to help inspired citizens organize protests. On February 27, fifty-one synchronized "tea parties" occurred in cities across the country, with an average attendance of just under six hundred at each. People brought flags and homemade signs with slogans like "Your Mortgage Is Not My Problem" and "Free Markets, Not Freeloaders." Something was brewing.[6]

Anger at the plan to rescue some people who were losing their homes proved ephemeral. But when news of the AIG bonuses broke in March 2009, all hell broke loose. The Connecticut headquarters of the guilty AIG division started receiving death threats, prompting some senior managers to resign from the firm, and others to post guards outside. "Never before or since have I seen vehement, universal public anger reach such a white-hot level," recalled Representative Barney Frank, then chair of the House Financial Services Committee, likening it to the torch-bearing mob of villagers marching on the laboratory in the 1931 movie *Frankenstein*. "I feared we were in danger of losing our capacity to govern—not just to enact a national financial reform bill but also to pass any legislation that required public trust in elected officials." Although TARP would succeed in its aims— and taxpayer loans would be completely repaid—AIG's actions discredited the bailout in the public eye, leading many to conclude that the government was coddling criminals and picking ordinary people's pockets to enrich them.[7]

Dick Armey himself said it was the "Wall Street bailout that ignited the firestorm." FreedomWorks, one of the few groups to have opposed TARP all along, was ready to capitalize on the rage. It was, as Armey later recalled, "at the center of the activism." The group's plan was to educate "Tea Party" participants in the long-standing laissez-faire agenda and then mobilize them to engineer a "hostile takeover" of the GOP. "By seizing control of the party, we can spend our time focused on ideas and use the party infrastructure that has been built over the past 156 years," he counseled in a self-described "Tea Party Manifesto" published in the summer of 2010. This effort to guide the ideological and strategic direction of the surging protest movement was largely though not completely successful, and led to the seizure of great swaths of the county- and state-level party machinery by Tea Party activists and the election of dozens of radical antigovernment ideologues to Congress.

FreedomWorks's role was facilitative, providing Web site tips on organizing and locating rallies and supporting and guiding the early activities of a grassroots umbrella organization, the Tea Party Patriots. Armey and other FreedomWorks officials served as spokesmen for the movement, shaping how the outside world perceived it. They formed alliances with Fox News and other conservative media outlets and even sponsored Glenn Beck's nationally syndicated radio show. (In 2012, the organization would pay Beck over $1 million to, as Armey later put it, say "nice things about FreedomWorks on the air," an arrangement that was later extended to Rush Limbaugh.) In March, FreedomWorks's staff of former corporate lobbyists—Armey himself had represented Raytheon and Verizon until 2009—began organizing Beck's "9/12" rally in Washington, D.C., applying for the appropriate permits while Beck promoted the event on air. The group also urged its followers to set aside social issues and embrace their libertarian economic platform, summed up in the group's motto: "Lower Taxes, Less Government, More Freedom."[8]

Beck also played a key role in the political education of his Tea Party admirers. His primary contribution was the tireless promotion of the works and ideas of W. Cleon Skousen, a right-wing extremist whose views were so fanatical he'd been ousted by the John Birch Society and placed under scrutiny by both J. Edgar Hoover's FBI and the Mormons' Quorum of Twelve Apostles. A Mormon and former FBI agent himself, Skousen had started developing complex conspiracy theories while serving as police chief of Salt Lake City in the 1950s. The Council on Foreign Relations, the American banking establishment, and the Rockefeller, Ford, and Carnegie foundations, he believed, were all in on "a paroxysm of world-wide political subversion" to "push the United States into a collectivist one-world society." The Rothschilds and Rockefellers were directing a grand conspiracy involving OSHA, the EPA, the fairness doctrine of the Federal Communications Commission, the Social Security Administration, and the United Nations, the unraveling of which became a central mission of his National Center for Constitution Studies. Skousen's seminal work, *The 5,000 Year Leap,* proclaimed that the U.S. Constitution was inspired not by the Enlightenment philosophers but by the Old and New testaments and that its divinely inspired authors believed in a minimal, laissez-faire government and a merging of church and state. Another of Skousen's books, *The Making of America,* argued that slave owners were the "worst victims" of the southern slave system, the slaves themselves being full of good cheer.[9]

Skousen had died in 2006, and his books and ideas had long since been forgotten. But in the aftermath of the financial meltdown, Beck began endorsing his work on air, touting *The 5,000 Year Leap* as "essential to understanding why our Founders built this Republic the way they did." Local Tea Party groups placed bulk orders for their Constitution study groups, sometimes bringing in "scholars" from the National Center for Constitution Studies to lead the sessions. The center's curriculum encouraged activists to embrace the view that the 1789 Constitution prohibited not only the institutions and programs of the New Deal and Great Society, but also federal income, corporate, and capital gains taxes, the national park and national forest systems, the separation of church and state on the state level, and the Sixteenth, Seventeenth, and Twenty-Fifth amendments, which provided for the popular election of U.S. senators, direct federal taxes, and clear procedures for replacing a dead or incapacitated president. Such a program would return the United States to the Gilded Age, with the added possibility of state theocracies. Beck wrote the foreword to the new edition of *The 5,000 Year Leap,* saying it was "divinely-inspired."[10] The book soon shot to number 1 on Amazon.com, selling a quarter million copies in the first half of 2009.

Grassroots Tea Party activists ultimately had to decide for themselves what they stood for. The propaganda they received from FreedomWorks (and an existing Republican PAC, rebranded the "Tea Party Express") was libertarian in the Goldwater-Gingrich sense, while the messages coming from Beck and Skousen's center were socially theocratic and economically libertarian. Not surprisingly, polls, interviews, and intensive scholarly studies have revealed a bifurcated Tea Party movement, with social conservatives of the Beck and Sarah Palin variety dominant in the Deep South, Tidewater, and Greater Appalachia, and libertarians of the Ron Paul and FreedomWorks variety holding the upper hand in the Far West and Yankeedom. Many local Tea Party groups experienced power struggles between these factions, especially in Yankeedom and the Far West, where libertarians often struggled to keep Christian conservatives from splitting the movement with regionally unpopular policies. However, members of both factions had a number of characteristics in common: They were overwhelmingly white, over forty-five years old, comfortably middle class, and self-identified as "extremely conservative." Polling and research showed the typical Tea Partiers took a Skousen-like view of the 1789 Constitution and a social Darwinist view of society that pits the worthy and hardworking (themselves) against the lazy and undeserving (the poor, the young, the uninsured). They departed from the teachings of both Clousen and FreedomWorks in that they felt the "deserving" were justly entitled to the big-government benefits of the New Deal and Great Society: Social Security, Medicare, and Veterans Affairs programs. In their view, they'd worked for them, they'd earned them, and the nation should provide them. "Almost all Tea Partiers favor generous social benefits for Americans who 'earn' them," Harvard University sociologists Theda Skocpol and Vanessa Williamson concluded in an in-depth study of the movement. "Yet in an era of rising federal deficits, they are very concerned about being stuck with the tax tab to pay for 'unearned' entitlements handed out to unworthy categories of people," including health insurance, student loans, and mortgage relief. They were twice as likely than other Americans to agree that providing government benefits to the poor "encourages them to remain poor" and significantly more likely to believe blacks and whites had equal opportunities to be successful.[11]

The movement grew rapidly, particularly after Obama announced an $800 billion economic stimulus package and a plan to extend health insurance to millions of uninsured Americans. Tax Day protests organized by FreedomWorks in April 2009 saw crowds of a few dozen to a few thousand gathering in 750 cities. In August, members of Congress confronted angry crowds of Tea Partiers at health care "town hall" meetings in their home districts who shouted them down as traitors and even executed some in effigy. Glenn Beck's "9/12" rally attracted between sixty and seventy thousand to the Washington Mall (although organizers would claim a million) to listen to Beck and Armey protest government overreach. In January 2010, Tea Party activists and donations propelled a Republican, Scott Brown, to an upset victory to take the U.S. Senate seat vacated by the death of national liberal lion Ted Kennedy of Massachusetts. The political establishment—both Democrats and Republicans of the Ronald Reagan and George W. Bush school—didn't know what had hit them.[12]

In keeping with Armey's vision, Tea Party activists began taking over the GOP apparatus from the bottom up. They signed up to be party precinct leaders, a low-level position that often remained vacant, but conferred the power to vote for party officials, approve platforms, and endorse candidates. Their mantra, *New York Times* reporter Kate Zernike reported, was, "Take the precinct, take the state, take the party." Coached by a group called the National Precinct Alliance, they seized control of the party in the Las Vegas area, the largest in Nevada, giving them the leverage to elect a Tea Party slate to the leadership of the state party. They followed the same program in the Phoenix area, leading not-always-libertarian senator John McCain to set up an entity to allow national party donors to bypass hostile state party officials and give directly to his reelection campaign. At Utah's state convention, Tea Partiers defeated the nomination of incumbent U.S. senator Bob Bennett—a conservative who had voted for TARP—in favor of one of their own, Mike Lee. In Maine, long a bastion of old-school national liberal consensus Republicans, Tea Partiers took over county committees and then the state convention to pass a platform calling for a "return to the principles of Austrian economics," the elimination of the Department of Education and Federal Reserve, prosecution of those participating in the "global warming myth," and resistance to the establishment of a "one-world government." "The people who come from the traditional conservative Reagan wing of the Republican Party have lost control of it," said moderate state senator Peter Mills, who was soundly defeated in the gubernatorial primary that year by Tea Party favorite Paul LePage. "Somehow Obama has morphed into George III, the Congress is the British Parliament, and the Tea Party is the Minutemen with their long rifles. I don't think people have thought through where that all leads."[13]

In the short term, the Tea Party's contribution was ambiguous, because support for its agenda was anything but broad-based. In the 2010 midterm elections, it failed to defeat a single Republican incumbent save Senator Bob Bennett. It nominated a cohort of radical laissez-faire candidates to the House and Senate, and won seats in the Deep South (including those of senators Jim DeMint of South Carolina and Marco Rubio of Florida), Far West (Mike Lee), and Greater Appalachia (Rand Paul). The Tea Party wave helped the GOP retake the House with a net sixty-three-seat gain, and unseated Democratic senators in Wisconsin and Arkansas. In Pennsylvania moderate Republican incumbent Arlen Specter switched parties to avoid a Tea Party primary challenge, only to lose the Democratic nomination; a Tea Party favorite, Pat Toomey, won the general election. At the same time, Tea Party activists nominated extreme Senate candidates in three states that otherwise would have almost certainly gone Republican—Delaware, Colorado, and Nevada— and forced the national party to divert resources to help rescue moderate incumbent Lisa Murkowski of Alaska from a Tea Party challenger.[14]

Indeed, while the Tea Party established a presence throughout the country, its success on the political stage was concentrated in certain regions. Of the sixty members of the House Tea Party caucus in the 112th Congress (2011–12), only three hailed from Yankeedom, and none from the Left Coast or New Netherland. The three

Yankees did not achieve victory easily; in the seven races they had collectively won, only twice had any of them achieved a margin of victory of greater than 5 percent (Minnesota's Michele Bachmann, in 2006 and 2010). One, Illinois freshman Joe Walsh, had won his seat by just 291 votes and was gerrymandered into lame-duck status by local Democrats. In Massachusetts, Scott Brown disappointed Tea Party activists by legislating as a Yankee moderate, while movement governors Paul LePage (in Maine) and Scott Walker (in Wisconsin) faced sustained resistance to their efforts to dismantle environmental, labor, and consumer safety protections. In 2012, the Republicans were swept in New England, losing every major federal and statewide contest, including Scott Brown's Senate seat, the lower chamber of the New Hampshire State House, and every one of the region's twenty-one House seats and electoral college votes for president; they also lost every Senate race in the rest of Yankeedom and a majority of Yankee-controlled House seats in Illinois, Minnesota, New York, and Iowa. From the Puritan migration of the 1630s to the debt ceiling debate, Yankees have championed individual self-denial for the common good, investment in strong public institutions, and governmental projects to improve society. The Tea Party was unable to take deep root in such inhospitable soil, and its partial takeover had driven the Republicans to near extinction in the region of their birth.[15]

By contrast, the Tea Party encountered little resistance to its agenda in the Dixie nations and the Far West, largely because its political agenda matched that of the Deep South: Reduce taxes for the wealthy and services for everyone else; crush the labor unions, public education, and the regulatory system; and suppress the turnout of immigrant, youth, and nonwhite voters. The four nations accounted for fifty-one of the sixty members of the House Tea Party caucus—85 percent of them—with the Deep South alone accounting for twenty-two. In the 2012 election, a referendum on Tea Party policy, Republicans had a net loss of eight seats in the House, but actually had a net gain of ten in the Deep South and Greater Appalachia.[16]

Once in office, Tea Party members of Congress quickly discredited the movement by threatening to destroy the world economy if their radical libertarian demands were not completely and immediately met. The first crisis came in the summer of 2011, when the Tea Party crowd announced they would block what had been a routine exercise to raise the ceiling on the national debt, enabling the United States to pay the bills Congress had already authorized in its budget. If the ceiling wasn't raised, the country would default on its national debt, an event most economists agreed would cause a world economic collapse that would have made the crash of 2008 seem trivial. Yet the Tea Party congressmen—especially the twenty freshmen who'd just been elected—announced they would not do so unless Congress cut spending by some $2 trillion to balance the budget without raising taxes. Obama, a pragmatic national liberal in the mold of Eisenhower, began secret negotiations with House Speaker John Boehner (Appalachian Ohio) and came up with a $4 trillion "grand bargain" that would have increased taxes, cut entitlement spending, and simplified the tax code.

While the compromise was a victory for deficit reduction, the Tea Party contingent refused to endorse Boehner's deal because it raised taxes on the wealthy, bringing the country within hours of a default, which downgraded the U.S. government's credit rating and cost taxpayers $1.3 billion in added interest.* "I think some of our members may have thought the default issue was a hostage you might take a chance at shooting," Senate minority leader Mitch McConnell said of the world economy. "Most of us didn't think that. What we did learn is this—it's a hostage that's worth ransoming."

---

* To avoid default, Congress agreed to create a bipartisan "super-committee" charged with reducing the deficit by $1.2 trillion over ten years, with automatic cuts to both military and social programs if they failed—which they did.

Indeed, after Obama decisively won reelection in 2012—over the overwhelming opposition in Greater Appalachia and the Deep South—the radicals repeated the exercise, bringing the country to the brink of default again in January 2013 in an attempt to force the defunding of the president's health care reform program. That fall, they forced a sixteen-day government shutdown, costing taxpayers another $2 billion and increasing the animosity directed toward the radicals. "We now have a group of US politicians seeking political purity, who seem to have much in common with the Taliban," wrote former Democratic representative Martin Frost during the 2011 debt ceiling crisis. "They are Tea Party members; and because of blind adherence to smaller government, they seem intent on risking destroying what American political leaders have constructed in more than two centuries of hard, often painful work."[17]

The effect of the movement's economic policies was clearest in places where they actually did control the government. In Kansas, Governor Sam Brownback in 2012 enacted a $1.1 billion tax cut benefiting the wealthy, while slashing spending on education, social services, and the arts and fully privatizing the Medicaid system. "We'll see how it works," he told CNN at the outset. "We'll have a real-live experiment." Two years later, the verdict was in: a $700 million plunge in state revenues in a single year and a staggering $1 billion revenue hole projected for the next two; a downgrading of the state's credit rating; lower job growth than any of its peer states; and public school cuts so severe that the state courts ruled them unconstitutional because they were "destructive of our children's future."

In North Carolina, meanwhile, Republicans took control of both the governor's mansion and the legislative branch for the first time since Reconstruction and enacted sweeping Tea Party reforms. Drastic cuts were made in unemployment benefits in a state with one of the highest unemployment rates in the country, because the state Chamber of Commerce objected to paying more taxes to keep the program solvent. Education budgets were stripped back, resulting in salary cuts to teachers, the elimination of ten thousand pre-kindergarten slots, and cuts in services to disabled children. Even though North Carolina's population had been rapidly increasing, lawmakers cut tens of millions from the budget for its court system, forcing 10 percent of its workforce to be laid off (including translators for Spanish-speaking defendants and victim's advocates) and a reduction in funds for public defenders. Lawmakers also scaled back early voting (popular among Democratic voters) and refused to expand Medicaid, even though 90 percent of its cost would be borne by the federal government. The *New York Times* editorial board called the moves "a demolition derby, tearing down years of progress in public education, tax policy, racial equality in the courtroom and access to the ballot."[18]

The movement espoused a radical form of libertarianism not seen since the late nineteenth century. In a particularly infamous incident in September 2011, Representative Ron Paul was asked at a CNN/Tea Party Express presidential debate in Tampa, Florida, how far his ethic of individual responsibility extended: If an uninsured thirty-year-old had a catastrophic illness requiring six months of intensive care, should society let him die? The crowd suddenly burst out in cheers, yelling, "Yeah!" Paul himself waffled, but essentially agreed: "That's what freedom is all about—taking your own risks." In another incident in October 2010, firefighters in rural Tennessee stood by while a man's house burned to the ground with all his possessions, a cat, and three dogs inside, because he hadn't paid a seventy-five-dollar annual fee. This position was denounced by the head of the national firefighters' association, and others pointed out that the department could have developed policies to recover their expenses and incentivize compliance while still saving the man's home, such as putting a lien on the property for the costs of response. Glenn Beck, however, took to the airwaves to defend the department's position, insisting that it was necessary to prevent people from "sponging off" their neighbors, while his on-air sidekick mocked the victim for begging firefighters to save his home. Social justice advocates, he said, would demand the department put out the fire. "They will push it up to a government responsibility instead of the individual's responsibility." Society, he said, was going to have to implement the fire department's tough-love approach to its job: "We are going to start to have to have these kinds of things." Tea Party Web sites and forums enthusiastically echoed his line.[19]

Tea Party politicians and activists also displayed an anger toward Obama's policies so vitriolic that it often defied logic. He was constantly attacked as a socialist, a Marxist, a dictator, or an alien hellbent on destroying America by turning it into a West European–style social democracy. In fact the president was, by West European standards, a center-right politician, and a liberal Republican by U.S. metrics, more akin to Eisenhower or the first Bush than to Vladimir Lenin, Che Guevara, or even Roosevelt, Kennedy, or Johnson. He continued the hawkish national-security-state policies of George W. Bush and Dick Cheney, devoted more than a third of his emergency stimulus bill to tax cuts (despite evidence that infrastructure spending is a far more effective form of stimulus), reduced the federal budget deficit from $1.4 trillion to $506 billion in his first five years in office, agreed to a compromise proposal with Boehner that would have slashed the social safety net, appointed moderate-to-conservative individuals to the Federal Reserve, Treasury, and National Economic Council, and was soundly criticized by liberals for letting Wall Street off the hook for the financial crisis. His only significant contribution to the New Deal agenda, a 2010 reform of the health insurance market, took the preferred national liberal solution of a universal Medicare-like "single payer" system off the table in favor of a market-based system modeled on the laissez-faire Heritage Foundation's 1989 proposal and the system created by his corporate Republican rival, Mitt Romney, when he was governor of Massachusetts. "Obama has governed as a moderate conservative," former Reagan aide Bruce Bartlett observed in late 2014. "He has been conservative to exactly the same degree that Richard Nixon basically governed as a moderate liberal." Indeed, actual left-liberals from the Kennedy-Johnson-McGovern tradition were generally unhappy with Obama's essential conservatism, and bona fide socialists were disgusted. "He posed as a progressive and turned out to be a counterfeit," political philosopher Cornel West, honorary chair of the Democratic Socialists of America, said of Obama in 2014. "We ended up with a Wall Street presidency, a drone presidency, a national security presidency. . . . [I]t turned out that he's just another neoliberal centrist."[20]

Finally, Tea Party ideas began to infect the Republican Party as a whole, prompting even its allegedly non–Tea Party leaders to adopt radical libertarian positions that would have given 1950s archconservative Robert Taft pause. In 2012, Republican representative Paul Ryan, chair of the House Budget Committee and self-described Ayn Rand devotee, proposed a budget featuring big tax cuts for the wealthy and draconian cuts in benefits and programs for middle- and lower-income people, excluding (in a nod to the Tea Party) retirees. The Urban Institute determined that its provisions would cause fourteen to twenty-seven million poor people to be dropped from Medicaid while cutting reimbursements to doctors and hospitals that treated those who remained by 31 percent. "We don't want to turn the safety net into a hammock that lulls able-bodied people into lives of complacency and dependence," Ryan explained, adding that his Catholic faith inspired the plan. The U.S. Conference of Bishops disagreed, writing Congress that the "central moral measure of any budget proposal is how it affects 'the least of these' . . . those who are hungry and homeless, without work or in poverty." Ryan's "budget resolution fails to meet these moral criteria." A group of Jesuit scholars and Georgetown University faculty members informed Ryan that his proposal "appeared to reflect the values of your favorite philosopher, Ayn Rand, rather than the Gospel of Jesus Christ."

The plan was thereafter embraced by Republican presidential nominee Mitt Romney, who picked Ryan as his running mate. So radical was the proposal that when the Democratic super PAC Priorities USA explained to focus groups what it actually entailed, the *New York Times* later reported, "respondents simply refused to believe any politician would do such a thing." At a nationally televised primary debate in August 2011, all eight Republican presidential candidates were asked to raise their hands if they'd refuse a deficit reduction deal that cut ten dollars in spending for every dollar in new taxes. All eight candidates—including Romney and alleged moderate Jon Huntsman, former governor of Utah—raised their hands.[21]

Much of the country did not support the Tea Party, as evidenced by Mitt Romney's selection as the party's presidential nominee in 2012 over a variety of Tea Party favorites; Obama's fairly easy defeat of Romney in the general election (again opposed by a majority of voters only in the Deep South, Greater Appalachia, and the Far West); Democratic gains in the 2012 congressional midterms; and establishment Republican victories in the 2014 congressional primaries. In national polls conducted over a span of thirty years, clear majorities of Americans have consistently expressed support for raising taxes on the wealthy, preventing cuts to Social Security benefits, the continued existence of labor unions to protect working people, and maintaining the government's role in assisting those who can't help themselves and ensuring that everyone has enough to eat and a place to sleep. In 2012—two years into the Tea Party ascendance—63 percent of Americans agreed that "a free market economy needs government regulation in order to best serve the public interest," a central plank of national liberalism; an even more striking finding was that 62 percent of self-described "non–Tea Party Republicans" felt the same, as opposed to just 29 percent of Tea Partiers. The same survey found that 72 percent of Americans believed that Wall Street "only cares about making money for itself," with little difference in the opinions of the working, middle, and upper middle classes. Furthermore, the trends were all against the laissez-faire movement. A 2014 Pew Research Center survey found that only 38 percent of millennials— people born after 1979—wanted a small government providing less services, and a majority believed it is government's responsibility to ensure all Americans have health insurance. David Frum, former speechwriter for George W. Bush, called them "the most pro-government generation the United States has seen since the generation that voted for President Franklin Roosevelt exited the stage."[22]

As the nation limped toward the 2016 presidential contest, its government was nearly paralyzed, starkly divided on a largely regional basis between radical libertarians and anyone who felt even a passing commitment to shared institutions and a sense of common purpose. Neither of its two main political formations, now starkly divided into ideological camps for the first time since the Jacksonian era, was able to muster the electoral supermajority required to overcome the other's resistance.

A new set of political ideals was desperately needed. The future of not only the United States but the world stood in the balance.

# CHAPTER 9

# A Lasting Union

W hen it comes to balancing the forces of individualism and collectivism, we don't need to guess at what works most effectively in America, despite our balkanized cultural geography. History offers a clear and consistent guide.

We are in aggregate one of the most individualistic political cultures on earth, the legacy of a revolution that was carried out at a time and place when the primary foe of liberty was a monarchical government, its primary beneficiary an enlightened aristocratic elite. Informed by John Locke, we put great faith in human capacity, innovation, and virtue, and remain vigilant against the rise of an overarching government that might deny us our individual potential. Socialism, which would place its trust in an all-knowing government of allegedly disinterested experts to control the economy and shape the social fabric, has always been a political nonstarter in America, whether one lives in community-minded Yankeedom or on the libertarian frontiers of Appalachia. Many liberal democracies have embraced social democracy to build capitalist-fueled welfare states that invariably top global rankings for wealth, happiness, and social trust; in aggregate, Americans have shown time and again that they don't want such a system. In the midst of a world war, Woodrow Wilson enacted a collectivist agenda that featured the criminalization of dissent; with peace, this agenda was soundly repudiated for swerving into tyranny. Even at the height of the New Deal, FDR encountered cross-country resistance to direct government participation in the workings of a peacetime economy, be it through central economic planning or the hiring of large numbers of laborers to build public works. Lyndon Johnson's experts made assurances that they had the knowledge to wage successful wars on poverty and North Vietnam; their failure to deliver on their promises brought down more than a presidential administration. There is an American consensus that government can't solve all problems and should limit its reach to those areas where it *can* succeed. We are a practical people; we want results and have little patience for failure.

That said, we are not a libertarian federation. Outside the Deep South and pre-1980s Tidewater, there has never been sustained public support for laissez-faire economics, the Far West and Greater Appalachia having a populist streak that quickly bristles against the oligarchic results that follow when these policies are put into practice. Each time we have been down the laissez-faire road, the trip ended in disaster. Twice in a century, economic libertarianism nearly brought down the world economy, threatening liberal democracy itself. In 2011 and 2013, its champions threatened to bring it down again if their demands weren't unconditionally met. They did so because their program lacked the political support to be enacted through nonauthoritarian channels. Decades of polling and voting have revealed that very few Americans actually want to return to the unfettered social Darwinism of the Gilded Age, as demonstrated by the election of Teddy Roosevelt in 1904 and Franklin Roosevelt in

1932, and the rejection of Newt Gingrich's revolutionaries in 1996 and George W. Bush's congressional enablers in 2006. As we've seen, despite the propaganda efforts of FreedomWorks and other champions of laissez-faire, even the Tea Party grassroots activists of 2009–12 vigorously supported guaranteed old-age pensions and government-administered health insurance for the elderly. Unlike socialism, however, the laissez-faire agenda does have the committed support of one of our most powerful regional cultures, and some measure of rhetorical sympathy in others, which is why it continues to periodically gain a foothold on our political landscape.

So the American consensus lies in the territory between the un-fettered capitalism of the late nineteenth century and turn-of-the-millennium West European social democratic states. If a politician or party leans too far in one direction or the other, Americans will vote them out of office. Somewhere within this space between Theodore Roosevelt's "New Nationalism" of 1910 and the national liberal consensus of 1965 lies an agenda that can again command a super-majority, that can again set the American Republic to the task the founders prescribed for it, the promotion of human happiness. Given the system of checks and balances that are embodied in our Constitution, it's perhaps the only way that we can move forward to confront the challenges the twenty-first century will bring our world.

✠

There are two reasons why the early twenty-first-century United States has found its governing institutions paralyzed, incapable of reliably performing such basic functions as passing budgets or approving the borrowing required to pay for those already passed.

The first, which should be abundantly clear to readers by now, is that we are not a nation-state in the European mold: a state governed by a particular nation with a distinct culture and values, like Germany, Austria, France, or Sweden. The United States is a federation comprised of several "nations" that share very little in terms of common ideals, goals, and views on the meaning of freedom. Throughout our history, our component regional cultures have fought with one another over whether freedom was to be understood only in terms of individual or "economic" liberty, or in terms of the promotion of the common good or the "freedom of the community."

We have been able to function within the constraints of this system for long periods because one political formation or another has been able to assemble a regional supermajority sufficient to control the levers of federal power: a majority in the electoral college and House of Representatives, and a filibuster-proof one in the Senate. This was the case during the Civil War, when a Yankee-led coalition had free rein in Congress, and again between 1877 and 1929, when laissez-faire-minded Republicans and conservative southern Democrats held sway. It was also the status quo during the national liberal period from 1932 to 1965, when progressive Democrats and Republicans built an active federal government. There were inklings of it in the early 1980s, when a new Dixie–Far West coalition put Reagan in the White House and brought a Republican-controlled Senate, but it was short-lived. In 2008, Democrats obtained control of all three bodies, leading many observers to write eulogies for the laissez-faire conservatives, only to see them seize the House in the very next election, propelled by a popular movement bearing a Deep Southern agenda. Looking back on the period since the collapse of the national liberal order, it's clear that neither the Deep Southerners' hierarchical libertarianism, nor the New Left's social libertarianism, nor the Christian right's social collectivism, nor the Dixie-led Democratic Leadership Council brand of triangulating neoliberalism is capable of building a governing supermajority.

Our cultural balkanization also helps account for why early twenty-first-century elections have become such suspenseful contests, decided by the shifting allegiances of a relatively minor number of voters from a small and recurring cohort of (mostly Midlander) battleground counties in a handful of swing states. Over the past half-century the regional blocs have remained stable. Yankeedom, New Netherland, and the Left Coast have faced off against the Deep South, Tidewater, Greater Appalachia, and the Far West over civil rights, the Vietnam and Iraq wars, the environmental and gay rights movements, health care and financial reform, and the last three presidential elections. (The exception: rapidly changing Tidewater, which became a "swing nation" from 2008.)

The northern alliance has been the champion of collective action for the common good, consistently favoring the maintenance of a strong central government, federal checks on corporate power, and the conservation of natural resources, regardless of which party was dominant in the region at any given time. (Recall that prior to the civil rights struggle of the 1960s, the Republicans were the party of Yankeedom.) The presidents it has produced—John F. Kennedy, Gerald Ford, George H. W. Bush, and Barack Obama—have all sought to better society through government programs, expanded civil rights protections, and environmental safeguards. All faced opposition from the Dixie-led nations even from within their own parties. With the southern takeover of the GOP, Yankeedom, New Netherland, and the Left Coast have become overwhelmingly Democratic in recent years.

The other coalition has been led by the Deep South, whose oligarchy's agenda has remained consistently laissez-faire and social Darwinist. Deep Southern leaders have fought to control and maintain a one-party state with a colonial-style economy based on large-scale agriculture and the extraction of primary resources by a compliant, low-wage workforce with as few labor, workplace safety, health care, and environmental regulations as possible and a tax structure that pushes much of the financial burden onto those least able to afford it. In office, the Deep South's leaders focus on cutting taxes for the rich, funneling massive subsidies to agribusiness and oil companies, rolling back labor and environmental initiatives, and creating "guest worker" programs and "right to work" laws to ensure a cheap, docile labor supply. Finding coalition partners for such an agenda hasn't been easy, so the Deep South has had to rely on a common strain of libertarianism as the basis for an expedient alliance with the far more populist-minded people of Greater Appalachia and the Far West. Even Tidewater, which once shared hierarchical libertarian notions with the Deep South, has been rapidly transforming into more of a Midland culture as the expanding federal halos around Washington, D.C., and Hampton Roads, Virginia (home to the world's largest naval base), have overcome vast stretches of the region. This "Dixie bloc" is much more vulnerable than its northern rivals, whose component nations have a far higher degree of cohesion.

Neither bloc, however, has the electoral power to maintain itself in office. Neither, on its own, holds an electoral college majority, or a filibuster-proof Senate one, or even a majority in the House without the temporary boost of radical partisan gerrymandering. Even as the U.S. population has generally shifted southward from Yankee and Midland states in recent decades, El Norte—not the "red coalition"—has digested many of the gains. As a result, both coalitions must woo the fickle "swing nations"—especially the Midlands—to win power.

If an American political formation is to build a lasting supermajority, therefore, it will need to alter its philosophy and vision to win over one or more of either the swing regions or the more weakly aligned regions of the opposing camp. Again, history is a guide as to how this can be accomplished. Policy challenges are ever-changing, and the relative strength of the country's nations have waxed and waned, but when it comes to the ideals each regional culture trea-sures, there has been remarkable continuity. By finding the common ground between the general characteristics of the aforementioned "zone of American consensus" and the particular characteristics of certain regional cultures, we can identify a set of political principles that can triumph.

Either political party can embrace the agenda that follows, or perhaps some group can beat the odds and build a viable new one to do so. At this writing, however, it's hard to imagine the Republican Party doing so, for several reasons. First, it has become the de facto vehicle of the Deep Southern agenda and relies on the libertarian-leaning regions of the country for electoral support; abandoning the Deep South would mean abandoning the party's base. Second, in recent decades the party has been completely purged of not only its national liberal wing (the one to which Dwight Eisenhower, Jacob Javits, and Harold Church belonged), but also its old establishment Yankee/Midlander one (the school of Herbert Hoover, Gerald Ford, George H. W. Bush, and Bob Dole). With the Tea Party takeover of great swaths of the party's local- and state-level infrastructure, it's hard to see the GOP being able to make the political sacrifices nec-essary to secure lasting power.

The Democrats, by contrast, have a considerable advantage. They could adopt this agenda without sacrificing any part of their current regional coalition: Yankeedom, New Netherland, and the Left Coast. El Norte already votes Democratic by default because the Republi-cans have made their party unwelcoming to nonwhites and immigrants; the agenda contains nothing that would change that. Meanwhile, the Democrats would likely consolidate control in the Midlands, win the defection of much of the Far West, and even make inroads in Greater Appalachia. The presidential election map might return to that of the 1950s, but with the colors reversed, the Democrats holding Ike's supermajority, and the Republicans isolated in Adlai Stevenson's old redoubts of the Deep South and parts of Greater Appalachia. If the Democrats captured hearts and minds in the Far West, the Senate would be theirs, what with each of those sparsely populated states represented by two of the chamber's members. If they won Midlander hearts as well, they would have a lock on the House. If they overreached or disappointed, however, they and the country would quickly return right back to where they started.

★

Regardless of what political formation seizes the opportunity, here is how the program would work. The American Way, the set of political values shared by the vast majority of Americans and the American Nations, is about pursuing happiness through a free and fair competition between individuals and the ideas, output, and institutions they produce. If someone becomes fantastically rich through hard work or brilliant innovation, most Americans applaud him or her. If someone squanders his or her opportunities by greed, sloth, or indulgence, most Americans have little sympathy. Rightly or wrongly, we as a country have great faith that when individuals are left to pursue their ambitions, their aggregate actions will contribute to the creation and sustenance of a happy, healthy, and adaptable society, one responsive to change and inhospitable to the seeds of tyranny: ignorance, hopelessness, fear, and persecution. There are other ways to build a contented, thriving society—witness the pre-contact Algonquians or contemporary Scandinavia—but their paths to achieving that state are ones we will never follow.

Notice, though, that I have argued that this competitive society needs to be not only free, but fair. Indeed, we've learned by painful experience that these two values are linked: An unfair society quickly ceases to be a free one. Once formed, monopolistic firms will use their control of their market to (unfairly) crush competitors and their innovations. If left entirely unchecked, the winners of a Darwinian social struggle will seize control not just of a nation's wealth, but of its government, courts, and internal security, becoming a hereditary oligarchy that (unfairly) prevents others from ever rising to challenge them. Both phenomena have happened time and again in both the United States and the wider world, from Standard Oil to Gazprom and the successful planter families of seventeenth-century Barbados and twentieth-century Guatemala. Free markets and free societies are not naturally occurring developments, like a mature forest. They're more like successful gardens, the product of sustained nourishment, attention, and, yes, protection.

It's through government that we protect our freedom, be it economic or civic. We use it to keep our external enemies at bay, of course, but also to ensure that our unending domestic competition remains fairly played. Our system requires a government that's strong enough to act as our collective referee, to prevent a slide into corporate or plutocratic oligarchy by stopping "cheaters" and the accretion of hereditary privilege and by maintaining the conditions for free and fair competition. (That we can't allow it to be so strong as to become itself a tyrannical force is obvious to most Americans, just as it was to the founders who built so many checks and balances into its blueprint.) The American Way isn't a matter of handouts or a government hand up, or a plutocracy's resources trickling down; it's a matter of a supportive government having your back as you make your way up in the world or keeping your power in check if you're one of the 0.1 percent who have reached the top.

These are the hallmarks of a tradition that has been with us since the founding of our country, and they are neither "liberal" nor "conservative," Democratic nor Republican. "In every wise struggle for human betterment one of the main objects, and often the only object, has been to achieve in large measure equality of opportunity," Teddy Roosevelt said in his famous 1910 "New Nationalism" speech, a battle cry for fairness at a time, much like our own, in which oligarchic forces were ascendant. "One of the chief factors in progress is the destruction of special privilege. The essence of any struggle for healthy liberty has always been, and must always be, to take from some one man or class of men the right to enjoy power, or wealth, or position, or immunity, which has not been earned by service to his or their fellows. That is what you fought for in the Civil War," he told the audience, which included many Union veterans of that conflict, "and that is what we strive for now."[1]

Herbert Hoover, no enemy of the free enterprise system, wrote a dozen years later during the Roaring Twenties:

> Our individualism differs from all others because it embraces these great ideals: that while we build our society upon the attainment of the individual, we shall safeguard to every individual an equality of opportunity to take that position in the community to which his intelligence, character, ability, and ambition entitle him; that we keep the social solution free from frozen strata of classes; that we shall stimulate effort of each individual to achievement . . . while he in turn must stand up to the emery wheel of competition. . . .
>
> We have also learned that fair division can only be obtained by certain restrictions on the strong and the dominant. . . . This guarding of our individualism against stratification insists . . . that the sons of the successful shall not by any mere right of birth or favor continue to occupy their fathers' places of power against the rise of a new generation in process of coming up from the bottom. . . . Otherwise our American fields of opportunity would have been clogged with long generations inheriting their fathers' privileges without their fathers' capacity for service.[2]

Eighty-nine years later, Barack Obama, a president well aligned with the old progressive Republican tradition, returned to the Kansas town where Teddy Roosevelt gave his "New Nationalism" speech to pay homage to the ideas therein. Roosevelt, he said,

> understood the free market only works when there are rules of the road that ensure competition is fair and open and honest. . . . Now, just as there was in Teddy Roosevelt's time, there is a certain crowd in Washington who, for the last few decades, have said . . . If we just cut more regulations and cut more taxes—especially for the wealthy— our economy will grow stronger. Sure, they say, there will be winners and losers. But if the winners do really well, then jobs and prosperity will eventually trickle down to everybody else. . . . But here's the problem: it doesn't work. It has never worked. . . . It results in an economy that invests too little in its people and in its future [and] . . . in a prosperity that's enjoyed by fewer and fewer of our citizens.

In 2014, Michael Gerson, chief speechwriter for George W. Bush, and his former deputy, Peter Wehner, who also served in the Reagan and George H. W. Bush administrations, laid out their "conservative vision of government":

> Conservatives believe not in equal results—a goal that leads to an excessive concentration of government power and to shared economic mediocrity—but in equality of opportunity. Government holds some responsibility for creating the ground for that equality of opportunity, which is not a natural condition. But government oversteps itself, creating corrosive resentments and economic havoc, when it tries to guarantee equality of results. . . .
>
> If conservatives are rightly at odds with liberals on this point, however, many conservatives fail to see the extent to which equal

opportunity itself, a central principle of our national self-understanding,
is becoming harder to achieve. . . . Dysfunctional institutions routinely
betray children and young adults. Children raised in communities of
chaos and disorder—where schools are broken and the streets are
violent and drug use is prevalent—face enormously difficult odds. . . .
Tremendous effort and creative policy will be required to fix the
institutions that can restore such communities and with them the
level playing field of equal opportunity.[3]

Indeed, this doctrine of fairness, of equality of opportunity and
intervention against oligarchy, can be traced in a line that stretches
from Abraham Lincoln to Dwight D. Eisenhower. It calls on government to take a stronger role in ensuring fairness than Herbert Hoover
was prepared to contemplate, but stops short of the technocratic over-
reach of FDR's National Recovery Administration or Lyndon Johnson's War on Poverty. It virulently defends fairness for all individuals,
and seeks to render irrelevant the group-based thinking that gave us
affirmative action for whites (the slave system, Jim Crow, the pre-
1964 New Deal) and, to make up for that failure, for nonwhites and
women. Building a fair society after centuries of injustice may require
proactive measures to address the problems to which it has given rise,
but ultimately neither accords with the country's ideals.

In the early twenty-first century, fairness must be reasserted as the
central issue of our political discourse and made the central value of a
new political coalition. It would be the foundation for championing individual achievement and investments in our shared institutions and
resources that foster more of it. It would be unapologetic in seeking to
protect the competitiveness and security of the market and the health of
consumers, workers, and the environment. And, yes, it would return the
tax code to a level at which the rich and ultra-rich pay a larger share of
the burden of maintaining a civilization that has served them so well.

This book seeks to articulate a successful political philosophy from which policies would organically flow, rather than propose the policies themselves, in part because the latter become quickly dated. However, in broad terms, here are some of the policies a new doctrine of fairness might argue for from the vantage point of the second decade of the twenty-first century.

In the current climate, shifting tax policies to require greater contributions from the wealthy is maligned as "redistributive," whereas adjustments in the other direction—through a so-called flat tax, for instance—are championed as "fair." All taxes are redistributive, of course, but those that divert some resources from the wealthy to provide physical and social infrastructure used by everyone are fair as well. The laissez-faire approach of the radical libertarians does not ensure equality of opportunity, because through no fault of their own people come into this world from radically unequal starting points. Left to its own, such a society turns into an oligarchy, because inherited advantages tend to accrete over time. Neoconservative political scientist Francis Fukuyama described the conundrum in his two-volume, multimillennia history of the state:

> Elites tend to get more entrenched because they can use their wealth, power, and social status to get access to the government, and to use the power of the state to protect themselves and their children. This process will continue until nonelites succeed in mobilizing politically to reverse it or otherwise protect themselves. . . . As in the case of redistribution, the trick is to prevent the overrepresentation of elites without punishing them for their ability to generate wealth.[4]

Liberal economist Paul Krugman presented statistics showing that the worst-performing eighth graders of 1988 from the wealthiest fifth of families—the "Rich Dumb Kids"—had a higher chance of graduating from college than the best-performing eighth graders from the poorest fifth. "What this tells us is that the idea that we have anything close to an equality of opportunity is clearly a fantasy," he wrote. "It would be closer to the truth . . . to say that in modern America, class—inherited class—usually trumps talent."[5]

Maintaining equality of opportunity requires rechanneling wealth—especially inherited wealth—back into institutions that level the playing field for those born without advantages: early childhood education, health insurance coverage, food assistance for poor families, and support for our public schools, community colleges, and universities, to be sure, but also the parks, libraries, recreational facilities, highways, and transportation systems that foster civic and individual well-being. In 2012, this principle inspired the world's third-richest man, Warren Buffett, to call on Congress to enact a minimum tax on the very rich: 30 percent of taxable income between $1 million and $10 million (to include dividends and capital gains) and 35 percent above that. "A plain and simple rule like that will block the efforts of lobbyists, lawyers and contribution-hungry legislators to keep the ultrarich paying rates well below those incurred by people with income just a tiny fraction of ours," he counseled, having previously noted that he paid taxes at a lower rate than his secretary. Meanwhile, the taxes paid by the highest income bracket—which in 2013 started at $450,000 a year for married couples—have plummeted, falling from 92 percent in 1952 to 70 percent in 1965 to 50 percent in 1986 to 39.6 percent in 2013; given that the economy remained thriving in the 1950s and 1960s, there's clearly some room to maneuver. The inheritance tax, which currently exempts the first $5.4 million in value per individual and $10.8 million for a married couple, stands at 40 percent, but is under attack from laissez-faire Republicans nonetheless; at a minimum, one would want to retain a tax that serves as a barrier to the creation and maintenance of a hereditary aristocracy.[6]

In the regulatory realm, the goal would be primarily defensive: to protect the accomplishments of the twentieth century from those who would have us return to the Gilded Age. One should always seek to make regulations more efficient, so long as they accomplish their goals, but the goals themselves should remain sacrosanct: conserving the nation's patrimony, protecting human health and the stability of the ecological systems that sustain us, and maintaining competitive marketplaces by preventing abusive and monopolistic business practices. Some outdated regulations were done away with during the period between 1980 and 2008 (few pine for the days of the Ma Bell telephone monopolies), but so were some that served important functions in maintaining fairness, like the Glass-Steagall Act and the campaign finance controls overturned by the Supreme Court's controversial *Citizens United* decision. Restoring a number of these would be both prudent and popular.

Investments in schools and the like would help keep the playing field even. There are others one would make for the reasons Lincoln would counsel: because they promote the happiness of the people but cannot be easily or effectively provided by the private sector. These would include increased investment in basic scientific research, because our innovation-driven economy depends on it, and because it has a high return on investment. Each dollar spent by the National Institutes of Health, for instance, typically generates $2.21 in additional economic output within the year. The $24 billion Apollo program put men on the Moon, but it also created over fifteen hundred commercial spin-offs that improved the quality of life and created entire industrial sectors, from solar panels and heart monitors to advanced insulation, quartz timepieces, and cordless drills. Similarly, investment in vital national infrastructure—bridges, tunnels, highways, airports, harbors, fast and high-speed railway lines, water treatment plants, and modern electrical grids—supports both our economy and our social fabric.

Numerous studies have found that such spending more than pays for itself, often generating two dollars in economic activity for every dollar spent. At the same time, one would seek not to invest in ventures that actually damage the country, like purchasing shockingly expensive and strategically inappropriate weapons systems the Pentagon itself doesn't want or providing subsidies to oil companies at a time when they are generating the highest profits in the history of the world. Oil industry subsidies—mostly in the form of tax breaks—come to nearly $5 billion a year, which represents the entire budget of the National Cancer Institute. Former representative Barney Frank, longtime chair of the House Budget Committee, estimated that something on the order of $1 trillion could be saved over ten years by dropping one of our three methods (missiles, bombers, and submarines) of delivering nuclear weapons on Doomsday and reducing our count of overseas bases. This would go a long way toward paying down the budget deficit run up by past supply-side administrations or providing proper care for soldiers injured serving the country in previous wars.[7]

Americans are practical-minded people. They may want government to have a limited scope of action, but they want it to function well in those areas where it operates. The doctrine of fairness gives it a clear mission that is consistent with the fundamental values of a supermajority of our regional cultures.

★

The reelection of George W. Bush in 2004 prompted a vigorous debate among Democrats about the best path forward to rebuild a regional governing coalition. Since the emergence of the Democratic Leadership Council (DLC) in the early 1990s, Democrats had sought to make themselves more competitive in the South by becoming more like the Republicans of the era: amenable to deregulating business and banking or scaling back social benefits for the poor; supportive of global trade agreements; and emphasizing individual responsibility. While these tactics enabled a Greater Appalachian native son, Bill Clinton, to narrowly capture and retain the White House in the 1990s, they also saw the collapse of the party's control of Congress and, in 2000, the humiliating loss of every single Dixie state save Florida by Clinton's successor and fellow Greater Appalachian, Al Gore. Instead of holding ground in the Deep South, Greater Appalachia, and Tidewater, the DLC era resulted in the rapid consolidation of Republican control there. Instead of drawing the wide center of the American electorate to their camp, the party's pro-business policies drove white working-class voters from their coalition, endangering the party's competitiveness in the key swing states of the Midlands. Given a choice between a Republican Party and a Republican Party Lite, most voters had decided to opt for the real thing. The DLC strategy had failed electorally, certainly, but by increasing inequality, vigorously supporting the disastrous war in Iraq, and creating the conditions for the financial meltdown of 2008, it had also failed to provide for the greater happiness of the people.

In the aftermath of 2004, when New Democrat John Kerry resoundingly lost "the South," the Far West, and the presidential election to George W. Bush, many Democratic strategists began calling on the party to return to its national liberal roots and embrace policies that actually help, rather than harm, working- and middle-class voters. These critics noted that when they ran candidates who did just that, the party had made gains in "red" areas of the country, because they were able to drive a wedge between socially conservative voters and the laissez-faire agenda of the early twenty-first-century GOP. "New Democrats, backed by huge corporate contributions, say that the party must reduce corporate regulation and embrace a free-trade policy that is wiping out local economies throughout the heartland," progressive operative David Sirota wrote in a widely discussed essay. "Yet these centrists get slaughtered at the ballot box, and their counterparts—the progressive economic populists—are racking up wins and relegating the DLC argument to the scrap heap."[8]

Proponents of this "back to national liberalism" point of view quickly broke into two camps. One, typified by University of Maryland, Baltimore County, political scientist Thomas Schaller, argued that the party should forget "the South" altogether, turning its attention instead to the regions I call the Far West and El Norte, where the fairness doctrine comports with underlying regional values. It's also a region that's socially libertarian, rather than socially conservative, wanting the government to leave alone not only gun ownership but also other arguably private social issues. "So, if a Democratic candidate approaches a Midwestern or western voter and says, 'Hey, I support the Second Amendment,' that voter may reply, 'Great, let's hear what you have to say about taxes, health care and education,'" Schaller wrote. "If a Democratic candidate says the same thing to a southern voter, the response is more likely to be, 'Great, but what are your views on abortion, teaching evolution in schools, or civil unions?'"[9]

Indeed, Schaller took his suggestion one step further, advising "economic populists" not just to ignore "the South" but to actively run against it. In his 2006 treatise, *Whistling Past Dixie,* however, it became clear that what he was really talking about running against was the *Deep* South. In developing his argument, he spends several pages describing South Carolina's track record of having "opposed or defied almost every beneficent social and political change in American history," racking up a "constitutional-historical . . . rap sheet: first to overturn a provincial government during the revolutionary period; last to abandon the Atlantic slave trade; first to call for nullifying the Constitution's federal authority; first to secede from the

Union; last to abolish the white primary; first to litigate against the integration of public schools and challenge the Voting Rights Act. Whenever America finds itself at some social or political crossroads and in need of direction, perhaps the best thing to do is ask, 'What would South Carolina do?' And then do the opposite."[10]

Other observers have cautioned against writing off the South, suggesting that doing so would be squandering a historic opportunity. Bob Moser, chief political reporter for *The Nation,* argued that a fairness doctrine–like platform could "translate the South's economic populist tradition into a forward-looking, class-based politics with broad appeal to blacks and whites alike." In *Blue Dixie,* published in 2008, he maintained that "a multiracial, post–religious right generation of Southerners has begun to emerge, with precious little patience for the politics of the past," that could be joined with "millions of middle- and working-class boomers who have lived through too many false economic dawns to keep believing the same old lines and by millions of laid-off and forgotten industrial workers." This new force, Moser argued, could be harnessed by candidates who "reasserted economic fairness as the central moral issue of politics."[11]

Revealingly, though, Moser's evidence for the efficacy of such an approach came almost entirely from Greater Appalachia, the only part of Dixie that has actually had an "economic populist tradition." He cited the Democratic fairness doctrine success stories of the first decade of the twenty-first century: Jim Webb, cultural champion of the Scots-Irish, who won a razor-thin upset victory in 2006 to represent Virginia in the U.S. Senate by making inroads into that state's Appalachian vote; John Yarmuth, who ousted an incumbent five-term congresswoman in a liberal northern Kentucky district; Larry Kissell, who took down a freshman Republican in 2008 to represent an Appalachian-dominated House district in North Carolina; and Heath Shuler, a Christian conservative who campaigned on economic and environmental "Mountain Values" to win a highland Appalachian seat in North Carolina. Moser followed Webb across Virginia as he articulated an economic populist message. "The natural base of the Democratic party, working-class folks, looked at both parties back in the '80s and saw they weren't going to get any help on economic issues," the candidate told him. "If we can get a number of these people to come back to the Democratic Party based on economic populism and fairness, rather than the way they've been maneuvered on issues like flag burning, God, guts, guns, gays—if they can be reached out to with respect, and in terms of fundamental fairness, I think a lot of them will come back to the Democratic Party." Webb found he could make gains in Appalachia by doing just that, although the core of his support came from the D.C. suburbs and other parts of rapidly changing Tidewater. In the Deep South, however, economic populists weren't winning any victories.[12]

The reality is that Schaller is correct not about "the South" but about the Deep South: It's a region whose values any supermajority-seeking party should run against. The Deep South's tradition of hierarchical libertarianism is profoundly un-American, being authoritarian in governance, oligarchic in economics, retrograde in human rights. At the same time, Moser's points are correct not in regard to "the South" but for Greater Appalachia: There is a strong populist and antioligarchic component to the culture that will respond to the doctrine of fairness, especially when conveyed by a social conservative.

Today, Appalachia and the Deep South are bonded together by a shared Protestant religious heritage that focuses on individual salvation in the next world and discourages efforts to perfect the current one. But in the realms of economics and power, Greater Appalachia is also a culture that prizes personal freedom and resents domination by outsiders, which is why it has had a near monopoly as the source of southern populists (LBJ, Ross Perot, Sam Rayburn, Mike Huckabee,

Jim Webb) and pro-business liberals (Cordell Hull, Bill Clinton, Al Gore). There are opportunities to make inroads into states dominated by Greater Appalachia—Kentucky, West Virginia, Indiana, or Tennessee—slowly transforming them from solid "red" partners of the Deep South to uncertain red-leaning ones. Small gains at the margins in places like south-central Pennsylvania, southern Ohio, or southern Missouri might tip the balance of an entire state in a presidential, gubernatorial, or Senate race. Because Tidewater is so rapidly changing, Virginia is already becoming a "blue" state, and the fairness doctrine could do the same for North Carolina, further eroding the "solid South."

In the Far West, the dividends of a fairness doctrine could be dramatic, potentially tipping many mountain states out of the laissez-faire camp. In both 2008 and 2012, Barack Obama, an outsider who spent nearly his entire adult life in Yankeedom, was able to defeat Republican rivals campaigning on a Dixie-bloc platform in Colorado and Nevada, and in 2008 nearly captured Montana as well. In the first fifteen years of the twenty-first century, Democrats won governors' races in Wyoming, Montana, and Arizona and Senate seats in Montana, Nevada, Colorado, both Dakotas, and Nebraska. Democrats have come to dominate the state legislatures of Nevada and Colorado and regularly hold one chamber in Montana. Gains in the Far West could also increase Democratic control in Oregon, Washington, and California, where the party currently relies on Left Coast sections for support.

From any perspective, the current Deep Southern–led "red" bloc is vulnerable. Tidewater has already left the coalition, Appalachia is potentially disloyal, and the Far West is susceptible to wooing. If fairness doctrine advocates were to campaign in these regions on promises to bring rogue bankers, mortgage lenders, mining interests, health insurers, seed companies, and monopolistic food processors to heel, they would have wide appeal; in egalitarian libertarian regions like Appalachia and the Far West, regulation can be sold as a matter of justice, the closing of tax loopholes a matter of fairness. Calls for new government programs are unlikely to win many hearts and minds in these two regions, but regulating to improve the efficiency and fairness of both the government and the marketplace can.

Simultaneously, such a strategy would also consolidate control over the two major "swing regions" of the national election map. In El Norte, Hispanics have reasserted political control after more than a century of subjugation. The Dixie agenda has always been unpopular there, while the Tea Party movement in the region has served as a vehicle for whites' fears that they are losing "their" country to Hispanic Americans and Mexican and Latin American immigration. ("Immigration attitudes are an important predictor of Tea Party movement support in the West," a 2011 study of polling data by two Sam Houston State University political scientists found, as were "economic issues related to minority relations.") So long as "blue bloc" political leaders continue to champion cultural inclusiveness—which the Dixie bloc does not—they can count on political and electoral support from this fast-growing region. The Hispanic population is expected to triple between 2010 and 2050—accounting for most of the nation's overall growth—and much of it is predicted to take place in El Norte. This will result in a commensurate decrease in radical libertarian influence in the legislatures and congressional delegations of Texas, California, Arizona, and New Mexico.[13]

The fairness doctrine would also rally the long-neglected white working and lower middle classes of the Midlands back to the "blue" camp, potentially turning this swing region into a solid member of the coalition. Midlanders are communitarian, not libertarian, in their outlook, with a strong commitment to fairness and a relatively tolerant social outlook; combine that perspective with an economic agenda that isn't explicitly hostile to the Rust Belt economy, and you have a strong standing here. The people of the Midlands also generally want their communities left alone so they can get on with their lives, but in the midst of a crisis they can be counted on to defend the federal union from authoritarianism, bigotry, or dismemberment. The region was generally apathetic about the Tea Party movement, providing just two members of its sixty-person House caucus in the high-water year of 2011. But were Republicans to actually execute the Deep South's agenda—slashing Social Security, Medicare, and federal spending on public education—Midlanders would rally to their northern neighbors.

In summary, a political movement championing the fairness doctrine could capture a reliable majority in seven of our nine major regional cultures—Yankeedom, New Netherland, the Midlands, Tidewater, El Norte, the Far West, and the Left Coast—together comprising nearly two-thirds of the population of the United States and guaranteeing an even larger proportion of the electoral college and Senate. It would also enable marginal—and possibly significant—gains in Greater Appalachia, essentially isolating the laissez-faire camp in the Deep South. It would be, in short, the basis for a governing supermajority capable of moving the country forward over the undoubtedly spirited objections of its most authoritarian region.

# Acknowledgments
## and Suggested Reading

*American Character* spans four centuries and a wide span of philosophical terrain and, as such, owes a debt to scores of historians and biographers, political essayists and philosophers, scientists and senators, presidents and priests, journalists and diarists, living and dead, who either chronicled their experiences and ideals or tried to make sense of the human experience.

Intellectuals have been writing about humans' existential nature since the advent of the written word, and even the post-Renaissance debate over its political implications would fill many bookshelves. Three more recent books further the discussion in a manner more immediately relevant to our own times. On the late eighteenth-century clash between the revolutionary advocates of egalitarian individualism and the defenders of a more traditional, community-oriented social order, there's Yuval Levin's *The Great Debate: Edmund Burke, Thomas Paine, and the Birth of Right and Left,* which focuses on the struggle between those two men before, during, and after the Terror in Revolutionary France. On the implications of actual scientific exploration of human biological and social evolution on the debate, E. O. Wilson's *The Social Conquest of Earth* is essential reading and a valuable corrective to the speculations of Enlightenment-era philosophers. For a comprehensive examination of how governmental systems and the state actually evolved, succeeded, and failed over human history—a story with stark implications for the debate over how to promote and maintain mass human freedom there is historian Francis Fukuyama's *The Origins of the Political Order: From Prehuman Times to the French Revolution* and its sequel, *Political Order and Political Decay: From the Industrial Revolution to the Globalization of Democracy.*

To understand how the founding fathers understood freedom, liberty, and republicanism, Gordon Wood's *The Radicalism of the American Revolution* remains essential reading, and his sequel, *Empire of Liberty: A History of the Early Republic, 1789–1815,* carries the story forward to the dawn of the Jacksonian era. For a full treatment of the profound regional differences in the debate over the meaning of freedom and the presentation of a framework for understanding regionalism on this continent, please read my *American Nations: A History of the Eleven Rival Regional Cultures of North America,* upon which many elements of this book have been built. For further reading on the clash between individualistic and more communitarian political camps in the first century of our republic, I suggest: Lynn Parsons's *The Birth of Modern Politics: Andrew Jackson, John Quincy Adams, and the Election of 1828;* Harry L. Watson's *Liberty and Power: The Politics of Jacksonian America* (a good introduction to the turbulent 1830s and 1840s); Eric Foner's *The Story of American Freedom* (especially on antebellum and Reconstruction-era events); and Bruce Levine's *The Fall of the House of Dixie: How the Civil War Remade the American South* (on how the Confederacy's oligarchic libertarianism creed trumped even the most fundamental collective undertaking: repelling a military invasion).

On the Gilded Age, H. W. Brands's *American Colossus: The Triumph of Capitalism* documents the rise of the greatest robber barons, while Frank Parsons's *The Railways, the Trusts, and the People* focuses on the corrosive political and economic effects of their ascendancy, and Richard Hofstadter's *Social Darwinism in American Thought* takes on their philosophical justifications. Neil Irvin Painter's *Standing at Armageddon: The United States, 1877–1919* focuses on the progressive Republican counterreaction, a topic for which Theodore Roosevelt's eponymous autobiography makes a good reading companion.

There is a voluminous literature on the rise and fall of the national liberal state. A good starting point is David M. Kennedy's *Freedom from Fear: The American People in Depression and War, 1929–1945*. FDR's devil's bargain with the Deep South is documented by Roger Biles in *The South and the New Deal*, and Ira Katznelson's *Fear Itself* contributes the effects of the wartime and Cold War mobilizations on the direction and purpose of the federal government. The resurgence and undoing of national liberal activism in the 1960s is tackled in *The Liberal Hour: Washington and the Politics of Change in the 1960s*, by political historians G. Calvin Mackenzie and Robert Weisbrot, and in Allen J. Matusow's *The Unraveling of America: A History of Liberalism in the 1960s*.

A number of scholars have grappled with the rise of what I would call resurgent laissez-faire individualism in the late twentieth century, but which is usually termed "movement conservatism" in an effort to distinguish it from the progressive conservatism of the early twentieth century and national liberal variety that was the dominant force in the Republican Party from the late 1940s to the late 1970s. Geoffrey Kabaservice's *Rule and Ruin: The Downfall of Moderation and the Destruction of the Republican Party, from Eisenhower to the Tea Party* focuses on the collapse of the GOP's moderate wing between 1960 and 1980, while Rick Perlstein's *The Invisible Bridge: The Fall of Nixon and the Rise of Reagan* examines the critical period between 1972 and 1976 in great detail. Kim Phillips-Fein's *Invisible Hands: The Making of the Conservative Movement from the New Deal to Reagan* provides indispensable background on how the marginalized laissez-faire conservatives of the 1940s and 1950s fostered and financed the movement, while Sam Tanenhaus's *The Death of Conservatism: A Movement and Its Consequences* provides a readable overview of the results. For blistering critiques of the movement from former national liberal conservatives, read Michael Lind's *Up from*

*Conservatism: Why the Right Is Wrong for America* (published during the Clinton administration) or Kevin Phillips's *American Theocracy: The Peril and Politics of Radical Religion, Oil, and Borrowed Money in the 21st Century*. For one from a progressive economist, there is Paul Krugman's *The Conscience of a Liberal*.

At this date, most of the best material on the rise of the radical libertarians is in article form—you will find references to them in the endnotes—but two sources of data and analysis are *The Tea Party and the Remaking of Republican Conservatism*, by Theda Skocpol and Vanessa Williamson, and *Steep: The Precipitous Rise of the Tea Party*, edited by Lawrence Rosenthal and Christine Trost.

While writing *American Character*, I had the good fortune to share ideas or gain insights from several individuals with expertise in one or another area of my studies. Among them, in loose chronological order: Sam Loewenberg, lately of Berlin; *Washington Monthly* editor Paul Glastris; former Maine congressman Tom Allen (on the divide in political practice); the late Andrew Ian Dodge of Maine (on Gladstonian liberals and the Tea Party movement); retired general Carl Reddel (on Eisenhower); Gleaves Whitney of the Hauenstein Center for Presidential Studies (on finding common ground between political traditions); and Wilton Dillon, emeritus professor at the Smithsonian Institution for his friendship and support. Jon Winsor of Reading, Massachusetts, was tremendously generous in calling my attention to a wide range of documentary sources while I was researching the book and reading early drafts of the manuscript; thanks kindly, Jon, for your suggestions and indefatigable interest in the topic. I owe a debt of gratitude to Cliff Schechtman and Steve Greenlee, editors extraordinaire at the *Portland Press Herald* and *Maine Sunday Telegram*, for letting me take the leave necessary to complete the book. Thanks also to Terry Monmaney at *Smithsonian* magazine and Garrett Graff of *Politico* for their encouragement and interest in the project, to designer Sean Wilkinson for the *American Nations* map, to

Viking's Brianna Harden (for the cover design), Amy Hill (for the interior design), Roland Ottewell (copy editor), Barbara Campo (production editor), and Diego Nunez (designated assists); and to the staff of Bowdoin College's Hawthorne-Longfellow Library, where I did much of my research.

As always, thanks are in order to my agent, Jill Grinberg of Jill Grinberg Literary Management, who also did yeoman service negotiating with NBC on the television deal for one of my previous books, *The Republic of Pirates*. I'm especially indebted to my longtime editor at Viking, Rick Kot, for his support and editorial guidance. My greatest debt, however, is to my wife, Sarah Skillin Woodard, who helped conceive of *American Character*, edited it while pregnant, and covered for me around the house; I love you, honey, and the book would be dedicated to you if it weren't for it being our firstborn's turn.

And thank you to you, dear reader, without whom none of this would be possible.

August 2015
Freeport, Maine

# Notes

## Chapter 1: Maintaining Freedom

1. Nick Bunker, *Making Haste from Babylon: The Mayflower Pilgrims and Their World* (New York: Knopf, 2010), 249–50, 268, 290–91.

2. Ibid., 285; William Bradford, *Of Plymouth Plantation* (Boston: Wright & Potter, 1898), 108–10; *Mourt's Relation* [1622] (Boston: Applewood Press, 1963), 15–18; John Locke, *Two Treatises of Government* (London: John Churchill, 1714), 2:185.

3. Bradford, *Of Plymouth Plantation*, 111; *Mourt's Relation*, 41–46, 81–82.

4. Transcript, *The Rush Limbaugh Show*, November 24, 2010, http://www .rushlimbaugh.com/daily/2010/11/24/the_true_story_of_thanksgiving3.

5. "Bradford Smith, Author, Teacher," *New York Times*, July 15, 1964; Bradford Smith, *Bradford of Plymouth* (Boston: Lippincott, 1951), 20–21, Bradford Smith, "The Pilgrims Tried Communism," *Rotarian*, November 1952, 48–50; Henry Hazlitt, "Instead of Famine—Thanksgiving!," *Freeman*, November 1968, 650–51; Jesse Helms, *Here's Where I Stand: A Memoir* (New York: Random House, 2005), 274–75.

6. Bunker, *Making Haste from Babylon*, 400–401.

7. Philip Vermeulen, *How Fat Is the Top Tail of the Wealth Distribution?*, Working Paper Series No. 1692 (Brussels: European Central Bank, July 2014), 29.

8. Thomas Hobbes, *Leviathan* [1651] (Cambridge: Cambridge University Press, 1904), 04.

9. E. O. Wilson, *The Social Conquest of Earth* (New York: Liveright, 2012), 241.

10. Ibid., 243.

11. Ibid., 31, 42–47, 226–27; Colin Woodard, "Clever Canines. Did Domestication Make Dogs Smarter?," *Chronicle of Higher Education*, April 15, 2005, A12; Colin Woodard, "The Intelligence of Beasts," *Chronicle of Higher Education*, June 26, 2011.

12. Cary J. Nederman, "Freedom, Community and Function: Communitarian Lessons of Medieval Political Theory," *American Political Science Review* 86, no. 4 (December 1992): 978–79; Robert Nisbet, *The Quest for Community: A Study in the Ethics of Order and Freedom* (San Francisco: Institute for Contemporary Studies Press, 1990), 74–79; Lee Boldeman, *The Cult of the Market: Economic Fundamentalism and Its Discontents* (Canberra: Australian National University, 2007), 106.

13. Hans Morgenthau, "The Dilemmas of Freedom," *American Political Science Review* 51, no. 3 (September 1957): 721–22.

14. Francis Fukuyama, *The Origins of the Political Order: From Prehuman Times to the French Revolution* (New York: Farrar, Straus & Giroux, 2011), 373–74.

15. Paul Heath Hoeffel, "The Eclipse of the Oligarchs," *New York Times Magazine,* September 6, 1981; Rory Carroll, "Victory Declared in Controversial Poll That Was Already a Win-Win for Honduras' Wealthy Elite," *Guardian,* November 30, 2009; Robert Levato, "Our Man in Honduras," *American Prospect,* July 22, 2009.

16. Alexander Hamilton, "No. 17," in *The Federalist Papers,* ed. Clinton Rossiter (New York: Mentor, 1961), 120–22.

17. James Madison, "No. 51," in ibid., 323–24.

18. Charles Francis Adams, ed., *The Works of John Adams* (Boston: Little Brown, 1851), 4:354–55, 585; Luke G. Mayville, "Fear of the Few: John Adams and the Power Elite," paper delivered at the annual meeting of the American Political Science Association, August 29, 2013, 23–28.

19. Madison, "No. 62" and "No. 45," in Rossiter, ed., *Federalist Papers,* 289, 380.

20. Eric Foner, *The Story of American Freedom* (New York: Norton, 1998), 6–10.

21. Fareed Zakaria, "The Rise of Illiberal Democracy," *Foreign Affairs,* November/December 1997.

22. Michael Gerson and Peter Wehner, "A Conservative Vision of Government," *National Affairs,* Winter 2014, 88.

23. Alexis de Tocqueville, *Democracy in America* [1835] (New York: Vintage, 1945), 1:328–29, 334.

24. John Stuart Mill, *Consideration of Representative Government* (London: Parker, Son & Bourn, 1861), 6.

25. James Gwartney et al., *Economic Freedom of the World: 2014 Annual Report* (Vancouver: Fraser Institute, 2014), 8–14, 31, 125, 130, 160; United Nations Development Program, *Human Development Report 2014: Sustaining Human Progress* (New York: UNDP, 2014), 160.

CHAPTER 2: Two Paths to Tyranny

1. Serge Schmemann, "East Berlin Tells Budapest to Halt Aid to Emigration," *New York Times,* September 13, 1989, A1, A8; Jill Smolowe et al., "Refugees: The Great Escape," *Time,* September 25, 1989; Terence Roth, "East Germans Fleeing to the West Double Last Year's Numbers," *Wall Street Journal,* August 14, 1989; Serge Schmemann, "Hungary Allows 7000 East Germans to Emigrate West," *New York Times,* September 11, 1989, A1, A12.

2. *RFE Weekly Record of Events in Eastern Europe,* September 7–13, 1989; September 21–28, 1989; Roth, "East Germans Fleeing"; John Tragliable, "Departing East Germans Say Country Is on the Brink of Collapse," *International Herald Tribune,* November 6, 1989.

3. Colin Woodard, *Ocean's End: Travels Through Endangered Seas* (New York: Basic Books, 2000), 17–23; Colin Woodard, "Fighting for the Scraps: Western Nuclear Companies Are on the Prowl in Eastern Europe," *Bulletin of the Atomic Scientists,* May/June 1996, 56–59; Author visit, Cernavoda Nuclear Power Plant, Cernavoda, Romania, September 1991.

4. Peter Sinai-Davis, *The Romanian Revolution of December 1989* (Ithaca, NY: Cornell University Press, 2005), 12.

5. Ibid.

6. Robert Cullen, "Down with the Tyrant," *New Yorker,* April 22, 1990, 97–98; Dinu Giurescu, *The Razing of Romania's Past* (Washington, DC: U.S. Council on Monuments and Sites, 1989), 67; Ion Mihai Pacepa, *Red Horizons* (Washington, DC: Regnery Gateway, 1987), 46–48, 211.

7. Václav Havel, "The Power of the Powerless" [October 1978], in *The Power of the Powerless: Citizens Against the State in Central-Eastern Europe* (New York: Routledge, 1985), 23–96.

8. John Kósa, *Two Generations of Soviet Man: A Study in the Psychology of Communism* (Chapel Hill: University of North Carolina Press, 1962), 20.

9. Klaus Mehnert, *Soviet Man and His World* (New York: Frederick A. Praeger, 1962), 61–62; Ann Livschiz, "Growing Up Soviet: Childhood in the Soviet Union, 1918–1958" (doctoral dissertation, Stanford University, September 2007), 58–60, 64.

10. Livschiz, "Growing Up Soviet," 206–8, 234, 255–56; Mehnert, *Soviet Man and His World,* 47.

11. Anne Applebaum, *Iron Curtain: The Crushing of Eastern Europe, 1944–1956* (New York: Doubleday, 2012), 153; Kósa, *Two Generations of Soviet Man,* 196.

12. Karl Schlögel, *Moscow, 1937* (Cambridge, UK: Polity, 2012), 120–24.

13. Milovan Djilas, *The New Class: An Analysis of the Communist System* (New York: Frederick A. Praeger, 1957), 44–47, 57–58, 69, 88–89.

14. Anne Conover Heller, *Ayn Rand and the World She Made* (New York: Nan E. Talese/Doubleday, 2009), 4–6, 9, 14–17, 26, 31–37, 51.

15. Maria Bustillos, "When Alan Met Ayn," *The Awl*, April 12, 2011; *The Mike Wallace Interview*, ABC-TV, February 25, 1959.

16. Gary Weiss, *Ayn Rand Nation: The Hidden Struggle for America's Soul* (New York: St. Martin's, 2012), 19–20; Whittaker Chambers, "Big Sister Is Watching You," *National Review*, December 28, 1957; Kevin Baker, "Ayn Rand's Rapture of the Rails: The Train Deaths of *Atlas Shrugged*," *Harper's* (online), June 16, 2014.

17. Daniel Schulman, *Sons of Wichita: How the Koch Brothers Became America's Most Powerful and Private Dynasty* (New York: Grand Central Publishing, 2014), 37–44.

18. Ibid., 42–55, 260–75.

19. Richard S. Dunn, *Sugar and Slaves: The Rise of the Planter Class in the English West Indies, 1624–1713* (Chapel Hill: University of North Carolina Press, 1972), 18–19, 46–48, 65, 72, 82; Hilary McD. Beckles, "'A Riotous and Unruly Lot': Irish Indentured Servants and Freedmen in the English West Indies, 1644–1713," *William and Mary Quarterly*, 3rd ser., 47, no. 4 (October 1990): 503–13; Edward B. Rugemer, "The Development of Mastery and Race in the Slave Codes of the Greater Caribbean During the Seventeenth Century," *William and Mary Quarterly* 70, no. 3 (July 2013): 435.

20. Alan Taylor, *American Colonies: The Settling of North America* (New York: Viking, 2001), 212–14.

21. Dunn, *Sugar and Slaves*, 89; Jack P. Greene, "Colonial South Carolina and the Caribbean Connection," *South Carolina Historical Magazine* 88, no. 4 (October 1987): 194.

22. Richard S. Dunn, "English Sugar Islands and the Founding of South Carolina," *South Carolina Historical Magazine* 101, no. 2 (April 1971): 153; Justin Roberts and Ian Beamish, "The Barbadian Diaspora and the Carolina Colony, 1650–1685," in *Creating and Contesting Carolina*, ed. Michelle LeMaster and Bradford J. Wood (Columbia: University of South Carolina Press, 2013): 49–72.

23. Robin L. Einhorn, *American Taxation, American Slavery* (Chicago: University of Chicago Press, 2008), 100–102, 106.

24. Clement Eaton, *Freedom of Thought in the Old South* (Durham, NC: Duke University Press, 1940), 67, 71–79; Forest Andrew Nabors, "The Problem of

Reconstruction: The Political Regime of the Antebellum Slave South" (doctoral dissertation, University of Oregon, June 2011), 256–58.

25. Nabors, "The Problem of Reconstruction," 429–31; James M. Denham and Randolph Roth, "Why Was Antebellum Florida Murderous? A Quantitative Analysis of Homicide in Florida, 1821–1861," *Florida Historical Quarterly* 86, no. 2 (Fall 2007): 226, 234–37; Edward Ayers, *Vengeance and Justice: Crime and Punishment in the 19th-Century American South* (New York: Oxford University Press, 1984), 49–50, 57–60, 122, 134.

26. Eaton, *Freedom of Thought in the Old South,* 128–29.

27. Bruce Levine, *Fall of the House of Dixie: How the Civil War Remade the American South* (New York: Random House, 2013), 82–87, 200–206; Thomas E. Scott, *Alexander H. Stephens of Georgia: A Biography* (Baton Rouge: Louisiana State University Press, 1988), 354.

28. John C. Calhoun quoted in Manisha Sinha, *The Counterrevolution of Slavery: Politics and Ideology in Antebellum South Carolina* (Chapel Hill: University of North Carolina Press, 2000), 87.

29. Ritchie Devon Watson, *Normans and Saxons: Southern Race Mythology and the Intellectual History of the American Civil War* (Baton Rouge: Louisiana State University Press, 2008), 37–40; William Gilmore Simms, "The Morals of Slavery," in *The Pro-Slavery Argument* (Philadelphia: Lippincott, Grambo, & Co., 1853), 273.

30. Eric Freedman and Stephen A. Jones, *African Americans in Congress; A Documentary History* (Washington, DC: CQ Press, 2008), 36–39, 66–67. The cited texts are: Frederick Douglass, "Speech to the Rochester Ladies Anti-Slavery Society," Rochester, NY, July 5, 1852; "Reply to the President by the Colored People of Newton, L.I.," *Liberator,* September 12, 1862, 248.

31. Sinha, *Counterrevolution of Slavery,* 13.

32. John Henry Hammond, *Two Letters on Slavery in the United States* (Columbia, SC: Allen, McCarter & Co, 1845), 10–20, 26.

CHAPTER 3: The Rival Americas

1. Colin Woodard, *American Nations: A History of the Eleven Rival Regional Cultures of North America* (New York: Viking, 2011).

2. Ibid., 57–64.

3. John Winthrop (1630) quoted in *Daily Life Through American History Through Primary Documents,* ed. Randall M. Miller et al. (Santa Barbara, CA: ABC-CLIO, 2012), 259.

4. Simon Middleton, "Order and Authority in New Netherland," *William and Mary Quarterly*, 3rd ser., 67, no. 1 (January 2010): 58–59.

5. Russell Shorto, *Island at the Center of the World: The Epic Story of Dutch Manhattan and the Forgotten Colony That Shaped America* (New York: Vintage, 2005), 215–18, 258, 266.

6. Milton H. Klein, "Origins of the Bill of Rights in Colonial New York," *New York History*, October 1991, 391–92, 397–404.

7. Woodard, *American Nations*, 71 note 10.

8. David Dean Bowldby, *The Garden and the Wilderness: Church and State in America to 1789* (Lanham, MD: Lexington Books, 2013), 90–91; Woodard, *American Nations*, 92–100.

9. Richard S. Dunn, "An Odd Couple: John Winthrop and William Penn," *Proceedings of the Massachusetts Historical Society*, 3rd ser., 99 (1987): 1–24; David Hackett Fischer, *Albion's Seed: Four British Folkways in North America* (New York: Oxford University Press, 1989), 594.

10. Jack P. Green, *Pursuits of Happiness: The Social Development of Early Modern British Colonies and the Formation of American Culture* (Chapel Hill: University of North Carolina Press, 1988), 126–27; Allan Kulifkoff, *From British Peasants to Colonial American Farmers* (Chapel Hill: University of North Carolina Press, 2000), 131–33.

11. Woodard, *American Nations*, 44–56.

12. Gordon Wood, *The Radicalism of the American Revolution* (New York: Knopf, 1992), 107–9.

13. Ibid., 230–47, 365; Herbert J. Storing, *What the Anti-Federalists Were For* (Chicago: University of Chicago Press, 2008), 72–73.

14. Ta-Nahesi Coates, "The Case for Reparations," *Atlantic*, June 2014, 54–71.

15. Fischer, *Albion's Seed*, 765–81; Gordon Godfrey Fralin, "Charles Lynch, Originator of the Term Lynch Law" (master's thesis, University of Richmond, 1955), 57–61.

16. Woodard, *American Nations*, 136–39.

17. David J. Weber, *The Mexican Frontier, 1821–1846* (Albuquerque: University of New Mexico Press, 1982), 15, 123; Juan Gómez-Quiñones, *Roots of Chicano Politics, 1600–1940* (Albuquerque: University of New Mexico Press, 1994), 99.

18. Weber, *Mexican Frontier*, 25–29, 32–41; Gómez-Quiñones, *Roots of Chicano Politics*, 126.

19. Gómez-Quiñones, *Roots of Chicano Politics*, 302–6.

20. Ibid., 408.

21. Woodard, *American Nations*, 216–23.

22. Ibid., 11–12, 281–82.

23. Ibid., 12, 243–53.

24. Ibid., 9–10, 13; Brian Lee Crowley, *Fearful Symmetry: The Fall and Rise of Canada's Founding Values* (Toronto: Key Porter, 2009), 72–76, 88–96; Colin Woodard, "As a Land Thaws, So Do Greenland's Aspirations for Independence," *Christian Science Monitor,* October 16, 2007.

25. Woodard, *American Nations,* 49–51, 115–40, 157–70.

CHAPTER 4: The Elite and the Masses (1607–1876)

1. Morgenthau, "Dilemmas of Freedom," 721.

2. David Ogg, *England in the Reigns of James II and William III* (London: Oxford University Press, 1969), 33–36; M. Dorothy George, *England in Transition* (Baltimore: Penguin, 1953), 12, 15; John Komlos, "On English Pygmies and Giants: The Physical Stature of English Youth in the Late 18th and Early 19th Centuries," discussion paper, Department of Economics, University of Munich, April 2005; Edmund S. Morgan, *American Slavery, American Freedom: The Ordeal of Colonial Virginia* (New York: Norton, 1975), 322–25.

3. Morgan, *American Slavery,* 381–83; Maurice Cranston, *John Locke: A Biography* (New York: MacMillan, 1957), 424–26.

4. Morgan, *American Slavery,* 381.

5. Woodard, *American Nations,* 120, 139–40.

6. Ibid., 123, 135–36.

7. Ibid., 128–29.

8. Ibid., 129–33.

9. Fischer, *Albion's Seed,* 787.

10. Woodard, *American Nations,* 136–38.

11. Merrill Jensen, "Democracy and the American Revolution," in *Essays on the American Revolution,* ed. David L. Jacobson (New York: Holt, Rinehart & Winston, 1971), 223, 226.

12. Terry Bouton, *Taming Democracy: "The People," the Founders, and the Troubled Ending of the American Revolution* (New York: Oxford University Press, 2007), 76–77, 83–87, 178–83, 197–215, 224–26; Woodard, *American Nations,* 160–62.

13. Orin Libby, "A Map Illustrating the Geographical Distribution of the Vote of the Thirteen States upon the Adoption of the Constitution of the United States, 1787–88," *Bulletin of the University of Wisconsin. Economics, political science, and history series,* 1, no. 1 (Madison: University of Wisconsin, 1894); Bouton, *Taming Democracy,* 181–85.

14. Joyce Appleby, *Liberalism and Republicanism in the Historical Imagination* (Cambridge, MA: Harvard University Press, 1992), 274–75; Wood, *The Radicalism of the American Revolution,* 262, 267, 281; Thomas Jefferson, "His First Inaugural Address," March 4, 1801, in *The World's Famous Orations,* vol. 8, *America: I (1761–1837),* ed. William Jennings Bryan (New York: Funk & Wagnalls, 1906).

15. Wood, *Radicalism of the American Revolution,* 262; Robert Kelley, "Ideology and Political Culture from Jefferson to Nixon," *American Historical Review* 82, no. 3 (Spring 1977): 535–39, 540; Gordon Wood, *Empire of Liberty: A History of the Early Republic, 1789–1815* (New York: Oxford University Press, 2009), 95–103.

16. Wood, *Empire of Liberty,* 114–17.

17. Ibid., 120–22.

18. Ibid., 368–70.

19. Ibid., 155.

20. Woodard, *American Nations,* 195–97.

21. Lynn Hudson Parsons, *The Birth of Modern Politics: Andrew Jackson, John Quincy Adams, and the Election of 1828* (New York: Oxford University Press, 2009), xv–xvi, 172, 185.

22. Harry L. Watson, *Liberty and Power: The Politics of Jacksonian America* (New York: Hill & Wang, 1990), 102–4.

23. Dean C. Hammer, "The Puritans as Founders: The Quest for Identity in Early Whig Rhetoric," *Religion and American Culture,* 6, no. 2 (Summer 1996): 167, 170–71, 175, 183.

24. Kelley, "Ideology and Political Culture," 541–43; Hammer, "Puritans as Founders," 175–77; Watson, *Liberty and Power,* 211–20.

25. Woodard, *American Nations,* 231–38.

26. Freedman and Jones, *African Americans in Congress,* 107–10; *Congressional Record,* 43rd Congress, 2nd Session, February 3, 1875, 943–47.

27. Kelley, "Ideology and Political Culture," 546; Mark Greenbaum, "The Do-Everything Congress," Opinionator (blog), *New York Times,* August 5, 2011.

28. Gerson and Wehner, "Conservative Vision of Government," 84–85.

29. Foner, *Story of American Freedom,* 106–7.

CHAPTER 5: The Rise and Fall of Laissez-Faire (1877–1930)

1. Jacob Hornberger, "Up from Serfdom" (blog post), Reason.com, April 9, 2010.

2. Robert F. Burk, *The Corporate State and the Broker State: The DuPonts and American National Politics, 1925–1940* (Cambridge, MA: Harvard University

Press, 1990), 281–83; Amity Shlaes, "Repeal the Minimum Wage," *National Review* (online), May 21, 2014.

3. Foner, *Story of American Freedom*, 116; Jack Beatty, *The Age of Betrayal: The Triumph of Money in America, 1865–1900* (New York: Knopf, 2007), 14–15.

4. H. W. Brands, *American Colossus: The Triumph of Capitalism, 1865–1900* (New York: Doubleday, 2010), 23–24; James Vickery and Richard W. Judd, "Agricultural Crisis and Adaptation, 1861–1900," in *Maine: The Pine Tree State from Prehistory to the Present*, ed. Richard Judd, Edwin Churchill, and Joe Eastman (Orono: University of Maine Press, 1995), 405–6.

5. Charles Lofgren, *The Plessy Case: A Legal-Historical Interpretation* (New York: Oxford University Press, 1987), 89–91; Foner, *Story of American Freedom*, 121–23; *Hammer v. Dagenhart*, 247 U.S. (1918), 271–80.

6. Chester McArthur Destler, "The Opposition of American Businessmen to Social Control During the 'Gilded Age,'" *Mississippi Valley Historical Review* 39, no. 4 (March 1953): 644, 670–73; "The Refined Lard Investigation," *National Livestock Journal*, March 27, 1888, 203; Michael McGerr, *A Fierce Discontent: The Rise and Fall of the Progressive Movement in America, 1870–1920* (New York: Free Press, 2003), 161–62; Bruce Watson, "The Poison Squad: An Incredible History" (blog post), *Esquire*, June 27, 2013; Samuel Hopkins Adams, "The Great American Fraud," *Collier's*, October 7, 1905, 14–15, 29.

7. Richard Hofstadter, *Social Darwinism in American Thought* (Boston: Beacon, 1955), 40–41, 56–60.

8. Ibid., 48–50; *Herbert Spencer on the Americans and the Americans on Herbert Spencer* (New York: D. Appleton & Co., 1883); Beverly Gage, "A Drunkard Is in the Gutter Where He Ought to Be," *Slate*, March 29, 2012.

9. McGerr, *A Fierce Discontent*, 17; Neil Irvin Painter, *Standing at Armageddon: The United States, 1877–1919* (New York: Norton, 1987), 185–86.

10. Beatty, *Age of Betrayal*, 200–203; *Pollock v. Farmers' Loan & Trust Company*, 157 U.S. 429 (1895).

11. Beatty, *Age of Betrayal*, 232–33; François Furstenberg, "What History Teaches Us About the Welfare State," *Washington Post*, July 1, 2011, A17.

12. Beatty, *Age of Betrayal*, 205–6; "Shall a New Kind of Slavery Be Established in the United States?," *Railway World*, July 28, 1877, 698–99.

13. Eleanor Hannah, *Manhood, Citizenship, and the National Guard: Illinois, 1870–1917* (Columbus: Ohio State University Press, 2007), 207; Martin Glaberman and Seymour Faber, *Working for Wages: Roots of Insurgency* (Lanham, MD: Rowman & Littlefield, 1998), 28; Sven Beckert, *The Monied Metropolis:*

*New York and the Consolidation of the American Bourgeoisie, 1850–1896* (New York: Cambridge University Press, 2003), 293–95; Beatty, *Age of Betrayal*, 206–7.

14. Frank Parsons, *The Railways, the Trusts, and the People* (Philadelphia: C. F. Taylor, 1906), 37, 57–60.

15. Ibid., 34–35.

16. Ibid., 63–66, 73; John Graham Brooks, *The Social Unrest: Studies in Labor and Socialist Movements* (New York: Macmillan, 1903), 47, 57.

17. David Alan Johnson, *Founding the Far West: California, Oregon, and Nevada, 1840–1890* (Berkeley: University of California Press, 1992), 325–34; Woodard, *American Nations*, 246–47, 250.

18. John Gunther, *Inside USA* (New York: Harper & Brothers, 1947), 166–74.

19. Parsons, *The Railways, the Trusts, and the People*, 66–68; Mark Twain, "Senator Clark of Montana (January 28, 1907)," in *Mark Twain in Eruption*, ed. Bernard DeVoto (New York: Harper & Brothers, 1940), 70–73.

20. Painter, *Standing at Armageddon*, 208–9.

21. Leslie V. Tischauser, *Jim Crow Laws* (Santa Barbara, CA: ABC-CLIO, 2012), 11–20; Richard Franklin Bensel, *Sectionalism and American Political Development, 1880–1980* (Madison: University of Wisconsin Press, 1984), 74–82.

22. Richard M. Abrams, *Conservatism in a Progressive Era: Massachusetts Politics, 1900–1912* (Cambridge, MA: Harvard University Press, 1964), 5–9, 11, 62, 131–32.

23. Ibid., viii, 2–3, 14, 18, 30, 35, 62, 288–89.

24. Lester F. Ward, *The Psychic Factors of Civilization* (Boston: Ginn & Company, 1893), 275–6. Emphasis in the original.

25. "Roosevelt Won't Drop Trust War," *New York Times*, August 21, 1907, 1.

26. Theodore Roosevelt, "The New Nationalism" (speech, Osawatomie, KS, August 31, 1910), available at http://www.pbs.org/wgbh/americanexperience/features/primary-resources/tr-nationalism/.

27. Woodard, *American Nations*, 297–98.

28. Ibid., 268–69.

29. Scott Galupo, "Tea Party, Glenn Beck Wrong on Woodrow Wilson's Progressivism," *U.S. News & World Report*, May 6, 2010.

30. McGerr, *A Fierce Discontent*, 280–99; Foner, *Story of American Freedom*, 177, 183.

31. McGerr, *A Fierce Discontent*, 300–312.

32. *Official Report of the Proceedings of the Seventeenth Republican National Convention* (New York: Tenny Press, 1920), 264, 269, 284; Herbert Hoover, *American Individualism* (New York: Doubleday, Page & Co., 1922), 10–13.

33. Brian R. Farmer, *American Conservatism: History, Theory and Practice* (Newcastle, UK: Cambridge Scholars Press, 2005), 215–21; David Cannadine, *Mellon: An American Life* (New York: Knopf, 2006), 287–92; David Kennedy, *Freedom from Fear: The American People in Depression and War, 1929–1945* (New York: Oxford University Press, 1999), 33–34.

34. Kennedy, *Freedom from Fear*, 39–41, 52–57; Amity Shlaes, *The Forgotten Man: A New History of the Great Depression* (New York: HarperCollins, 2007), 96.

35. Kennedy, *Freedom from Fear*, 65, 69, 87; Shlaes, *Forgotten Man*, 112.

36. Kennedy, *Freedom from Fear*, 87–88; T. H. Watkins, *The Hungry Years: A Narrative History of the Great Depression in America* (New York: Henry Holt, 1999), 55.

37. Kennedy, *Freedom from Fear*, 79, 91; Cannadine, *Mellon*, 448–49.

38. Watkins, *The Hungry Years*, 53, 61–62.

CHAPTER 6: The Rise and Fall of National Liberalism (1933–1967)

1. Kennedy, *Freedom from Fear*, 162–63.

2. Harry L. Hopkins, *Spending to Save: The Complete Story of Relief* (New York: Norton, 1936), 76–77, 86–87; Jonathan Alter, *The Defining Moment: FDR's Hundred Days and the Triumph of Hope* (New York: Simon & Schuster, 2007), 1–4; Earle Looker, *The American Way: Franklin Roosevelt in Action* (New York: John Day, 1933), 4–5.

3. Mordaunt Hall, "Walter Huston as a President of the United States who Proclaims Himself Dictator" (film review), *New York Times*, April 1, 1933; Alter, *Defining Moment*, 4–8; John Shelton Lawrence and Robert Jewett, *The Myth of the American Superhero* (Grand Rapids, MI: Wm. B. Eerdmans, 2002), 133–36.

4. *The Public Papers and Addresses of Franklin D. Roosevelt*, vol. 1, *The Genesis of the New Deal, 1928–1932* (New York: Random House, 1938), 76.

5. Kennedy, *Freedom from Fear*, 246–47.

6. Ibid., 276; *The Public Papers and Addresses of Franklin D. Roosevelt*, vol. 4, *The Court Disapproves, 1935* (New York: Random House, 1938), 272.

7. Roger Biles, *The South and the New Deal* (Lexington: University Press of Kentucky, 2006), 127–28; Kennedy, *Freedom from Fear*, 125–27.

8. Ira Katznelson, *Fear Itself: The New Deal and the Origins of Our Time* (New York: Liveright, 2013), 127–28, 163; Jefferson Cowie and Nick Salvatore, "The Long Exception: Rethinking the Place of the New Deal in American History," *International Labor and Working-Class History* 74 (Fall 2008): 3–32.

9. Katznelson, *Fear Itself,* 259–60; Ira Katznelson, *When Affirmative Action Was White* (New York: Norton, 2006), 45–49; Foner, *Story of American Freedom,* 208.

10. Kennedy, *Freedom from Fear,* 209–10; Ira Katznelson, *Fear Itself,* 166–67.

11. Biles, *The South and the New Deal,* 139–40; Jane Walker Herndon, "Ed Rivers and Georgia's 'Little New Deal,'" *Atlanta Historical Journal* 30, no. 1 (Spring 1986), 97–105; Kennedy, *Freedom from Fear,* 340–41.

12. Katznelson, *Fear Itself,* 170–73.

13. Kennedy, *Freedom from Fear,* 348–49.

14. Ibid., 326–38.

15. Ibid., 661, 664–65.

16. Ibid., 644–45, 649–55; "An Up and Coming Leader in the U.S. Chamber of Commerce," *Salt Lake Tribune,* August 26, 1943, 8.

17. Franklin D. Roosevelt, "State of the Union Message to Congress," January 11, 1944, available at http://www.fdrlibrary.marist.edu/archives/address_text .html.

18. Foner, *Story of American Freedom,* 234–35; Kennedy, *Freedom from Fear,* 782–83; on the Full Employment Bill, see G. J. Santoni, "The Employment Act of 1946: Some History Notes" (white paper), Federal Reserve Bank of Saint Louis, November 1946; Kim Phillips-Fein, *Invisible Hands: The Making of the Conservative Movement from the New Deal to Reagan* (New York: Norton, 2009), 31–32; Paul Krugman, *The Conscience of a Liberal* (New York: Norton, 2007), 59, 67–68.

19. Geoffrey Kabaservice, *Rule and Ruin: The Downfall of Moderation and the Destruction of the Republican Party, from Eisenhower to the Tea Party* (New York: Oxford University Press, 2012), 14.

20. Author interview with Carl Reddel, executive director, Eisenhower Memorial Commission, Washington, D.C., January 29, 2015.

21. U.S. Senate Committee on Labor and Public Welfare, *The National Defense Education Act of 1958: A Summary and Analysis of the Act Prepared by the Staff* (Washington, DC: Government Printing Office, 1958), 1–8; Daniel J. Glavin, *Presidential Party Building: From Dwight D. Eisenhower to George W. Bush* (Princeton, NJ: Princeton University Press, 2009), 51.

22. Kabaservice, *Rule and Ruin,* 18; John W. Jeffries, "The 'Quest for National Purpose' of 1960," *American Quarterly* 30, no. 4 (Autumn 1978): 462–63.

23. Krugman, *Conscience of a Liberal,* 38–39, 47–49, 57.

24. Phillips-Fein, *Invisible Hands,* 16–19, 26–27, 54; Kabaservice, *Rule and Ruin,* 6; "Speech to Mortgage Bankers Association of America," January 25, 1949, in

*Papers of Robert A. Taft*, vol. 4, *1949–1953*, ed. Clarence E. Wunderlin Jr. (Kent, OH: Kent State University Press, 2006), 19.

25. Tony Judt, *Ill Fares the Land* (New York: Penguin Press, 2010), 98–105; Phillips-Fein, *Invisible Hands*, 39; F. A. Hayek, *The Road to Serfdom* (New York: Routledge, 2008), 196.

26. Phillips-Fein, *Invisible Hands*, 34–36, 39–46, 52; Hayek, *Road to Serfdom*, 87, 136.

27. Janann Sherman, *No Place for a Woman: A Life of Senator Margaret Chase Smith* (New Brunswick, NJ: Rutgers University Press, 2001), 110–11; Robert Griffith, *The Politics of Fear: Joseph R. McCarthy in the Senate* (Amherst: University of Massachusetts Press, 1970), 264; Chip Berlet and Matthew Lyons, *Right Wing Populism in America* (New York: Guilford, 2000), 196–98.

28. Djilas, *New Class*, 44–46.

29. Irving Kristol, "On Corporate Capitalism in America," *Public Interest*, Fall 1975, 134.

30. G. Calvin MacKenzie and Robert Weisbrot, *The Liberal Hour: Washington and the Politics of Change in the 1960s* (New York: Penguin Press, 2008), 14–15; Allen J. Matusow, *The Unraveling of America: A History of Liberalism in the 1960s* (Athens: University of Georgia Press, 2009), 6–9.

31. Bill Moyers, *Moyers on America: A Journalist and His Times* (New York: New Press, 2013), 167.

32. *National Review* quoted in Krugman, *Conscience of a Liberal*, 102.

33. Phillips-Fein, *Invisible Hands*, 118–19; Barry Goldwater, *The Conscience of a Conservative* (Shepherdsville, KY: Victor Publishing Co., 1960), 37, 66, 69–70.

34. Kabaservice, *Rule and Ruin*, 120–22; MacKenzie and Weisbrot, *Liberal Hour*, 109.

35. "Annual Message to Congress on the State of the Union," January 4, 1965, in *Public Papers of the Presidents of the United States: Lyndon Johnson, 1965* (Washington, DC: Government Printing Office, 1966), 2–5.

36. David Zarefsky, *President Johnson's War on Poverty: Rhetoric and History* (Tuscaloosa: University of Alabama Press, 2005), xiii, 21, 38–41, 48–49; Cowie and Salvatore, "The Long Exception," 16.

37. "Commencement Address at Yale University," June 11, 1962, in *Public Papers of the Presidents of the United States: John F. Kennedy, 1962* (Washington, DC: Government Printing Office, 1963), 470–75; Theodore H. White, "The Action Intellectuals: A Brotherhood of Scholars Forms the Most Powerful Community in Our Society," *Life*, June 9, 1967, 44–45, 52–65.

38. MacKenzie and Weisbrot, *Liberal Hour*, 361; Zarefsky, *President Johnson's War on Poverty*, 58–59, 96; Catherine Caufield, *Masters of Illusion: The World Bank and the Poverty of Nations* (New York: Henry Holt, 1996), 117–99, 173–75.

39. Governor's Commission on the Los Angeles Riots, "Violence in the City: An End or a Beginning?," December 2, 1965, Overview; Zarefsky, *President Johnson's War on Poverty*, 71–72; Valerie Reitman and Mitchell Landsberg, "Watts Riots, 40 Years Later," *Los Angeles Times*, August 11, 2005.

40. Tom Wicker, "President Johnson Forewarned of 'Another Deprived Nation'" (syndicated *New York Times* column), *Oxnard* (CA) *Press-Courier*, August 18, 1965, 8.

41. Rick Perlstein, "1966—When Everything Changed" (online article), History News Network, June 5, 2008; "1966 Civil Rights Act Dies in Senate," *CQ Almanac 1966*, available at http://library.cqpress.com/cqalmanac/document .php?id=cqal66-1301767.

42. Foner, *Story of American Freedom*, 288.

43. Ibid., 289–95; Judt, *Ill Fares the Land*, 86–90.

CHAPTER 7: Dixie Takes Over (1968–2008)

1. Albert Bergesen, "Race Riots of 1967: An Analysis of Police Violence in Detroit and Newark," *Journal of Black Studies* 12, no. 3 (March 1982): 261–74; Matusow, *Unraveling of America*, 416–22 (on Chicago).

2. Kabaservice, *Rule and Ruin*, 214–21, 223; Rick Perlstein, *Nixonland: The Rise of a President and the Fracturing of America* (New York: Scribner, 2008), 72, 90–91.

3. Perlstein, *Nixonland*, 277–78, 334; Ian Haney-Lopez, "How the GOP Became the 'White Man's Party,'" *Salon*, December 22, 2013.

4. Kabaservice, *Rule and Ruin*, 268–70, 327, 330–31.

5. Ibid., 337, 342.

6. Douglas Brinkley and Luke Nichter, *The Nixon Tapes: 1971–72* (New York: Houghton Mifflin Harcourt, 2014), 702–3; "Nixon's Failed Attempts at 'Poisoning the Press,'" *Fresh Air*, National Public Radio, September 30, 2010; Rick Perlstein, *The Invisible Bridge: The Fall of Nixon and the Rise of Reagan* (New York: Simon & Schuster, 2014), 137–38, 141–43, 281; James M. Naughton et al., "How a Fragile Centrist Bloc Emerged as House Panel Weighed Impeachment," *New York Times*, August 5, 1974.

7. Perlstein, *Invisible Bridge*, 57, 177, 265, 309.

8. John Robert Greene, *The Presidency of Gerald R. Ford* (Lawrence: University Press of Kansas, 1994), 53, 59, 71.

9. Ibid., 75–77, 157; Perlstein, *Invisible Bridge*, 674–77, 796, 800.

10. Perlstein, *Invisible Bridge*, 612, 653, 661–62.

11. Phillips-Fein, *Invisible Hands,* 169–72; Sidney Blumenthal, *The Rise of the Counter-Establishment: From Conservative Ideology to Political Power* (New York: Union Square Press, 2008), 45, 49; Perlstein, *Invisible Bridge*, 306.

12. William Trombley, "Reagan Library Strains Link Between Stanford and Hoover Institution," *Los Angeles Times*, March 8, 1987; Blumenthal, *Rise of the Counter-Establishment*, 35; Perlstein, *Invisible Bridge*, 457; Colin Woodard, "The Profit Motive behind Virtual Schools in Maine," *Maine Sunday Telegram*, September 2, 2012, p. Al.

13. Blumenthal, *Rise of the Counter-Establishment,* 41; Irving Kristol, "On Corporate Philanthropy," *Wall Street Journal*, March 21, 1977.

14. Phillips-Fein, *Invisible Hands*, 174; Perlstein, *Invisible Bridge*, 306.

15. Phillips-Fein, *Invisible Hands*, 228–29, 232.

16. Woodard, *American Nations*, 278; Phillips-Fein, *Invisible Hands*, 230.

17. Michael B. Berkman, *The State Roots of National Politics: Congress and the Tax Agenda, 1978–1986* (Pittsburgh: University of Pittsburgh Press, 1994), 48–49; William C. Berman, *America's Right Turn: From Nixon to Bush* (Baltimore: Johns Hopkins University Press, 1994), 46–49, 53.

18. Ronald Reagan, speech delivered at the Detroit Economic Club, May 15, 1980, text available at http://www.kwrendell.com/full-description.aspx ?ItemID=20202017.

19. Kevin Phillips, *The Emerging Republican Majority* (New York: Arlington House, 1969), 15; William Rusher, "A New Party Eventually: Why Not Now?," *National Review*, May 23, 1975, 550–51.

20. The $111 billion figure is in 1968 dollars; it would be $738 billion when adjusted to 2010 dollars. Stephen Daggett, "Cost of Major U.S. Wars," *Congressional Research Service Report to Congress*, June 29, 2010, 2; "Transcript of Ronald Reagan's 1980 Neshoba County Fair Speech," *Neshoba Democrat*, November 15, 2007.

21. David Stockman, *The Triumph of Politics: Why the Reagan Revolution Failed* (New York: Harper & Row, 1986), 72.

22. Ibid.

23. William Greider, "The Education of David Stockman," *Atlantic*, December 1981, 27–54.

24. Glenn Kessler, "The Historical Myth That Reagan Raised $1 in Taxes for Every $3 in Spending Cuts," The Fact Checker (blog), *Washington Post*, December 14, 2012; Stockman, *Triumph of Politics*, 374.

25. Bill Bradley, "Tax Reform's Lessons for Health Care Reform," *New York Times*, August 29, 2009, WK-9; Janet Novack, "10 Reasons Why Reagan Could Cut the Top Tax Rate to 28 Percent but Romney Can't," *Forbes* (online), October 22, 2012; David Altig and Charles Carlstrom, "Marginal Tax Rates and Income

Inequality in a Life-Cycle Model," *American Economic Review* 89, no. 5 (December 1999): 1213; Peter Dreier, "Reagan's Real Legacy," *Nation*, February 4, 2011.

26. "Persons Below Poverty Level in the U.S., 1975–2010," Information Please Database, http://www.infoplease.com/ipa/A0104525.html; Martha M. Burt, *Over the Edge: The Growth of Homelessness in the 1980s* (New York: Russell Sage Foundation, 1992), 140, 211; Edward N. Wolff, "Recent Trends in Household Wealth in the United States," Levy Economics Institute at Barnard College Working Paper No. 589, March 2010, 44; Leonard Silk, "Economic Scene; How Well Off Are Workers?," *New York Times*, September 2, 1988, D2.

27. Gallup presidential approval trends, http://www.gallup.com/poll/116677/presidential-approval-ratings-gallup-historical-statistics-trends.aspx; Leslie McCall and Lane Kenworthy, "Americans' Social Policy Preferences in the Era of Rising Inequality," *Perspectives on Politics* 7, no. 3 (Spring 2009): 464–70.

28. Timothy Naftali quoted in "George H. W. Bush," *American Experience*, WGBH/PBS.

29. Mary Kate Cary, "A Courageous President," *U.S. News & World Report*, April 9, 2014; "Remarks on Signing the Americans with Disabilities Act of 1990," July 26, 1990, in *Public Papers of the Presidents of the United States: George Bush, 1990* (Washington, DC: Government Printing Office, 1991), 1069.

30. Richard Viguerie quoted in "George H. W. Bush," *American Experience*, WGBH/PBS; Kevin Phillips quoted in R. W. Apple, Jr., "Riots and Ballots," *New York Times*, May 2, 1992, A9.

31. Steven M. Gillon, *The Pact: Bill Clinton, Newt Gingrich and the Rivalry That Defined a Generation* (New York: Oxford University Press, 2008), 78–84; Bill Clinton, *My Life*, vol. 1, *The Early Years* (New York: Vintage, 2005), 430–31.

32. Mark Tran, "Popularity Rating That Belies the Clinton Record," *Guardian*, October 24, 1994, 12; Phillips-Fein, *Invisible Hands*, 265.

33. Mike Lofgren, *The Party Is Over: How Republicans Went Crazy, Democrats Became Useless and the Middle Class Got Shafted* (New York: Viking, 2012), 35–36; Alex Seitz-Wald, "How Gingrich Crippled Congress," *Nation*, January 30, 2012; Michael Kranish, "Republican Old Guard Takes Aim at Gingrich," *Boston Globe*, December 9, 2011.

34. Michael Lind, *Up from Conservatism: Why the Right Is Wrong for America* (New York: Free Press, 1996), 129–30, 136.

35. Televised interview, December 1994, in *The Big Guy: Tom DeLay's Stolen Congress*, directed by Mark Birnbaum and Jim Schermbeck (Culver City, CA: Brave New Films, 2006).

36. Fred Barnes, "Revenge of the Squares: Newt Gingrich and Pals Rewrite the '60s," *New Republic*, March 13, 1995, 23–28.

37. Gillon, *The Pact*, 59.

38. Ibid., 58, 122; James Fallows, "The Republican Promise," *New York Review of Books*, January 12, 1995; George Stephanopoulos, *All Too Human: A Political Education* (New York: Little, Brown, 1999), 344.

39. "GOP Throws Down Budget Gauntlet," *CQ Almanac 1995* (Washington, DC: Congressional Quarterly, 1996); Stephanopoulos, *All Too Human*, 360.

40. Gillon, *The Pact*, 169–72.

41. Stephanopoulos, *All Too Human*, 411–12; Thomas Frank, *What's the Matter with Kansas?* (New York: Metropolitan Books, 2004), 242–45; Al From, "Recruiting Bill Clinton," *The Atlantic* (online), December 3, 2013.

42. Barney Frank, *Frank: A Life in Politics from the Great Society to Same-Sex Marriage* (New York: Farrar, Straus & Giroux, 2015), 179; Gillon, *The Pact*, 178; David Leonhardt, "Washington's Invisible Hand," *New York Times Magazine*, September 26, 2008, 32; Michael Hirsh, "The Case Against Larry Summers," *National Journal*, September 12, 2013; Gail Russell Chaddock, "What It Took to Enact Banking Reform," *Christian Science Monitor*, October 21, 1994.

43. Alexander Lane, "Nader Almost Said Gore=Bush, but Not Quite," PolitiFact, *Tampa Bay Times*, June 30, 2008.

44. Bruce Bartlett, *Impostor: How George W. Bush Bankrupted America and Betrayed the Reagan Legacy* (New York: Doubleday, 2006), 1, 120.

45. Tim Dickinson, "How the GOP Became the Party of the Rich," *Rolling Stone*, November 9, 2011; Tom Allen, *Dangerous Convictions: What's Really Wrong with the U.S. Congress* (New York: Oxford University Press, 2013), 46; Lofgren, *The Party Is Over*, 169.

46. Dickinson "How the GOP Became the Party of the Rich"; Allen, *Dangerous Convictions*, 47–48; John Cassidy, "Taxing," *New Yorker*, January 26, 2004.

47. William Greider, "Rolling Back the Twentieth Century," *Nation*, May 12, 2003; Bob Dreyfuss, "Grover Norquist: 'Field Marshal' of the Bush Plan," *Nation*, May 14, 2001; Allen, *Dangerous Convictions*, 58–59; Bruce Bartlett, *The Benefit and the Burden: Tax Reform—Why We Need It and What It Will Take* (New York: Simon & Schuster, 2012), 49.

48. Allen, *Dangerous Convictions*, 89–94.

49. Lofgren, *The Party Is Over*, 187.

50. Thomas Frank, *What's the Matter with Kansas?*, 106–13; "Will Anyone Pay for Abu Ghraib?" (editorial), *New York Times*, February 5, 2015, A26; Scott Shane

and Ron Nixon, "Contractors Becoming a Fourth Branch of Government," *New York Times,* February 4, 2007.

51. Paul Krugman, "The DeLay Principle," *New York Times,* June 9, 2006, A27.

CHAPTER 8: Rise of the Radicals (2008–)

1. Jonathan Stempel, "One in Five Homeowners with Mortgages Under Water," Reuters, October 31, 2008; Larry Elliott and Jill Treanor, "Lehman Brothers Collapse Five Years On: 'We Had Almost No Control,'" *Guardian,* September 13, 2013.

2. Andrew Ross Sorkin, "Lehman Files for Bankruptcy, Merrill Is Sold," *New York Times,* September 14, 2008, A1; Alex Berenson, "Wall Street's Turmoil Sends Stocks Reeling," *New York Times,* September 15, 2008, C7; Bob Ivry et al., "Secret Fed Loans Gave Banks $13 Billion Undisclosed to Congress," Bloomberg, November 27, 2011; "The Financial Crisis: The *Frontline* Interviews" (online oral history resource), PBS, http://www.pbs.org/wgbh/pages /frontline/oral-history/financial-crisis/.

3. Edmund L. Andrews and Peter Baker, "A.I.G. Planning Huge Bonuses After $170 Billion Bailout," *New York Times,* March 14, 2009, A1; *The Situation Room,* CNN, March 16, 2009, transcript available at http://www.cnn.com /TRANSCRIPTS/0903/16/sitroom.03.html.

4. Phillip Swagel, *The Impact of the September 2008 Collapse* (Washington, DC: Pew Economic Policy Group, April 28, 2010); "Bush Approval Rating Doldrums Continue," Gallup, October 20, 2008; Kara Scannell and Sudeep Reddy, "Greenspan Admits Errors to Hostile House Panel," *Wall Street Journal,* October 24, 2008.

5. Jim F. Couch et al., "An Analysis of the Financial Services Bailout Vote," *Cato Journal* 31, no. 1 (Winter 2011): 121–22.

6. Kate Zernike, *Boiling Mad: Inside Tea Party America* (New York: Henry Holt, 2010), 22–23; Rick Santelli's rant can be seen at http://video.cnbc.com /gallery/?video=1039849853; Dick Armey and Matt Kibbe, *Give Us Liberty: A Tea Party Manifesto* (New York: William Morrow, 2010), 57.

7. Brandy Dennis and David Cho, "Rage at AIG Swells as Bonuses Go Out," *Washington Post,* March 17, 2009; Frank, *What's the Matter with Kansas?,* 298–301; Russell Goldman, "Employees Fear for Their Lives: The Other AIG Outrage," ABC News, March 27, 2009.

8. Theda Skocpol and Vanessa Williamson, *The Tea Party and the Remaking of Republican Conservatism* (New York: Oxford University Press, 2013), 104–5;

Joe Strupp, "Dick Armey Dishes on FreedomWorks' Deals with Beck & Limbaugh," *Media Matters,* January 4, 2013.

9. W. Cleon Skousen, *The Naked Communist* (Salt Lake City: Ensign Publishing, 1958); Alexander Zaitchik, "Meet the Man Who Changed Glenn Beck's Life," *Salon,* September 16, 2009.

10. W. Cleon Skousen, *The American Heritage & Constitution Study Course* (Provo, UT: Freeman Institute, c. 1980); Zaitchik, "Meet the Man Who Changed Glenn Beck's Life"; Zernike, *Boiling Mad,* 73–77; Sean Wilentz, "Confounding Fathers," *New Yorker,* October 18, 2010.

11. Skocpol and Williamson, *The Tea Party and the Remaking of Republican Conservatism,* 56–61; Nate Silver, "Were the Tea Parties Really a Libertarian Thing?," FiveThirtyEight.com, April 26, 2009; Colin Woodard, "The Soul of the Tea Party," *Newsweek* (online), December 1, 2010; Zaitchik, "Meet the Man Who Changed Glenn Beck's Life"; Lisa Disch, "A 'White Citizenship' Movement?," in *Steep: The Precipitous Rise of the Tea Party,* ed. Lawrence Rosenthal and Christine Trost (Berkeley: University of California Press, 2012), 136–37, 143.

12. Ian Urbina, "Beyond the Beltway, Health Debate Turns Hostile," *New York Times,* August 7, 2009, A1; Lizz Robbins, "Tax Day Is Met with Tea Parties," *New York Times,* April 15, 2009, A16; Jeff Zeleny, "Thousands Rally in Capital to Protest Big Government," *New York Times,* September 12, 2009, A37.

13. Zernike, *Boiling Mad,* 105–7; Marc Cooper, "John McCain's Last Stand," *Nation,* August 16, 2010, 11–12; Colin Woodard, "Tea Party–Backed Platform Sails Through Maine GOP Convention," *Christian Science Monitor,* May 10, 2010; Colin Woodard, "Brewing Up a Storm," *Down East,* September 2010.

14. William J. Miller and Jeremy D. Walling, *Tea Party Effects on 2010 U.S. Senate Elections: Stuck in the Middle to Lose* (Lanham, MD: Lexington Books, 2011), 351–52.

15. Colin Woodard, "A Geography Lesson for the Tea Party," *Washington Monthly,* November/December 2011, 11, 16; Colin Woodard, "Republicans Have a Yankee Problem," *Maine Sunday Telegram,* December 16, 2012, E1.

16. Woodard, "Geography Lesson for the Tea Party," 16.

17. Lofgren, *The Party Is Over,* 68; Martin Frost, "The Tea Party Taliban," *Politico,* July 29, 2011; Woodard, "A Geography Lesson for the Tea Party," 11.

18. Mark Binelli, "The Great Kansas Tea Party Disaster," *Rolling Stone,* November 6, 2014, 46–51; Brad Cooper, "Kansas Revenues Will Fall $1 Billion Short of 2015 and 2016 Expenses, Fiscal Experts Say," *Kansas City Star,* November 10, 2014; David Sciara and Wade Henderson, "What's the Matter with Kansas'

Schools?," *New York Times,* January 8, 2014, A23; "The Decline of North Carolina" (editorial), *New York Times,* July 9, 2013; "Funding Cuts Hobble NC Courts" (editorial), *Raleigh News and Observer,* November 22, 2014.

19. Jacob Weisberg, "Let Him Die," *Slate,* September 13, 2011; T. Jefferson, "Glenn Beck: Firemen Let House Burn over $75," interview transcript, Glennbeck.com, October 5, 2010; Adam Cohen, "Should Tennessee Firemen Have Let the House Burn?," *Time,* October 13, 2010.

20. Bruce Bartlett, "Obama Is a Republican," *American Conservative,* November/December 2014, 12–16; Thomas Frank, "Cornel West: 'He Posed as a Progressive and Turned Out to Be Counterfeit,'" *Salon,* August 24, 2014.

21. Tami Luhbi, "Romney-Ryan Would Aim to Overhaul Medicaid," CNNMoney, August 13, 2012; Laurie Goodstein, "Georgetown Faculty Latest to Chide Ryan," The Caucus (blog), *New York Times,* April 24, 2012; U.S. Conference of Catholic Bishops, Catholic Charities USA and Catholic Relief Services to House and Senate Appropriations Committees, Washington, DC, March 19, 2015; U.S. Conference of Catholic Bishops to Congressional Members, Washington, DC, March 6, 2012; Robert Draper, "Can the Democrats Catch Up in the Super PAC Game?," *New York Times Magazine,* July 5, 2012; Steve Benen, "Ten-to-One Isn't Good Enough for the GOP," Political Animal (blog), *Washington Monthly,* August 12, 2011.

22. Pew Research Center, "Trends in American Values: 1987–2012," June 4, 2012, 55, 57, 63–65; Pew Research Center, "Millennials in Adulthood: Detached from Institutions, Networked with Friends," March 7, 2014, 35–37; David Frum, "Crashing the Party," *Foreign Affairs,* September/October 2014.

CHAPTER 9:  A Lasting Union

1. Roosevelt, "New Nationalism."

2. Hoover, *American Individualism,* 9–11, 20–21.

3. Gerson and Wehner, "Conservative Vision of Government," 88–89.

4. Francis Fukuyama, *Political Order and Political Decay: From the Industrial Revolution to the Globalization of Democracy* (New York: Farrar, Straus & Giroux, 2014), 57.

5. Krugman, *Conscience of a Liberal,* 248.

6. Warren Buffett, "A Minimum Tax for the Wealthy," *New York Times,* November 26, 2012, A27; Warren Buffett, "Stop Coddling the Super-Rich," *New York Times,* August 14, 2011, A21; Tax Foundation, *U.S. Federal Individual Income Tax Rates History, 1862–2013* (downloadable tables); Richard Rubin, "Paul

Ryan Plans Panel Vote Next Week to Repeal U.S. Estate Tax," Bloomberg, March 18, 2015.

7. Colin Macilwain, "Science Economics: What Is Science Really Worth?," *Nature* 465 (2010): 682–84; NASA, "Benefits of Apollo: Giant Leaps in Technology," Document FS-2004-07-002-JSC, July 2004; Diana G. Carew and Michael Mandel, *Infrastructure Investment and Economic Growth: Surveying New Post-Crisis Evidence* (Washington, DC: Progressive Policy Institute, March 2014), 6–7; Frank, *Frank,* 346–47; Andy Kroll, "Triumph of the Drill," *Mother Jones,* April 2014.

8. David Sirota, "The Democrats' Da Vinci Code," *American Prospect,* December 8, 2004.

9. Thomas F. Schaller, *Whistling Past Dixie: How Democrats Can Win Without the South* (New York: Simon & Schuster, 2006), 282–83.

10. Ibid., 275–76.

11. Bob Moser, *Blue Dixie: Awakening the South's Democratic Majority* (New York: Henry Holt, 2008), 92, 235.

12. Ibid., 80–83.

13. Woodard, "Geography Lesson," 17.

# Index

32953012490142